Master Bombers

MASTER
BOMBERS

The Experiences of a
Pathfinder Squadron at War 1944-1945

Sean Feast

GRUB STREET · LONDON

Published by
Grub Street Publishing
4 Rainham Close
London
SW11 6SS

British Library Cataloguing in Publication Data
Feast, Sean
    Master bombers : the experiences of a Pathfinder squadron at war, 1944-1945
    1. Great Britain. Royal Air Force. Bomber Command. Group, No. 8
    2. World War, 1939-1945 – Aerial operations, British
    3. World War, 1939-1945 – Regimental histories – Great Britain
    I. Title
    940.5′44′941

ISBN-13: 9781906502010

Cover design by Lizzie B design

Formatted by Pearl Graphics, Hemel Hempstead

Printed and bound by MPG Ltd, Bodmin, Cornwall

Grub Street only uses
FSC (Forest Stewardship Council) paper for its books.

Contents

Foreword   7
Introduction   9

Chapter 1   **A Squadron is Born**   11
            April 1944
            Philip Patrick MBE, DFC   20

Chapter 2   **A Squadron at War**   29
            April – June 1944
            Heaven Can Wait – Les Hood   36
            The Mile High Club – George Hall DFC & Bar   44
            One More for Luck – Roy Pengilley DFC & Bar   53

Chapter 3   **A Squadron at War**   61
            July – September 1944
            Teenage Pathfinder – Roy Last   71
            The Luck of the Irish – John Torrans   79
            One of the Many – Allan Farrington   85
            Master Navigator – Bill Heane DFC   94
            The Flying Controller – Vera Jacobs   102
            Double Jeopardy – Tommy MacLachlan   108

Chapter 4   **A Squadron at War**   115
            October – December 1944
            Johnny's War – John Smith DFM   124
            Lucky Thirteen – Bill Hough   132
            Two of a Kind – David Spier and Bob Pearce   139

Chapter 5   **A Squadron at War**   148
            January – April 1945
            Life in Both Hands – Frank Lloyd DFC   155
            Leading the Way – Reg Cann DFC   163
            Pathfinder VC – Ted Swales VC   171
            100 Up! – Ted Stocker DSO, DFC   179
            Squadron Commander – Stafford Coulson   189
              DSO, DFC

Chapter 6   **A Squadron at Peace**   200
            May – September 1945

Appendix One   Roll of Honour   203

Appendix Two   Aircraft Losses   208

Appendix Three The Loss of the Star Tiger   210

Glossary   213

Sources   215

Personal thanks   217

Index   218

Foreword

I am honoured to write the foreword to *Master Bombers*, a comprehensive review of 582 Squadron's activities during the Second World War. This book covers not only the work of the aircrew, but also of supporting staff and WAAF personnel.

When I received my wings and commission at Cranwell, I was rated an 'above average' pilot and was sent to Central Flying School to train as a flying instructor. After a time I was posted to Bomber Command, joining 149 Squadron to fly Stirlings where I met my crew. Our longest flight, I remember, was nine hours and twenty-five minutes, to Stettin on the Baltic coast. We completed our first tour and then separated to our different occupations.'

When I was posted to 7 Squadron, Oakington, at the start of my second tour in November 1943 my crew joined me again, with the exception of the navigator who was replaced by an Australian, Gordon Goodwin, who after the war became head of navigation for Qantas. My abiding memory of this time is of the station commander and squadron commander standing by the caravan at take-off point and saluting each aircraft as it rolled forward.

My tour with 7 Squadron ended in March 1944, by which time I had flown to Berlin on no fewer than ten occasions, and had been promoted flight commander. I was then asked to take my Flight as the nucleus for a new unit, 582 Squadron, then being formed at Little Staughton in Bedfordshire as part of Pathfinder force.

The operations of the Pathfinders involved a variety of highly specialist (and often highly dangerous) tasks including route-marking and target-marking which were vital to the success of the main force bombing. During my time on 582 Squadron we were heavily involved in the invasion operations, attacking railway marshalling yards, airfields, coastal gun batteries and buzz-bomb (V1) assembly sites that could have caused serious damage to our invasion forces.

The story of 582 Squadron has never before been told, and the combination of extensive research and personal interviews with those of us who were there at the time makes *Master Bombers* a most informative and lively read.

Wing Commander Philip Patrick MBE, DFC
Officer IC training, 582 Squadron PFF

Introduction

This is the story of a group of men and women described by the commander-in-chief of Bomber Command, Arthur Harris, as the 'corps d'élite', and for very good reason. The Pathfinders, quite literally, led the way in virtually every major bomber operation for the last three years of the war. It was they who took the greatest risks, and often took the greatest casualties.

Pathfinders were a mixed bag of talent, but whether they were career-minded, pre-war 'regulars' or unashamed enthusiastic amateurs in for the duration, all shared a common desire: to be the best. And they were the best. Master bombers in every sense. But whilst much has been written about such famous squadrons as 617, the Dambusters (and understandably so) it seems that the countless heroic deeds of the Pathfinders have failed to ignite the public's imagination in the same way.

This first struck me whilst researching my previous book *Heroic Endeavour* (Grub Street, 2006). Here was the story of a raid by a handful of Pathfinders in broad daylight on a vital target against incredible odds, in which they took a large number of casualties and in which the leader – Bob Palmer – won the Victoria Cross for a supreme act of gallantry for which he lost his life.

The parallel between the Pathfinders and the Dambusters – and between Palmer and Guy Gibson specifically – is remarkable, albeit that Palmer was killed in winning his VC, and did not have a dog with an unfortunate name! And yet whilst there have been four books on the life of Gibson alone, and countless others about the Dambusters per se, stories about the Pathfinders are still (relatively) thin on the ground.

Master Bombers focuses on the men and women of one particular squadron – 582 – but it is not a squadron history as such. It is rather a book full of personal experiences and reminiscences from those who were there at the time, and therefore those that count. Their memories are placed in the context of the squadron's operational life, to give greater continuity to the story, and hopefully a better understanding of their contribution.

What is important to stress, however, is that their stories are no different from any other Pathfinder squadron aircrew serving in

Pathfinder force at that time. They are not claiming to be an elite within an elite, but rather 'representative' of what the whole PFF stood for and achieved.

Whilst most of those featured in the book are aircrew, this should not be taken as failing to acknowledge or appreciate the vital efforts played by their colleagues who packed the parachutes, serviced the aircraft or cooked the teas. Unfortunately the passage of time hampered my attempts to find sufficient numbers of those men and women 'who also served'.

Stafford Coulson, the squadron's last wartime commanding officer, told me that he had always been concerned that no one had ever really understood how difficult a job it was to be a Pathfinder. He believed that their real contribution to the war effort had never been fully realised. He also thought that the contribution of the groundcrews was too rarely mentioned. At reunions, he asked veterans not to wear any medals, out of respect to their colleagues who helped keep them in the air, and for those whose gallant deeds had otherwise gone unrewarded. Sadly Stafford died during the preparation of this book, but it is to his memory, and to the memory of all those Pathfinder aircrew and ground crew that died during the war and since, that this book is dedicated.

Sean Feast
Sarratt

Chapter One

A Squadron is Born

April 1944

The Royal Air Force seemed to like April Fools Day. It was, after all, the date chosen for the birth of the RAF in 1918 when it emerged from the shadows of the Royal Flying Corps, and it was the date also, in 1944, that it chose to announce a new squadron, No. 582, to join the illustrious ranks of the Pathfinders.

The Pathfinders were the corps d'élite of Bomber Command, the command that had been leading the fight-back against Germany ever since the fall of France in 1940, and even before. For four long years, Bomber Command, led from February 1942 by the bullish Air Chief Marshal Sir Arthur Harris, had been waging war with Hitler's armies and civilian populations in the hope of bombing them into submission. And with some effect. Cities had been pounded, and the mighty manufacturing facilities of the Ruhr Valley – responsible for churning out the thousands of tanks, guns and munitions on which a German victory depended – had been severely disrupted. Bomber Command had been honed into a splendid fighting machine, a far cry from the first heroic but sadly pathetic attempts of the early bomber boys to scare their enemies into submission by dropping leaflets rather than bombs.

A primary reason for the greater efficiency of Bomber Command, and its greater successes, was the Pathfinder force, a force that quite literally 'led the way'. Before they came into being, only one third of those who claimed to have bombed a target at night got to within a five-mile radius of the aiming point. In fact, only one in five actually bombed within 75 square miles of the intended target, and it was this dismal record of success above all that precipitated the need for some special 'target-marking' force to be created. The story of how the Pathfinders came into being has been told many times before, but suffice to say its formation was not a universally popular decision, not even with Harris. Some background, however, is necessary.

There was an argument that forming 'elite' squadrons to mark targets and lead the bulk of the bomber formations to bomb the right place at the right time would strip the main force squadrons of their best men, thereby making them less effective. There was an argument also that elite squadrons at the vanguard of a bombing operation would be singled out for special attention by the German defenders, and take a much higher percentage of casualties. Harris' plan was to train and form target-marking squadrons in each group, rather than have a separate force. This, he argued, would generate healthy competition and allow new ideas to be tried and shared. His view was reflected by his group commanders, some of whom were already developing their own target-marking tactics, and objected strongly to the idea of having their best squadrons disrupted or their future leaders poached.

Despite his objections, Harris was directly overruled by the air ministry, and so he set about finding an appropriate commander. He settled upon the mercurial Australian, Donald Bennett, as 'the obvious man'. Harris had known Bennett since 1931, and although very young to become a group commander (Bennett was 31 whereas the average age of his contemporaries was 56), his technical knowledge and personal operational ability was described by Harris as 'altogether exceptional'.

Although popular with his commander-in-chief, Bennett did little to endear himself to others, never hiding his disdain for operational commanders who had themselves never taken part in operations. He once famously said of Ralph Cochrane, commander of 5 Group from February 1943: "He would have been the best group commander in Bomber Command had he done 10 trips – or if he had done any trips. But his knowledge of flying and of operations was nil." Bennett's own credentials, on the other hand, both as a flyer and as a commander were impeccable. A brilliant navigator (he quite literally wrote the text book on air navigation, some say on his honeymoon!), by 1942 he was in command of 10 Squadron leading one of the early attacks on the battleship *Tirpitz*. Shot down over Trondheim, he successfully evaded capture, and made his way home to England via Sweden.

The Pathfinders officially began life on July 5, 1942 as a unit reporting directly to C-in-C Bomber Command. For aircraft and crews it poached four squadrons from within the existing group structure: No. 7 from 3 Group (John Baldwin), No. 35 from 4 Group (Roddy Carr), No. 83 from 5 Group (at that time still commanded by Cochrane's predecessor Alec Coryton), and No. 156 from 1 Group (Edward Rice). It also had a further squadron, No. 109, designated for 'special purposes' that was not yet affiliated to any particular group.

After an inauspicious, not to say disastrous, start to a raid on Flensburg in which the majority failed to find the target, PFF began to steadily prove its mettle, helped by rapid developments in target finding and marking techniques. New technologies came into play such as H2S – a ground-scanning radar that could pick out certain geographical features under favourable conditions thus enabling much improved navigation – and Oboe that allowed for the precise identification of specific aiming points.

New tactics and techniques were also evolved, all to ensure greater accuracy to the navigation and bombing, and to allow a higher number of bombers over the target in a much quicker time. These bombing techniques were given codenames: Newhaven, for example, was the name given to visual ground marking – that is, a target identified visually by a pathfinder aircraft and marked subsequently with coloured indicators (Target Indicators or TIs) for the main force to attack. If the target was obscured by cloud or smoke, such that Newhaven might not be practical, the crews reverted to a blind-marking tactic known as Parramatta, using their H2S radars. When the more precise Oboe blind-bombing device was being used, the raid was known as a Musical Parramatta, and in the event that the target was totally obscured by cloud, a last-resort technique known as Wanganui was employed. This involved using sky-markers to give an approximation of where to bomb through the cloud in order to hit the target. The strange names came from the hometowns in Australia and New Zealand of some of Bennett's staff.

With the new technologies and new tactics came the new crews. A 'normal' Bomber Command crew signed up for a tour of 30 operations, after which they were 'rested', often at an operational training unit (OTU) helping others to prepare for combat. A second tour of 20 operations would then follow. Pathfinders, however, were different. Because of the intense training required and the ultimate expertise of the crews, it was decided that to lose such experience after 'only' 30 trips would impact significantly on the progress of the war. Better by far, it was decided, to set the minimum 'tariff' for pathfinder crews at 45.

Although Harris had openly opposed the formation of PFF, this did not mean he was deliberately hostile towards it. Indeed it was on Harris' insistence, and no one else's, that Pathfinder aircrew be given a special badge to distinguish them from 'ordinary' Bomber Command men. This badge took the form of the Royal Air Force eagle to be worn beneath the left breast pocket, and was awarded to aircrew 'temporarily' after a certain amount of 'proving' sorties had been completed, and then 'permanently' at the end of their tour. It was also on Harris' insistence that promotions to PFF aircrew would be accelerated, partly in recognition of the much higher risks that they faced.

Whilst the Pathfinders were no doubt the elite, it is a myth, however, that all pathfinder aircrew were already seasoned veterans with a tour or two under their belts before they volunteered. Certainly there were a good number whose quest to be the best had driven them from main force to PFF, already with a chest-full of medals and of significant officer rank. Then there were those plucked from other groups who had just started out on their tour, but who had already shown early promise. And there were those who had yet to fly their first operation but had passed out top of the class at pilot or navigation school. There were also a number posted to PFF by a handful of squadron commanders who saw the Pathfinders as a suitable dumping ground for their 'waste'; needless to say, they rarely if ever made it through without being quickly posted out.

Even the veteran crews who had survived a tour found themselves novices in the eyes of the experienced Pathfinders, and soon discovered that previous 'achievement' or indeed rank counted for little until they had proven themselves to their new peers. The entry-level pathfinder crew undertook the role of 'supporter' for the first few operations. Supporters were used to ensure that aircraft were on scene at the right time to start bombing once the target had been marked, and to help saturate the defences. From a supporter a crew might be promoted to a 'backer-up', an aircraft tasked with estimating the mean point of impact (MPI) of all of the primary markers and then placing their TIs at that point with the aid of their MkXVI bombsight. They were also responsible for ensuring the target was constantly illuminated. Having proven themselves in this capacity a crew might be asked to perform a number of other tasks. 'Recenterers', for example, were responsible for keeping the attack on the aiming point; 'route markers' dropped TIs at important turning points to help the main force maintain a 'stream'; 'blind illuminators' used H2S to navigate to the target and then drop flares to help the visual markers in Newhaven attacks. Arguably the most difficult job of all, and one given to only a handful of selected crews, was the role of 'primary visual marker'. It was the primary visual marker's task to put his target indicators on the target at the very beginning of a raid, and accuracy both in timing and precision was essential.

Even amongst the elite there were gods, and these took the form of the master bombers. The master bomber, as the name suggests, was the aircraft in charge of the whole attack. It was the master bomber who determined the accuracy of the target indicators dropped by the primary visual markers, and what further marking or illumination was required. It was the master bomber that would transmit instructions over VHF radio to the main force telling them which coloured markers to ignore and which to bomb, exhorting them on to greater consistency. It took the proverbial nerves of steel to orbit high above the bomber stream over the target area, in constant fear of attack from fighters or flak, sometimes for over an hour. Unsurprisingly the master had a designated deputy master to assist, and to take over in time of trouble. If the role of the primary visual marker was the most difficult, then the role of the master bomber was the most dangerous.

The Pathfinders' success had been considerable, the results proven, and the losses – whilst always regrettable – not as dramatic as had been predicted. In recognition of its success, PFF had been granted full 'group' status as 8 Group, headquartered in Huntingdon, with its leader, Bennett, promoted. The size of the force began to expand commensurate with the increase in pace of Harris' attacks against Germany, and so new squadrons had to be formed.

Pathfinder force had started with five squadrons using four different aircraft: Wellingtons (156 and 109 Squadrons), Halifaxes (35 Squadron), Stirlings (7 Squadron) and Lancasters (83 Squadron). Steadily this was rationalised to Lancasters and Mosquitoes only. By the beginning of 1944, the five founding squadrons had been joined by 97 Squadron and 405 Squadron (Royal Canadian Air Force) flying Lancasters, and 105, 139 and 627 Squadrons on Mosquitoes.

The practice at the time in forming new squadrons was to take at least one flight (i.e. a group of between 12-16 aircraft and crews) from an existing squadron to form the nucleus of the new unit. A Bomber Command squadron at this stage would have usually comprised three flights – designated A, B and C – with each flight commanded, confusingly, by a squadron leader whereas the squadron itself was commanded by a wing commander!

A meeting of senior officials held early in the New Year (1944) decided that with effect from March 7, 35 Squadron was to lose its Halifax IIIs in favour of 30 Lancaster Is and IIIs. In the same meeting, authority was given for the reduction in aircraft establishment of four Lancaster squadrons in order to create two new Lancaster Pathfinder squadrons.

Paragraph four of SD 155/1944 (604-605) states:

> "With effect from March 20, 1944, Nos 35 and 97 Squadrons are to be reduced from an aircraft establishment of 24+6 to 16+4 Lancaster I/III and, with effect from April 1, 1944, Nos 7 and 156 Squadrons are to be reduced from an aircraft establishment of 24+6 to 16+4 Lancaster I/III. Nos 9007, 9035, 9097, and 9156 Servicing Echelons are to be reduced in conformity with their respective squadrons."

The result of this instruction was the formation of two new squadrons. From 35 and 97 Squadrons, No. 635 Squadron was to be formed and based at RAF Downham Market with effect from

March 20, 1944. It would have 16+4 Lancaster I/IIIs and a new servicing echelon – Nos 9635 – with a note that 'The aircraft, personnel and equipment thrown up by the reduction in establishment of 7, 35, 97 and 156 Squadrons, and their respective servicing echelons, are to be utilised as the nucleus for the formation of 635 Squadron and the servicing echelon of that squadron.'

The second of the new squadrons to be formed, which would have the same number of Lancasters and its own servicing echelon drawn from the planned re-organisation of its sister units, would come into being on April 1, 1944, and be based at RAF Little Staughton in Bedfordshire. Its crews and aircraft would be taken primarily from 7 and 156 Squadrons.

The new squadron was designated No. 582 Squadron of No. 8 (PFF) Group Bomber Command. Its motto: *Praecolamus Designantes*. We fly before marking.

Originally, Little Staughton had been built as a base for the USAAF as the 2nd Advanced Air Depot for repair of B-17s of the 1st Bomb Wing, but on March 1, 1944, it had been handed over to Bomber Command, and the command in turn had allocated it to PFF. The station commander was one of the pioneer Pathfinders, Group Captain Raymond Collings.

Collings, nick-named 'Fatty' on account of his somewhat rotund figure, was a pre-war regular, who had joined the RAF in the mid-1920s. Rising through the ranks, he spent time as a test pilot with 'A' Flight, Performance Testing Squadron at the Aircraft & Armament Experimental Establishment (A&AEE), Boscombe Down. As CO of 35 Squadron from November 1940 he was instrumental in the development and eventual introduction of the Halifax into military service. He had an impressive record of ops, and still flew whenever he could. Most recently he had been commanding officer of 156 Squadron, adding the DSO to an earlier AFC and a Mention in Despatches for his 'great skill, excellent judgement and unswerving devotion to duty'. He was an iconic figure, greatly admired by his men.

The crews began arriving at Little Staughton by road and air on the first day of the new squadron's formation. The majority had been taken from the 'C' Flights of 7 Squadron from Oakington and 156 Squadron – Collings' old squadron – from Upwood, both relatively local to their new home. Within 24 hours, squadron strength was reported to be up to 50 officers and the unit was beginning to assume shape. The new adjutant, Flight Lieutenant H G 'Timber' Woods wrote in the squadron's operations record book (ORB):

"Occupation of squadron headquarters, flight offices, commodious crew rooms and specialist offices was carried out, and various necessary adjustments and alterations to existing buildings were effected."

To command the squadron, Bennett selected Squadron Leader (Acting Wing Commander) Charles McKenzie Dunnicliffe, a man of exceptional experience. Unusually, Charles Dunnicliffe was not a volunteer reserve (RAFVR), but rather regular RAF who had risen through the non-commissioned ranks to attain commanding officer status. He had flown his first operational sortie, a daylight attack on Heligoland in October 1939, only a month after war had been declared. This was followed by a succession of reconnaissance missions, anti-invasion patrols and bombing attacks throughout the early stages of the Battle of Britain, completing his first tour in August 1940.

He returned to operational flying in 1943 with 97 (Straits Settlements) Squadron, a recent addition to PFF, as a flight commander noted for his high degree of organising capability. Despite being a pilot, his tour included no fewer than eight trips as a bomb aimer to 'Pat' Daniels, a legendary Pathfinder and original master bomber who later went on to complete three tours and twice win both the Distinguished Service Order and Distinguished Flying Cross. Dunnicliffe too was recommended for the DFC in December 1943, the particulars stating:

> "Of this officer's total of 46 operational sorties, 11 have been with Pathfinder force, nine of these as Marker. He served with a bomber squadron early in the war and carried out many sorties over enemy territory as the captain of a Blenheim aircraft. On joining 97 Squadron he functioned first as a bomb aimer in one of the leading crews of the squadron and later as pilot and captain. In both the roles he has filled and on all operations in which he has been engaged he has shown pronounced ability and has achieved noteworthy success. His cheerful mien in face of known hazards, his high sense of duty and his all-round ability set a fine example to his flight in particular and the squadron in general."

Dunnicliffe survived the Battle of Berlin at a time when many exceptional crews were lost. He also had the necessary 'management' experience, assuming command of 97 Squadron for a brief period at the end of 1943 from Group Captain Noel 'Press-on' Fresson GC, DFC upon the latter's posting to RAF Snaith, and before the arrival of the new CO, Wing Commander Edward Carter DFC.

In keeping with many COs, Dunnicliffe brought with him to Little Staughton several members of his former squadron and crew, including his regular navigator, Squadron Leader Ross Ingalls DFC and his wireless operator, Flight Lieutenant Charles Chetham DFC.* These two men he made 'leaders' of their respective disciplines, effectively in charge of all of the other navigators and wireless operators on the squadron. Amongst the other 'trades' (as they were called), bombing leader was Flight Lieutenant Arthur Feeley DFC, gunnery leader was Flight Lieutenant Leslie Booth DFC, and Flying Officer Harold Siddons DFC (later a post-war actor) was placed in charge – officially at least – of flight engineers, albeit that the task actually fell to the more experienced Flight Lieutenant Ted Stocker DFC.

Amongst the crews there was an eclectic mix of novices and consummate pathfinding professionals, and whilst the majority of the new squadron was made up of crews taken from 7 and 156 Squadrons, it was not exclusively so. Pilot Officer Roy Pengilley, for example, joined from 625 Squadron with his crew having only flown a total of nine trips; Flying Officer George Hall arrived from 101 Squadron, a special duties squadron that carried an eighth German-speaking crew member operating a nightfighter radio jamming device, with only six trips under his belt (one of those was to Nuremberg on the night the RAF suffered its heaviest casualties losing 95 aircraft).

At the other end of the scale there were men like Squadron Leader Bob Wareing, a second-tour man who had already won the DFC & Bar. He had received his first 'gong' as a pilot officer with 106 Squadron in April 1941 attacking two enemy battle cruisers in the port of Brest, and a second on completing his tour in December. All but one of his crew were similarly on their second tour of operations.

Squadron Leader John Weightman DFC was an even earlier starter, winning his award one night in July 1940 as pilot and captain of a Hudson undertaking a reconnaissance mission over the Norwegian coast. Attacked by two Messerschmitt 110s (twin-engined fighter aircraft), he managed to make his escape, but not before his gunner had badly damaged one of their opponents. At the time of his award, he had already flown 92 operational flights over the sea amounting to more than 360 hours flying time.

Flight Lieutenant Clive Walker had survived a tour on Boston light bombers with 107 Squadron in 1942 when very few did; he then survived more than a year instructing which was perhaps more incredible still. Pilot Officer 'Splinters' Spierenberg was another remarkable case, arriving at 582 from 115 Squadron, part of 3 Group. His case was remarkable, not so much because of his flying

---

* Sadly for two others from Dunnicliffe's regular crew – Martin Bryan-Smith DFC & Bar, and Herbert Rieger, a 21-year-old Canadian – both men were killed on the night of D-Day flying with the 97 Squadron CO Edward Carter. They have no known grave.

experience, but because he had originally joined the Dutch merchant navy and had two ships torpedoed from under him!

Not surprisingly, arguably the most experienced men were the two flight commanders, Derrick 'Dickie' Walbourn and Brian McMillan. Both had exceptional flying records, and their credentials were beyond reproach. Walbourn, I/C 'A' Flight – designated a 'blind' bombing flight, had been one of the few pre-war pilots to attain the Air Efficiency medal (AE) whilst as a test pilot for De Havillands. McMillan, I/C 'B' Flight – comprising visual bombing specialists – was a New Zealander and skier of international standard. A member of the Reserve of Air Force Officers (RAFO), he had been awarded the Air Force Cross (AFC) for his airmanship in June 1943.

As a supernumerary flight commander, and an officer officially placed in charge of training, they were assisted by another seasoned veteran, whose curriculum vitae included a DFC awarded for successfully completing a tour on Stirlings in 1942. More recently he had led a flight at 7 Squadron. His name was Wing Commander Philip Patrick.

The story of

Philip Patrick MBE, DFC, 582 Squadron

Philip Patrick had always wanted to fly. A Scotsman born in Edinburgh in March 1915, he joined the RAF on September 3, 1940 – exactly one year after Britain had declared war on Germany – undertaking the obligatory training without incident or mishap at 3 ITW, then on to 6 EFTS at Sywell, Lincolnshire. His skill as a pilot, and aptitude for multi-engined aircraft in particular singled him out for training as an instructor, and soon after being awarded his wings, he was posted to Central Flying School (CFS) Cranwell instructing on twin-engined Oxfords.

Fortunately for a man keen to get on to operations, his stint as a flying instructor did not last too long. From Cranwell he went to 11 OTU, Bassingbourn, spending five months, between January – June 1942, flying and teaching others to fly the Barnes Wallis-designed Vickers Wellington. Finally he joined the 149 Squadron Conversion Unit, from where he flew his first operation on June 27 to Bremen.

The conversion unit was designed to help pilots 'convert' from two-engined aircraft such as the Wellington to four-engined aircraft such as the one then being used by 149 Squadron – the mighty Stirling. The Stirling, manufactured by Shorts Brothers of Belfast, was the first of the RAF's four-engined 'heavies' to enter service, and at that point in the war, the network of heavy conversion units (HCUs) that many subsequent pilots and crews enjoyed did not exist.

Having successfully completed his conversion from two to four engines, Philip joined 149 (East India) Squadron proper at Lakenheath the following month, and flew his second operation (his first with the squadron) on July 8 to Wilhelmshafen. The squadron at that time was commanded by Wing Commander Cecil Charlton-Jones (later to be replaced by Wing Commander Kenneth Wasse).

There then followed the relentlessness of squadron life, ticking off German cities as they were systematically bombed, one by one: Duisberg, Hamburg, Lübeck.

"My first trip to Hamburg was particularly fraught," Philip recalls. "The aircraft iced up over the North Sea, increasing weight and drag and impacting on the performance of the aircraft so severely that we doubted whether we could go on. With a little bit of skill and a great deal of luck we somehow managed to maintain height, and by the time we arrived over Hamburg we had made 10,000ft but could go no higher.

"Almost immediately we were coned by searchlights, a terrifying experience, and then attacked by a nightfighter that succeeded in scoring a number of hits on our aircraft. Our luck held, however, and we limped back to base. It had been a disastrous night all round. I believe some 300 aircraft had set out, and in the end only about 50 managed to find the target."

But it wasn't just to Germany that Philip dragged his aircraft and his crew night after night. Bomber Command was equally keen to show its Allies – and its public – that no Axis city was safe from British attack, and that included those under the jurisdiction of Il Duce Mussolini. And so they raided Genoa, Milan, Turin – all long hauls of eight hours or more. "On the way back from Milan," Philip says, "we were attacked by a single-engined Me109 at the French coast, but succeeded in giving it the slip."

One other flight of note occurred on November 11, Armistice Day, when Philip had as a passenger the distinguished figure of none other than Air Vice-Marshal The Hon Sir Ralph Cochrane. At the time, Cochrane was air officer commanding 3 Group, but would achieve fame – and some notoriety – from February 1943 onwards when he took command of 5 Group following the dismissal of Air Vice-Marshal Coryton by Harris.

"When Cochrane and I became acquainted, it was because he wanted to see for himself what it was like to take part in a low-level bombing operation – albeit a training one." Philip remembers:

"The squadron had its fair share of characters. Jock Watt, one of the flight commanders was a particularly 'press on' type who wanted to do every op, and had to be restrained, sometimes almost physically, from taking part. He would wait up all night for his crews to return, such was his feelings towards his men. I was also a contemporary and good friend of Ron Middleton, a quiet, earnest man whose steely determination proved instrumental in the award of his Victoria Cross."

Rawdon Hume Middleton, known simply as Ron, was a 26-year old from Waverley, Sydney. He was a keen cricketer and footballer, despite being slightly built. "He was a good-looking young man, very quiet and a little moody, with a strong streak of honest determination," according to Philip.

On October 14, 1940 Middleton enlisted in the Royal Australian Air Force under the Empire Air Training Scheme. He learned to fly at Narromine and received further instruction in Canada. Arriving in Britain in September 1941, he was promoted flight sergeant in December and posted to 149 Squadron in February 1942. After gaining experience as second pilot on Stirlings, he became first pilot and captain in July. Next month he was posted to 7 Squadron, RAF, but returned to 149 in September.

By November 28, 1942 Middleton had completed 28 operational flights. Three of his crew had already flown their quota of 30 and could have left, but decided to stay through loyalty to their skipper. Their sortie that night was to Turin, Italy. Over the target they were hit by flak. One shell exploded in the cockpit wounding Middleton. His right eye was destroyed and the bone above it exposed; he was probably also wounded in the body and legs.

With his aeroplane severely damaged, Middleton rejected the options of flying to Africa or baling out over German-occupied France and insisted on returning to England for the sake of the crew. The flight lasted more than four hours, during which he was in constant agony. He could barely see and suffered further pain when he spoke. On reaching the English coast, he flew over land so that his comrades could parachute safely. Five of them reached the ground and survived. He then turned back towards the English Channel to avoid crashing in a populated area. Two of the crew remained with their captain, parachuted into the sea and drowned. Middleton was too weak to leave the Stirling that crashed into the sea on the morning of November 29, 1942, taking him to his death. He was posthumously awarded the Victoria Cross and promoted pilot officer (with effect from November 15). Middleton's body was washed ashore at Shakespeare Beach, Dover, in February 1943 and buried in St John's churchyard, Beck Row, Suffolk, with full military honours. He won the first VC awarded to a member of the RAAF in World War II.

By the time that Philip's first tour ended, he had taken part in 31 operations, 29 as captain, of which 28 had been successfully completed. He was assessed by Wing Commander Wasse as an 'above average' heavy bomber pilot, and awarded the Distinguished Flying Cross for his troubles.

During all of this time, he flew with the same crew, and three of them – Sergeants Lee, Brown and Sage – would follow him on to his next squadron.

"From 149 Squadron, I was again posted as an instructor, joining 1651 Stirling Conversion Unit where my flying skills were tested to the limit by a number of exciting and excitable students. The Stirling was a beautiful aircraft to fly once in the air, but getting it off the ground and bringing it back down again required considerable skill.

Sitting in the flight offices, it was not unusual to hear a loud thump every now and again as another pupil brought in an aircraft for a rather heavy landing!

"Two students I remember in particular. One was a Pole, Pilot Officer Plonczynski, a pre-war civilian airline pilot. Once we landed, I remarked that there was nothing I could teach him that he didn't already know; in fact it was probably the other way around! The second was a young leading aircraftsman by the name of Beesey. Within two years, Beesey would have risen from LAC to squadron leader, and earned the DSO into the bargain."

It was not long before Philip's talents as a bomber pilot were again called for, and he was invited to join the Pathfinders, completing his PFF NTU in November 1943 under the watchful eye of Ernest Rodley (another of the Pathfinder 'greats'), and then on to 7 Squadron at Oakington under the command of Group Captain Kenneth Rampling. By this time he had gone from 'above average' to 'exceptional' as a heavy bomber pilot – a rating very rarely given.

His first operation with 7 Squadron was to Berlin on December 2, a major raid involving some 458 aircraft of which 40 were lost. For once the Germans had guessed accurately the target and managed to marshal their nightfighters above the city in time. Philip subsequently flew on nine further trips to Berlin, something of a squadron record.

Now flying Lancasters, on January 21/22, the crew completed an extremely eventful trip to Magdeberg, the first major raid on the city involving some 648 aircraft, as Philip describes:

"Flying over the target, the rear gunner – Jimmy Brown – could clearly see a fellow Lancaster about to be bounced by a German nightfighter. The Junkers Ju88 (a twin-engined nightfighter) swooped from above, setting the Lancaster on fire, but as it dived past, it flew directly into Brown's line of sight. He didn't hesitate. Bringing his guns to bear, he put in a long burst and had the satisfaction of seeing the fighter stagger and then burst into flames, its starboard engine billowing black smoke. He kept watching as the aircraft dived into the ground."

But the night was not yet over.

"As we flew over the sea on the return leg, we spotted another Lancaster far below in trouble, seeing her ditch in the Channel. The wireless op sent out a signal, giving the aircraft's last known position. Later, we were delighted to hear that the dinghy had been sighted and, not long after, the crew successfully picked up. It was a most satisfying end to a most exciting trip."

The Patrick crew seemed to attract trouble like the proverbial magnet. They were attacked again on their next trip to Berlin, successfully beating off two separate assaults from a Ju88 and an Fw190. Over Augsburg, their luck – or at least a large slice of it – finally ran out.

The date was February 25, 1944. The target, Augsburg. Augsburg had been the scene earlier in the war of one of Bomber Command's most ambitious raids, an unescorted daylight attack by 12 Lancasters from 44 and 97 Squadrons. Perhaps not surprisingly, the raid did not go according to plan. Perhaps also not surprisingly, the raid's leader – Squadron Leader John Nettleton – earned the Victoria Cross. Now they had learned their lesson, and were returning at night, a Lancaster's more natural environment, and this time with nearly 600 aircraft.

"Over the target, a Ju88 swooped, opened fire and struck a near fatal blow. Hydraulic lines were punctured and began spewing their contents into the insides of the aircraft. Oil too began spilling into the main fuselage which suddenly burst into flames.

"I began calling my crew to report in, but they heard nothing. The intercom had gone. That night we were flying with a second pilot, giving him his first taste of operational flying. I instructed him to go aft and report on the state of the mid-upper and rear gunners, Jimmy Brown and Jimmy Smith, since I had heard nothing from them since the fighter attacked.

"A rather ashen-faced deputy returned a few minutes later to report that there was good news, and there was bad. The good news was that the fire was out. The bad news was that so too were the mid-upper and rear gunners! They had baled out, certain, no doubt, that with the silence their skipper must have been killed, and that the aircraft was done for.

"We flew the return leg of the trip without hydraulics, and with the flaps locked in the down position, unable to move. Somehow we got back, albeit with two less crew than we started out. I had the sad duty of informing Jimmy Brown's wife in Perth that I had had to leave Jimmy behind."

By April 3, 1944, Philip had flown a further 21 operations to add to his tally of 28, and was now a flight commander. He maintained his 'exceptional heavy bomber pilot' rating, a certificate endorsed by the new squadron commander, Wing Commander Guy Lockhart.

Given his experience, it was perhaps not surprising when he was asked to be in the vanguard of forming a new squadron – 582 Squadron – then coming together at Little Staughton. The 'A' and 'B' Flight commanders – Squadron Leaders Walbourn and McMillan respectively – had already been chosen, but with his expertise, and his rank, he was placed in a supernumerary capacity in charge of training.

"The flight commanders' role included looking after the welfare of their men, and in particular keeping up squadron morale. It was not always easy. When operations were 'on', the flight commanders selected the crews to take part, and their names were chalked on the board hanging outside the flight office. If a crew failed to return, the name was rubbed out, and a new name written in its place.

"Against that background, it was not easy to keep people's spirits up, and sometimes they failed. It was not unheard of for a skipper or even an entire crew to have had enough. The flight commander might try and persuade them otherwise, but his words would fall on deaf ears. Then there was nothing they could do to prevent them being labelled 'LMF' – lacking in moral fibre, a coward by any other name. Then it was Sheffield, where all of the bad boys were sent, and then – who knows? No one seemed to know or care. They didn't have the time.

"The flight commanders were also responsible for organising specific training; cross-country, low flying, night flying, fighter affiliation, landings (standard beam approach or SBA flights), practice bombing, air-firing, 'Y' training (the codename for the ground radar H2S) etc."

This was where Philip came into his own, supporting the flight commanders in making sure the appropriate training was available and given. But it didn't stop him from flying on operations, or leading from the front.

Philip had with him two members of his very first crew at 149: Johnny Sage and Wally Lee. His regular navigator at 7 Squadron, Gordon Goodwin, had also been replaced. The balance of the crew now comprised Alan Drew (nav one), Alan Coleman (nav two – the H2S set operator), Jim Humphrey (bomb aimer), 'Taffy' Jacobs in the rear turret, and 'Hoppy' Dawson mid-upper gunner.

The crew took part in a number of the early sorties carried out by 582, including a highly successful trip to bomb the railway marshalling yards at Noisy-Le-Sec on April 18/19 where they obtained an excellent aiming point photograph. Two further trips to Düsseldorf and Karlsruhe were followed by their first trip as master bomber to attack more railway yards at Aulnoye.

Many of the attacks during this period were focused on

destroying the vast communications networks that criss-crossed
Europe allowing the Germans to move men and munitions great
distances at will. With the invasion of Europe only weeks away,
Harris was ordered to switch his tactics from carpet-bombing
German cities and industry to specific targets such as railway
marshalling yards that would prevent the enemy from rushing
troops to the front. As a result, rather than single, heavy raids of
more than 500 aircraft at a time, multiple, smaller raids, many with
less than 100 aircraft, now became the norm. It meant the
Pathfinders, however, became desperately stretched, having to
provide target-marking aircraft and master bombers for each raid.
At Aulnoye, on April 27, it became Philip's turn to take up the reins:

> "As master bomber, you needed all of your experience,
> guile, and luck. We would mark the target, and then circle
> to assess the results. If I was satisfied, I would instruct the
> main force to come in and bomb on my flares. If my aim
> was a little awry and off-target, I would instruct main force
> accordingly, telling them to bomb to the right or left or to
> undershoot or overshoot by seconds in relation to the
> markers."

At Aulnoye, his aim was bang on, and the target was almost
completely wiped out. Even though a handful of the main force
began bombing before receiving instructions to do so, the majority
concentrated their attack on the green TIs that had been dropped.
Philip stayed over the target area at some 4,000ft for 16 minutes,
continually issuing instructions, especially as the smoke from the
target indicators began to obscure the aiming point. His deputy
master bomber, the 'A' Flight commander Dickie Walbourn
continued to support Philip's efforts by dropping further flares. It
was an excellent example of master bombing, his deputy and main
force combined to achieve remarkable success. 582 Squadron
contributed 10 crews (out of a total force of 223 aircraft) to the
attack – a considerable achievement given that as a result of
operations to Essen the previous night, it could muster only seven
Lancasters the following morning, and had five listed as requiring
serious (category 'A') repairs. Extraordinary efforts on the part of
the ground crews, supported by 9582 Servicing Echelon, resulted in
the dispatch of the full quota of aircraft that evening – the 10 to
Aulnoye, and a further 14 to Friedrichshafen. All returned safely.

  If Aulnoye was a spectacular success, then Philip's next attack
was a dismal failure. The squadron put up 14 aircraft for an Oboe-
led raid on the Somain marshalling yards in northern France. Philip
was again master bomber, taking with him the bombing leader
Arthur Feeley. This time his deputy was a very experienced New
Zealander, Squadron Leader Harold Heney. Philip recalls:

"The initial Oboe marking from the attendant Mosquitoes was inaccurate, forcing me to instruct main force to wait and orbit – something they never liked doing. I descended to 3,000ft to be certain of the aiming point, and then marked it with a salvo of mixed green and yellow TIs, dropping my bombs at the same time. Ordering the main force to aim at the mixed yellows and greens, I also instructed Heney to 'back up' with his own TIs which he successfully did. Despite our best efforts, however, I had the impression at the time that the bombing was wildly inaccurate."

His impression was right. Most of the Halifaxes that comprised the majority of the main force either didn't hear or more likely chose to ignore Philip's orders and their bombs missed the target. Although some damage was inflicted on the yards, most of the bombs fell in open country.

Philip completed a further six trips with 582 Squadron, including one more as master bomber, achieving partial success with an attack on Louvain, hampered by severe interference on his radio transmission (R/T) as well as some clever 'spoof' broadcasts by the Germans urging his force in English to 'return to base'. He was also flying the night that Squadron Leader Heney DSO went missing, and on the morning of D-Day when the squadron lost yet another veteran, Squadron Leader Arthur Raybould DSO, DFM.

"On our way back from attacking the Montfleury light coastal battery I remember looking down and the whole channel seemed to be covered in ships. It was quite a sight."

On June 7/8 he arrived two minutes late over the target, having been stalked by an enemy fighter for about five minutes. He lost it by popping into a cloud and making a wide orbit. The following evening, whilst attacking Rennes airfield, it seemed somehow fitting that Philip ended his operational flying in the manner to which he had become accustomed – by being attacked by a fighter, this time another (unidentified) single-engined type. The gunners fired back and claimed several strikes, but nothing was confirmed.

Throughout all of his operational flying, Philip had the support of a good crew, some of whom stayed with him for two tours. Eric 'Hoppy' Dawson, his mid-upper gunner who had the privilege of being given his DFC by the King's own hand, was killed later in the year having completed over 100 operations; Jim Humphrey, the bomb aimer, opted to fly with Roy Pengilley; Wally Lee went on to fly Butch Harris' Dakota. 'Taffy' Jacobs, who had taken over in the rear turret, was especially sorry when Philip's tour came to an end, and was later shot down and became a POW following the near-disastrous raid on Castrop-Rauxel. Most, if not all of his loyal companions were decorated. Strangely, and perhaps perfectly illustrating the lottery and inconsistency in the distribution of awards, Philip received no recognition for his work on Pathfinders beyond his permanent Pathfinder badge, given to him on June 23, 1944. While others received DSOs or Bars to DFCs for their efforts, Philip went unrewarded. He suggests that his might have got lost in the post.

What does he think made a good crew?

"Mutual trust, and a confidence in one another's abilities. You had to; your life was quite literally in their hands. We didn't natter, we kept our comments to anything that was directly relevant to the job. How could you concentrate otherwise? My first trip before captaining my own aircraft was with a Canadian crew that did not stop talking. I vowed then that with my crew it would be different. And it was... What made a good captain was the ability to exert enough authority, whilst keeping everyone happy. In my case, I was very fortunate."

Chapter Two

A Squadron at War

April – June 1944

By the end of the second week of April, 1944, 582 Squadron could boast 36 fully operational crews. By the end of July, less than four months later, 11 of those crews were missing, either killed in action, evading, or prisoners of war. The end of the war – and safety – was still far away.

The squadron had become operational almost immediately, sending seven crews to the Lille marshalling yards on the night of April 9/10. The honour of dropping the first bombs went to Flying Officer Clyde Magee, a Torontonian who had originally enlisted as a gunner and who remustered as a pilot later in the war. The raid, which involved 239 aircraft in all, was only partially successful, and although two-thirds of the goods wagons were destroyed, a great number of local Frenchmen and women were killed and their houses destroyed.

Further attacks followed on Lâon, Aachen, Noisy-Le-Sec, and Cologne, until the night of April 22/23 when the squadron strength was divided, with seven aircraft detailed to attack Lâon, and seven to attack Düsseldorf. Lâon was the much smaller of the two raids, involving some 181 aircraft – a fairly even split between Halifaxes, Lancasters and Stirlings, supported by 12 Mosquitoes. Whilst the damage inflicted on the yards was considerable, the raid also accounted for the loss of the master bomber, the 30-year-old Wing Commander Alan Cousens DSO, DFC, MC (Czech) of 635 Squadron. A closer loss to 582 Squadron was the news that Flight Sergeant Bernard Wallis and his crew had failed to return. The 20-year-old Kiwi's aircraft, JA933 – which had logged some 352 hours – was shot down by a nightfighter and exploded, crashing in flames at Dives, north east of Compiègne, killing all on board. This included two 19-year olds, Henry Collins and Joseph McGinn.

The squadron was lucky not to lose another crew that same day when Lancaster ND737 'hit some houses' on take-off and crash-landed, being written-off. Behind that bland statement 'hit some houses', however, lies a rather more involved and interesting story involving the Church and GOD.

GOD was the nickname of the pilot of ND737 'E' Easy, Flying Officer Godfrey O'Donovan, a man loved by his all-NCO crew but, it appears, a character few others found so endearing. O'Donovan, also known as 'OD', was an ex-156 Squadron type, and a master flyer. That day, however, he got it all wrong. The morning was bright and sunny, and the crew was joined by an experienced set operator, Syd Johnson, tasked with teaching them about the latest H2S variant, the Mark III. For reasons best known to O'Donovan, at the intersection of the two runways he turned the aircraft so that it was facing the wrong way, i.e. lined up with the shortest part of the runway from which to take off. It may have been a deliberate move because of the wind, or it may simply have been that O'Donovan was already a little flak happy. Whatever the reason, rather than turn about he called for 'full power' and they were rolling. Remarkably the Lancaster managed to gain enough speed to make it into the air but within moments there was a sickening crash as the undercarriage wheel clipped the top of a church steeple.

O'Donovan immediately tried to lock the whole undercart down; the port wheel locked but the starboard wheel swung lifelessly in the slipstream. Rather than try to land with only one wheel in the correct position, he attempted to retract the port wheel, but without success. Stubbornly he repeated the exercise and equally stubbornly the wheels refused to play ball. Flying Control was by now well aware of their predicament, and directed O'Donovan to make for the emergency landing ground at Woodbridge, near Ipswich. GOD consulted with the rest of his crew, giving them the option of baling out. All agreed to stay put, one even answering 'what for?' Approaching Woodbridge, they opened the escape hatches and assumed crash positions. Bringing the Lancaster in for final approach, the aircraft was just a few feet above the ground when it stalled. O'Donovan managed to hold the unsupported starboard wing above the tarmac in a brilliant piece of airmanship before the whole aircraft finally fell to earth. The port wing reared, and the Lancaster did a complete about-face. The crew expected fire, but none came. It was the end, however, for 'E' Easy. God seemed to be very much on GOD's side!

O'Donovan was lucky again a few days later over Essen. 14 aircraft were detailed for operations; 13 took off and two returned early. Of the others that made it back, many were damaged by heavy flak. O'Donovan's aircraft received damage to the astrodome, the rear part of the cabin, the roof, starboard outer, and No. 2 fuel tank. His wireless operator, Sergeant Taylor, was also wounded in the right hand.

Warrant Officer Ray Rember also received the unwelcome attention of the German flak batteries, taking hits to the trailing edge of his starboard wing. Flying Officer John Goddard's Lancaster ND623 was also struck, with shrapnel piercing the bomb aimer's perspex, no doubt to the latter's consternation. An Australian, Pilot Officer Smith, another from 156 Squadron who had only recently been commissioned, had a dreadful night. His aircraft, for reasons unknown, was not able to gain operational height, leaving him to bomb from only 11,000 feet – some 7,000 or even 8,000 feet lower than his colleagues. Not surprisingly he was hit by flak, with the rear turret blown off. His rear gunner, however, escaped unscathed.

May started where April had ended. Badly. Indeed doubly so.

The target was a relatively innocuous one. A Luftwaffe airfield at Montdidier. The raid was only a small one: 84 Lancasters and eight Mosquitoes. Four of the Lancasters were lost. Two of them flown by Canadian pilots from 582 Squadron. Flight Lieutenant Freddie Bertelsen's aircraft was intercepted by a German nightfighter and shortly afterwards was seen to explode. The crew, mainly ex-7 Squadron and which included three Canadians and an Australian, all perished. The second aircraft, flown by Pilot Officer Charles O'Neill came down at Beaulieu-les-Fontaines, north-west of Noyon. O'Neill, who had arrived at 582 via 576 and 156 Squadrons was killed with most of his crew. His nav two, Flying Officer Armstrong, got out in one piece and was picked up by three local Frenchmen and was taken to their home for the night. The following morning, Monsieur Norbert Corrion, chief of the Resistance for the area, took him to his home in Lassigny where he stayed for three weeks before being moved on to the village of Canny. There he remained until 3rd September in the care of a Belgian, Monsieur Can Laere, and his son Jean who was engaged in numerous acts of sabotage. He was liberated soon after.

The attack on Montdidier occurred on the night of May 3/4, 1944. A much larger raid was undertaken that night by a force of almost 350 Lancasters and 14 Mosquitoes on a German troop concentration at Mailly-le-Camp. It was a disaster of epic proportions with 42 of the Lancasters shot down, including the deputy master bomber. It was little consolation to 582, but had they gone to Mailly-le-Camp their casualties might have been higher.

As May progressed, the targets became more obviously related to the planned invasion of Europe: the marshalling yards at Nantes-Grasssicourt, Louvain, Boulogne, Tergnier and Aachen; the airfields at Chateau Bougon and St Jacques; gun emplacements at Cap Griz Nez and Mardyck; a radar-jamming station at Mont Couple. The major cities, however, could not be ignored for long, with attacks recorded on Duisberg (a Wanganui attack comprising flares of red with yellow stars because of the weather) and Dortmund being singled out for special attention.

Over Nantes-Grasssicourt, Flight Sergeant Freddie Gipson reported seeing a Lancaster hit by a bomb from another aircraft that

immediately blew up. Gipson's Lancaster was in turn hit by
fragments of bomb casing increasing the ventilation in his own
aircraft but fortunately not seriously so.

Over Aachen on May 24/25 the squadron lost yet another crew,
this one skippered by yet another experienced Canadian, Flight
Lieutenant Stuart Little DFC. 'Sam' Little joined 156 from 166
Squadron in December 1943, and had completed 18 Pathfinder
sorties by the time he arrived at 582. At 30, Sam was a little older
than his contemporaries, and was a popular man on the squadron.
His loss was keenly felt by all, none more so than by his regular mid-
upper gunner, Tommy MacLachlan who had been granted
compassionate leave to visit his terminally ill father, and so was not
flying that night. His place had been taken by a 20-year-old gunner,
Bernard Webb, who died with the rest of the crew when the aircraft
was hit by flak and fell onto Schutzenstrasse in the centre of Aachen.
Tommy went on to be crewed with 'Joe' Street.

An even greater tragedy, if such things can be measured, was the
loss of the New Zealand Squadron Leader Harold Heney two nights
later, killed whilst attacking the airfield at St Jacques. The loss is
given even greater poignancy by the entry in the operations record
book (ORB) on May 27 that records the award of Heney's
immediate DSO on the same day that he was shot down and killed.

Heney, sometimes known as 'Pat', had completed no fewer than
59 trips, and had attained master bomber status. Indeed he had
recently led the raid on Cap Griz Nez. He won his DSO for a
magnificent display of airmanship during his bombing run over
Dortmund on the night of May 22/23 when his aircraft was hit by
incendiaries dropped from above. One struck his port rudder, and a
second lodged in his port outer engine, where it exploded, setting the
engine ablaze. Despite the fire, Heney completed his bombing run,
took the necessary photograph, and then feathered the engine. He
ordered the crew to stand-by to bale out, by which time flames were
streaking back 50 yards behind his aircraft.

As if things couldn't get any worse, their Lancaster was then
picked out by searchlights. Heney threw the aircraft into a dive,
trying to lose the beam and extinguish the flames. It didn't work, at
least not immediately.

By this time he was down to 13,000ft, trying to get clear of the
target. Then, almost as suddenly as they started, the flames seemed
to go out, although his problems were far from over. Whilst flying
through the Ruhr, between Cologne and Munchengladbach, he fell
victim to predicted flak, striking the aircraft several times. Steadily
losing height, Heney's Lancaster managed to avoid further damage,
eventually making the English coast. Even then he was far from safe.
At about 2,500ft above the airfield at Mepal in Cambridgeshire he
came under attack from a German intruder below and from the rear.
With his rear turret out of action, he was effectively a sitting duck,

but somehow managed a corkscrew to starboard and out of harm's way, but not before the Lancaster had again been raked from stem to stern. Fortunately no one was injured. With his hydraulics shot away, Heney was forced into carrying out emergency landing procedures, manually bringing down the undercarriage and flaps, and making it safely home to base, even, as it transpired later, with a 500-pound bomb hung up in his bomb bay. The aircraft was a 'cat E' – damaged beyond repair.

Heney was recommended for an immediate DSO, his citation making reference to the large number of sorties in which he had participated. Interestingly it does not mention how Heney's aircraft came to catch fire as such 'accidents' should not be seen to happen in the eyes of the general public.

The incident seems to have affected Heney considerably. The CO, Charles Dunnicliffe, in announcing the award to the assembled squadron, chose to make a joke of the event, suggesting that Heney shouldn't have been where he was in the first place. Heney, white faced and visibly shaking, got up and went to walk out, only to be hastily asked to return by an embarrassed CO who went on to tell him about his DSO. It was a misjudgment, but an understandable one. Few can have perhaps understood just how red raw Heney's emotions must have been after such an encounter.

Pat Heney's luck ran out over Rennes. Heney was flying as deputy to Dickie Walbourn, and had just been asked to re-inforce the red TIs when there was a break in transmission. His aircraft appeared to be enveloped in a mass of red and green as it exploded, coming down on the western edge of the target area. There were no survivors.

Four crews were lost in May; 28 good men. June was no better.

Whereas the previous six weeks had seen several attacks on targets in preparation for the Allied assault on Europe, when the invasion became a reality such attacks were given even greater pertinence. There was great pride amongst the crews (and not just within PFF) to fly on D-Day, but it also spelled the end for another 582 Squadron crew, skippered by Squadron Leader Arthur Raybould DSO, DFM.

Again the operation was only comparatively small, and the services of the squadron split between assaults on various coastal batteries, both light and heavy, including Montfleury and Longues. Raybould and 10 other 582 aircraft were tasked with taking out a light coastal battery at Longues, taking off a little after three o'clock in the morning of June 6. Each aircraft carried the same payload: two 500-pound general purpose bombs and 11 1,000-pounders. The attack achieved only partial success.

Raybould, a veteran of 78 trips, was lost without trace, and with it his experience. He had won the Distinguished Flying Medal whilst as an NCO flying with 101 Squadron in 1942; he added a DSO as a flight lieutenant with 105 Squadron, the citation describing him as: 'an outstanding captain, whose gallant example, dogged determination and unfailing devotion to duty have set an example of the highest order.' It also made reference to his participating in attacking 'a wide variety of targets, including Essen, Hamburg, Dortmund and Cologne.'

And it wasn't just Raybould's experience that was lost that night. Three of his crew, Henry Kitto, John Papworth, and Dennis Johnson held either the DFC or DFM, and Johnson, a pre-war regular, was a flight lieutenant – a lofty rank indeed for a rear gunner. Also missing was the squadron bombing leader, Arthur Feeley DFC who had won his DFC in 1943 with 83 Squadron. Flight Lieutenant Coleman was posted in to replace him.

The squadron was on ops again the following evening, when the CO survived a brief skirmish with fighters, and Flight Lieutenant Robert Sexton's gunners similarly fought off a determined attack by a Me110. Sexton's mid-upper gunner, Flight Sergeant Wright was wounded in the foot in the exchange of fire, and his Australian skipper was forced to put down at Manston.

They flew again on the 9th and 11th, but operations on the 12th and 13th were later cancelled. The next two days called for attacks against Douai and Lens, and two more 582 aircraft were lost, those being flown by Flight Lieutenant John Hewitt DFC, and the 21-year-old Pilot Officer Norman Tutt.

Hewitt took off at 00.24 to bomb a locomotive depot in Douai. He was master bomber. Intercepted by German nightfighters over the target, his Lancaster was shot out of the sky, coming down near Adinkerke in Belgium with the loss of his whole crew, nearly all of whom had been decorated. The crew included two ex-156 NCOs, Pilot Officer Harry Wilson and Pilot Officer Vincent Crosby, both of whom had had their DFMs gazetted on June 2 – less than two weeks earlier. Crosby, who was 33 – positively ancient in aircrew terms – came from Sligo in the Irish Republic. Other casualties in the crew included Pilot Officer Robert Clenahan DFC, Pilot Officer Denis Flynn DFC, Warrant Officer Walter Smith DFC, Flight Sergeant Albert Bouch DFM, and Flight Sergeant Gilbert Cottrell.

Clyde Magee, the Canadian who had dropped 582 Squadron's first bombs in anger, also almost came to grief. Attacked by a Messerschmitt 410, Germany's answer to the De Havilland Mosquito but nothing like as successful, he was not able to assess the accuracy of the bombing and had his aerial shot away.

Norman Tutt was also shot down by a nightfighter whilst attacking the marshalling yards at Lens, the wreckage coming down in the north-west suburbs of Arras. Tutt, like Hewitt, had been amongst the first crews posted to 582 Squadron. He had been 'lucky' over Duisberg the previous month when his aircraft was hit by heavy flak, blowing the Perspex cover off the H2S scanner. Now his luck had run out. Within his crew, only the wireless operator, Flight Sergeant Boots, made it out in one piece and survived, while the rest perished in the flames.

The month ended on a sad note with the loss of the Spierenberg crew, although there was some comfort weeks later when three of the crew turned up alive and well, and their skipper was confirmed as a POW.

The loss of so many men in such a short space of time – 57 killed, prisoners, or on the run in less than six weeks – meant new crews had to be drafted in to replace them. Amongst those airman arriving in June were a number whose stories are yet to be told, including two South Africans with their distinctive khaki uniforms and South African Air Force (SAAF) insignia – 'Tiny' Shurlock and Ted Swales.

New crews were also matched with new targets, and a new menace – the Vergeltungswaffe 1 – the first of Hitler's 'Vengeance' weapons that could help win him the war; a crude, but nonetheless lethal, cruise missile.

For the time being, however, the squadron already had enough to worry about.

HEAVEN CAN WAIT

The story of Revd (former Flight Sergeant) Les Hood, nav two, 582 Squadron

Les Hood wanted to fly from the day he could walk, but his mother wouldn't let him. It took a certain Adolf Hitler to enable Les to fulfil his boyhood dream. It was the start of an adventure that would take him to France and back by air and by foot, and he in time became one of the happy few who joined both the Caterpillar Club for the successful evacuation of an aircraft by parachute, and the order of the Flying Boot for evading capture and making it home to fight another day.

> "One of the first Frenchmen I spoke to early on that morning in June 1944 was a keen gardener. I know he was keen because the sun had just come up and it was approaching five o'clock! He looked up, saw an English airman, hatless, without badges of rank or a brevet and with flying boots tucked inside his trouser legs, and said nothing. In my best schoolboy French I asked how far it was to Paris. He replied: 'Quatre-vingt dix kilometres,' and resumed his digging. By then I had walked west-south-west during the hours of darkness since two o'clock, taking directions from the stars – which I learned to do in the cubs – and making for Paris."

Not for the first time that day, his thoughts turned to home, and how a young mining engineer who had been 'through the shop' experiencing every part of pit life had now come to find himself sitting in a ditch, somewhere in France, with no boots on having an incongruous conversation with a French jardinier.

Born in Seaham, Les' love of flying had led him to become a founding member of Seaham Air Training Corps in April 1941, and he volunteered for the RAF a month later. Even though mining was a reserved occupation, making him exempt from military duty, it was a privilege he chose to ignore. Like thousands before him, and many after, he journeyed down to London and the Aircrew

Reception Centre (ACRC) then situated at Lord's cricket ground, billeted in some comfort in the surrounding apartments. Having been formally accepted, he was subsequently despatched via troopship to Durban, travelling onwards to Rhodesia for pilot training.

"I remember well our arrival in Durban. We were greeted by 'The Woman in White' singing patriotic songs. Apparently she was there for the arrival of every troopship. It was a very emotional moment. It was the first time for many of us that we had been away – and such a long way – from home."

Les passed through EFTS (flying Tiger Moth biplanes) without a problem, but at SFTS, trying to master the twin-engined Oxfords, the powers-that-be decided Les would make a better navigator than pilot. Remustered, he was passed on to 24 Combined Air Observer School (CAOS) at RAF Moffat:

"I was disappointed not to make pilot. I was one of three being assessed, and there were only two who were going to be put forward. I missed out, and it broke my heart, but I really took to navigating and enjoyed it. We were all so young and keen, we wanted to get on and be the best."

Before leaving for Rhodesia, Les had met and fallen in love with a local girl, Olive. Given advanced pay, he decided to blow it all on a ring. Arriving back in England on November 18 , he went on leave on the 23rd and married Olive on the 27th. Shortly after he was posted to an advanced (acclimatisation) flying unit at RAF Mileham to complete his training, passing out at the top of his class.

"A pal of mine, Dennis King (who ultimately went on to 405 Squadron), and I passed out as the top two in our class and were told we were going on to Pathfinders. At first I refused, but then I found out that the others were being posted to a glider towing unit so quickly changed my mind. Originally I was informed I was going to 7 Squadron, but ended up at NTU at Warboys, and was then posted to 582 Squadron."

Arriving at 582 Squadron the week after its formation, Les was temporarily a 'spare bod' without a permanent crew, although this was quickly to change. Whilst in the mess one evening, he met Splinter Spierenberg, a Dutch pilot and squadron 'entertainments officer' who was short of a nav two. They instantly hit it off.

Splinter (also known as 'Don') had been born in The Hague and upon leaving school he attended the Netherlands merchant navy college. Serving on tankers, he twice had ships torpedoed from under him before deciding instead to join the RAF. He reached 582 Squadron in April 1944 via 115 Squadron (3 Group), by which time he had become an experienced operator.

Their first trip as a new crew was to Noisy-Le-Sec. This was as uneventful as their next operation was dramatic, filing the squadron's first combat report with nightfighters on the night of April 22/23 whilst attacking Düsseldorf:

> "Rear gunner (Sergeant Coole) sighted enemy aircraft on starboard quarter up, at approximately 400 yard range, identified as Ju88. Rear gunner gave pilot immediate orders to corkscrew starboard. This was carried out with both gunners opening fire. No hits claimed on enemy aircraft which then broke away to starboard quarter up. Another attack was made by same aircraft from port quarter up, at a range of 500 yards. Lancaster went into port corkscrew, with both gunners opening fire. Hits were claimed in nose of enemy aircraft which broke away to port beam down, coming round to make another attack from starboard quarter up. Lancaster 'R' (JD417) carried out a further corkscrew to starboard when enemy aircraft was at 500 yards range. Both gunners opened fire at range of approximately 450 yards. No hits were claimed on enemy aircraft, but Lancaster 'R' sustained damage to starboard fin and starboard side of bomb bay. Enemy aircraft then broke away to port quarter up, only to come round to starboard quarter to make fourth attack. This attack again commenced at approximately 500 yards range. Lancaster went into another starboard corkscrew at the same time that both gunners gave long bursts, claiming hits on port engine of enemy aircraft. Enemy aircraft broke away to starboard quarter down with flames pouring from port engine. It was last seen doing a vertical dive into cloud below with port engine on fire and was not seen again."

Sergeant Douggie Coole and Sergeant Bobby Chelu – the mid-upper gunner – between them fired some 700 rounds.

Apart from their next trip to Essen, where they were hit by heavy flak, the Spierenberg crew (which as well as Splinter, Les, Douggie and Bobby included Bill Foley – nav one – and wireless operator 'Johnny' Austin) logged a further 10 operations without incident. They were next briefed for an attack on Blainville sur l'Eau on the evening of June 28/29, flying with Harold Siddons as flight engineer, and on the way to the target fell foul of a German nightfighter flown by a recognised 'ace' Oberleutnant Drünkler of I/NJG5 chalking up his 17th kill. In the first attack the enemy aircraft shot the rudder away. Although Splinter managed to right the machine, part of the wing had also been hit, the intercom had gone dead and so he gave the order to bale out. Les recounts:

"We were attacked three or four times shortly after crossing the coast. We knew we'd been hit and in the last attack, hit badly. Our gunners were good but couldn't have seen him. I pulled the curtain back that covered our navigator's compartment and could see flames coming out of the engines on the starboard side. The aircraft began to vibrate and shudder violently. The skipper asked for help up front and to prepare to abandon aircraft.

"I quickly chewed and swallowed the rice paper with the secret codes on them, and although I was meant to blow up the H2S set, I didn't. I was sitting closest to Don and he used to fly with a rabbit's tail on the back of his helmet. I distinctly remember seeing this tail swinging around on the back of his head. I helped Don out of his Sutton harness so he could make his escape. I didn't have my own helmet on so couldn't hear any instructions to bale out but Bill tapped me on the shoulder and pointed to the hatch. We had been told in training that it took eight seconds to get out of a Lancaster. It seemed much longer.

"We didn't have any parachute instruction but I went out head first. It may sound daft but I wanted to be on my back before I pulled the cord. It was a chest-type parachute and I didn't want to get hurt. I remember the moon coming over the side of me, then my feet, then my head as I was clearly falling head over heels. There was total silence, and no sense of falling.

"I pulled the D-ring and the parachute opened with a crack and pulled me up sharply in my tracks. It was quite a jerk. I could see an aircraft on fire, seemingly miles away but actually I was going to land in the same field. Below me I thought I was landing in the middle of a German camp, as I could see what looked like lots of small huts. The huts turned out to be small haystacks.

"I hit the ground and rolled over. All I could see were these huge flames, high in the air, and realised it was our own. I then remembered that our bombs and target indicators were still on board, and as I ran away I could see the green TIs igniting."

Les ran across the field, taking off his parachute and harness and hiding them under one of the haystacks. He also removed all insignia and badges of rank, and sat for a moment, catching his breath. His first thought was of the others in his crew, but he could see no one. He therefore decided to put as much distance between himself and the burning aircraft as possible, and set off before the German search parties arrived.

At daybreak he found a small wood in which to hide and tried to sleep. Sleep proved impossible, of course, and there was an urgent restlessness to be active and on his way, hence his meeting with the French gardener. It was to be the first of several encounters that day, all of them, fortunately, helpful. He breakfasted with a family in a little cottage outside a small village near Coincy, and in the afternoon a farmer's wife on her doorstep gave him something to eat and drink. Later that afternoon, using his escape map, he came to a crossroads, and sat down under some bushes to plan his next move:

> "I was surprised to hear voices and, hoping for help, raised my head to look along the road where – to my great surprise and horror – two German soldiers were cycling towards me. If they were a search party they were very casual for they rode straight on quietly chatting and smoking whilst I, hugging the ground closely, was really afraid that they would hear my heart beating. Then it began to rain and I was soaked to the skin."

Les made his way back to the farm and asked the farmer's wife to dry his clothes. She sent him upstairs but soon after asked him to leave as her baby grand-daughter had arrived with her mother, and she feared for their safety should a German patrol arrive. Unhappily, but understanding their predicament, Les put his wet clothes back on and set off for Monteuil-aux-lions.

By a village pond a few kilometres further on, he was recognised as a British airman by a group of women who gave him milk and some eggs. He was followed as he set off again by a young boy on a bicycle who, after a few cautious attempts, finally made contact and escorted Les to a farm where he was to remain for the next few days. He was at last in touch with the French underground.

At the farm he was given labourer's clothes and taught how to milk a cow. He was constantly kept busy; he was also constantly watched, until one day three men arrived to interrogate him:

> "They thought I was a German trying to infiltrate their evasion line. They asked where I had hidden my parachute so I told them. They then went off to look for it as they did not believe that I had covered 30km in a single day, even though I was able to recite the names of the villages I had passed. They found my 'chute, but didn't tell me. Thank goodness they did, because in the next room was a fourth man with a loaded revolver ready to shoot me if my story

didn't check out. I was also asked to ride a bike around the courtyard. Apparently that was another test; every Englishman knows how to ride a bike!"

Later that same week, Les was taken by pony and trap to a safe house in Charly-sur-Marne. He had company: an American airman who had broken his ankle and could not be moved. A Dutchman, who he later found out was called Aandre, came to see him and said that he would be taken to Paris in a 'trunk'. To Les' relief, he actually meant a 'truck', although in the end Aandre turned up with a motorcycle. Bundled into a large overcoat, Les was taken to Livry-Gargan, slightly to the east of Paris, and to the headquarters of the local Resistance:

> "Our hosts were the family of the chief, Monsieur Nicholas, who was an amazing character, partly paralysed, but very active and resourceful. I was moved to a house on the outskirts of the town that belonged to the manager of a plaster of Paris factory. He was then sheltering four pilots – three English and one American. The latter was moved to another larger house nearby and was replaced by an English pilot who arrived on a stretcher by ambulance one Sunday afternoon, disguised as an accident victim."

Les stayed with M. et Mme. Renault, his new hosts, for the remainder of the time he was in hiding, albeit that they had some freedom of movement, even visiting the nearby American evaders for tea. Jeff Morris, a Spitfire pilot, made a chess set from odds and ends of wood and a cigarette rolling machine to help pass the time. André and Micheline Couvert brought Les some Gauloises; M. Renault grew his own tobacco in the garden, but it was better not to smoke it.

> "Providing food for us must have been very difficult; I know that the Renaults sold their car to help. We made coffee for ourselves by long-roasting grain and other stuff meant for the hens. When it went black it was ground, and the brew was drunk with closed eyes.
>
> "July 14 was a special day when all in town, by common consent, decided to do no work. M. Nicholas, supported by Jeff and me on either side, went to the town square where some Frenchmen were working on the German HQ building. M. Nicholas was furious and berated them at the top of his voice, he was soon joined by others who were equally incensed. The commotion grew until the Germans called out the guard who faced us with rifles levelled. The uneasy silence was broken by a little

white dog whose tail had been painted red, white and blue which ran yapping among the crowd and the soldiers who all began laughing. M. Renault arrived in time to hurry M. Nicholas and we two away."

Final salvation came in the form of the American military, but not before one last adventure:

"Early one morning the Germans arrived and ordered everyone out as they wanted to use the house as a strong point. M. Renault asked for time to remove his valuables and was given half an hour. His 'valuables' were fast asleep having heard nothing, but we quickly made our way to the canal. Jeff and I sat on the bank and fished all day, watching a Tiger tank that was stationed on the bridge not far away. The other two – Bill Geeson*, a Lancaster pilot and Jack Brandt, the CO of a Typhoon squadron – went to the local co-op store and spent all day on its roof where we joined them at dusk. The following day after more false alarms and reports, a tank nosed around the corner of the square. It was American."

Les was repatriated, and gave an account of his escape to MI9 on his return. It was also the first time he would hear of the fate of the others in his crew. Bobby Chelu, Douggie Coole and Johnny Austin had all been killed. They had had the terrible bad luck of landing amongst the wreckage of the crashed bomber. Harold Siddons, the flight engineer who had been first through the hatch, was already home.

  Bill Foley, a 30-year-old Australian schoolteacher in civilian life, baled out and landed near Armentières. Hiding his parachute, harness and Mae West (life preserver) he began walking south-west, and then hid in a wood until the afternoon. Setting off again, at dusk he arrived in a village and spent that night and the following day in a shed. On the evening of June 30 he called at a house in the village and struck lucky. He was given help, and heard that Splinter Spierenberg had called at the same house but two nights previously. The following day, a man arrived and took him to a further safehouse where he remained for the next fortnight. Whilst there, he heard that Bobby and Douggie were dead, and a third body, that of a Canadian airman named Brevis had also been found. The Resistance took him to another farm and then on to their headquarters in Beuvardes. Conveyed further down the line, he made contact with the Allied forces and returned to the UK by boat.

* Flying Officer W P Geeson, a pilot with 625 Squadron, had been shot down on an operation to bomb rail facilities at Achères on the night of June 10/11. He and four others within his crew evaded capture.

Despite the initial optimism about Splinter, the good news soon turned to bad. Although picked up and making it as far as Paris, his luck ran out whilst hiding in the Hotel Etoile. A contact arrived and told him to get ready for a journey to Lyons. Splinter followed the man downstairs and into the waiting car, where he instantly knew something was wrong, and sure enough he had been betrayed. First taken to the Palais de Securité, he then spent four brutal months in the hands of the SS and Gestapo, firstly at the infamous Fresnes prison in Paris and then onto the equally infamous Buchenwald concentration camp. 'Rescued' from Buchenwald by the Luftwaffe Polizei, he was transferred to Stalag Luft III, Sagan, the scene of the 'Great Escape' earlier that year, where he made his own escape from a wood-cutting party with a Squadron Leader Mathers. Despite being free for five days, they were eventually recaptured and taken to Milag Nord in Bremen, where three weeks later they were liberated by the Guards armoured brigade.

After he was shot down, a letter was sent to Les' mother from the air ministry informing her that he was 'missing'. A more personal letter was despatched to his wife by the squadron CO, Charles Dunnicliffe, describing him as a 'popular member of the squadron'. A further letter was sent to his mother soon after to say that he was safe and on the run, but that she was not to say anything in case it prejudiced his escape.

"It was already too late," Les concludes. "My mother just ran out into the street and shouted it from the roof tops!"

THE MILE HIGH CLUB

The story of Flight Lieutenant George Hall DFC & Bar, DFC (US), pilot, 582 Squadron

George Hall arrived at 582 Squadron, one of the first crews to be posted in, as a virtual novice. He left a seasoned veteran, flying on operations continually for nine months without respite, completing 56 operations including a number of trips as master bomber for which he won the DFC & Bar. He was also awarded the DFC by the United States. He's still not quite sure why!

One evening, coming back from an exhausting operation, tired, and with the strain of combat beginning to tell, George Hall lined his Lancaster up for final approach, as he had done countless times before. But this time it was different.

> "Something was wrong. As we descended, I could see the runway clearly marked. Too clearly, perhaps. Rather than the usual lights, the whole area seemed to be illuminated by two sheets of flame. I couldn't believe it at first. It took just a brief second for me to realise this was a FIDO* runway, with my landing delineated by thousands of gallons of burning fuel. But we didn't have FIDO. A second after that and I thought 'this must be Graveley', and not my home of Little Staughton. Within moments I had the wheels up, throttles 'through the gate' (i.e. fully forward into the 'extra boost' position for maximum revs) and the landing was aborted and my potential embarrassment saved."

This incident is typical of a pilot kept on operations for so long – perhaps even too long – without rest, but by the end of 1944, with the end in sight, the urge to go on was still very powerful, even though the odds were stacked heavily against pilots with George's experience making it through in one piece. Even if the German flak

---

* FIDO stood for Fog Investigation and Dispersal Operation and was a method of clearing fog by burning thousands of gallons of petrol along specially-designed perforated tubes set alongside the runway. Only a handful of airfields were thus equipped.

or fighters didn't get him, the risk of accidents brought on by mechanical failure or even pilot error remained very real indeed.

George Hall had joined the volunteer reserve of the RAF – with its distinctive 'VR' flash on his uniform lapel – in February 1941. A grammar school boy, at that time he was working at the local authority in the health department – the same local authority where his father, a veteran of the First World War, had worked for 50 years in the town clerk's office. Passing his preliminary tests at Padgate in April, he was finally called up in August 1941 to train as a pilot, with the first leg of his journey starting at Lord's at much the same time as Les Hood:

> "We were billeted in beautiful new flats that had been built but never occupied. That didn't mean we lived in any great comfort, however. We had to sleep on the floor, on 'biscuits' as we called them – straw-filled mattresses."

Initial training wing was in Scarborough which, being a 'local' lad from the north-east, proved the perfect posting. Whereas to many the 'frozen north' was a misery, particularly on the coast, to George, with relatives living in the town and his parents not so far away, it proved ideal. Indeed it allowed his family to be around him to celebrate his 21st birthday.

> "From ITW I was sent to 4EFTS in Brough (May 6, 1942), and went solo within seven hours. The first time I was sent off on my own – and was allowed to leave the circuit, I thought I'd take it up to 4,000ft and put her into a spin. We had been told in lectures how to get out of it – full opposite rudder and stick forward – so I gave it a go. The fact that I am here today meant that I must have got it right!"

Having successfully completed the first part of his pilot training, George kicked his heels at the RAF central repository for unwanted airmen, Heaton Park, before receiving news that he would shortly be on his way to the United States via Canada. But then the air ministry intervened.

> "At that stage of the war, too many of our aircrew under training were being washed out for minor disciplinary offences – uniform not clean, ties not straight that sort of thing. They decided therefore that I was to stay in Canada and train with the Royal Canadian Air Force. The result was that six weeks after arriving in Moncton (31 Personnel Despatch) I was 'absorbed' into the RCAF and then posted to 19 EFTS at Verdon in the province of Manitoba."

By now it was August 1942. Two months later his sojourn abroad was coming to an end, having passed every exam the authorities could throw at him at 10 SFTS Dauphin. It was then back to 31 PD, and the long journey back to England, arriving at 7 Personnel Despatch Centre (PDC) Harrogate on March 17, 1943 and on to 15 EFTS Carlisle (April 8, 1943).

Now the pace of training accelerated. Within a month he was at 6 Advanced Flying Unit (AFU) Little Rissington and its satellite (Windrush), learning to acclimatise to the blacked-out conditions of England, before moving on to 30 OTU at Hixon. From Hixon, piloting a twin-engined Wellington, George flew his first operational sortie. It was not untypical for crews to fly Nickel sorties whilst still training – stooging around the French coast to disrupt and confuse the German counter offensive to the bomber threat. George, however, went one better, dropping eight, 500-pound bombs on a German long-range gun battery in Boulogne:

> "It was the first and only time we were ever coned by searchlights," he recalls. "It was like walking along Piccadilly in broad daylight with no clothes on."

George's sustained period of training was nearly over. Sent to 1667 HCU Faldingworth on Halifaxes he added a flight engineer and additional gunner to complete his crew which now comprised three Canadians: Len Stewart, Lloyd Taggart and Art Day; and three Brits: Phil Tovey, Les Bellinger and Tommy Nichol. George found some of the flying at Faldingworth amongst the most 'hairy' he had experienced to date. Many of the aircraft had already far exceeded their sell-by date, and, George suspected, were using very low octane fuel.

> "It was a wonder that they managed to get off the ground at all, some of them. I believe that had an engine failed on take-off, it would have gone straight in."

With the pilot and crew now converted onto four engines, it was finally necessary for them to convert to the actual aircraft they would be using on operations: the Lancaster. With Lancasters then still in short supply, and squadrons already overburdened, the solution was to form specific training units, known as Lancaster Finishing Schools, to which crews being posted to Lancaster squadrons could be sent to gain more intimate knowledge of the type. At No 1 LFS Hemswell, George took the pilot's seat for the first time:

> "The Lancaster was an excellent aircraft to fly. Very responsive. Very well balanced, with the weight of the

bombs evenly distributed compared to the Halifax. After only six hours in the type, they seemed happy with me, and I received my first operational posting to 101 Squadron based at Ludford Magna."

At 101 Squadron, George was to have an eighth member of the crew – a Pilot Officer King – who was known as a special duties operator (SDO). An SDO operated a secret device, called Airborne Cigar (or ABC), that enabled him to jam multiple transmissions from German ground defences attempting to vector their nightfighters onto a target. Billeted separately from the rest of the crew, lest they talked in their sleep, the sole qualification for an SDO appeared to be the ability to distinguish German from any other European language they might pick up on their sets. They did not need to be fluent in German, neither did they transmit any false information. George was virtually in the dark: he suspected King talked to the Germans, vectoring them onto false targets, but never really knew what he did.

The Hall crew flew their first operation at 101, and the first since September the previous year on March 15, as part of a force of 863 aircraft sent to bomb Stuttgart. The German fighter controller did well, his aircraft intercepting the stream just before Stuttgart was reached and accounting for 27 Lancasters and 10 Halifaxes. The Pathfinders did not do so well, and whilst some of the bombs fell in the city, the vast majority threatened only the livestock in open country to the south-west of the city. George came through his second trip unscathed.

Although none of them knew it at the time, by March 1944 Bomber Command was coming to the end of the period known as the Battle of Berlin. There were no 'soft' targets, as George was to discover, attacking Frankfurt (twice), Berlin and Essen in his next four sorties. The operation on the night of March 30/31 to Nuremberg is one he will never forget.

"It was a dreadful night for 101 Squadron, I believe we suffered the highest loss in one night of any squadron in Bomber Command (the squadron lost no fewer than seven aircraft and 56 men). It was a terrible mistake. We were flying straight and level for too long – a very long leg that passed over all of the German fighter radars. I never used to write much in my log book, but that night I wrote the words: 'Lots of chop'. 96 aircraft were shot down."

Despite settling in well with 101, George was keen to be further tested. The obvious challenge was the Pathfinders – the elite, and a visit by one of Bennett's recruitment officers and a call for volunteers from the 101 Squadron CO Bob Alexander sealed their decision:

"The others were desperate to get into Pathfinders and so was I. We liked to believe we were good, but the only way we would know is if we took on another challenge. Most people on 101 thought we were absolutely out of our silly minds and we did think about it but there you are. To us, a move to Pathfinders was one further step up the ladder."

The 'step up the ladder' meant training at PFF NTU Warboys under the tutelage of a legendary instructor, Squadron Leader Geoghan, and then a posting to 582 Squadron on April 16, 1944 – two weeks after the squadron came into being. They joined Dickie Walbourn's 'A' Flight, and by May 3 were already on operations, briefed to attack Montdidier for the trip on which Freddie Bertelsen was lost. Seven further trips were completed without incident, and on June 6 they attacked Longues:

"This of course was D-Day, which we knew was coming, and the squadron bombed a number of targets along the coast. On the way back, dawn was breaking, and Lloyd (Taggart) reported seeing funny little white patches on the sea below us. As we got lower, and it got lighter, the 'patches' transformed into the wakes of hundreds of ships, and then we knew for definite that the invasion was 'on'."

The first request for Bomber Command to assist Allied troops in a purely tactical attack came on June 30, when 266 aircraft were asked to bomb a road junction (referred to in the briefing as a 'choke point') at Villers Bocage through which the tanks of two German Panzer divisions would have to pass in order to attack Allied forces. For a pinpoint target, it was a comparatively large raid, with 582 Squadron putting up 14 aircraft including Lancaster ND812 'M' Mother flown by Flying Officer Hall and crew. It was the largest daylight operation to date, and so nearly their last.

The attack was a controlled Oboe raid, and the master bomber, the 'B' Flight commander Brian McMillan instructed the main force to reduce height to 4,000ft to make certain they could see the target indicators clearly through the wispy cloud and the smoke from the exploding bombs. The majority, of course, steadfastly refused to come down so low, but with a target no bigger than the size of Wembley stadium, McMillan nonetheless marshalled his force well. Despite being hit by light flak – one shell coming right through the wireless operator's table – McMillan calmly continued to issue new instructions as each group of markers was dropped. George puts the dangers into context:

"On night operations we flew at 20,000 feet upwards but

when we started bombing tactical targets in daylight we were down at about 6,000 feet and lower which made a difference in a Lancaster. It's a considerably bigger target at 6,000ft than at 20,000 feet. And the other thing is of course that at 20,000 feet you were shot at by 88mm guns, the same as the things they had in the Tiger tanks. But at 6,000 feet all of the light flak that was there was aimed at you – 30mm stuff and you could even see the people who were firing at you."

As 'M' Mother approached from the Channel, the red TIs were barely visible, and on McMillan's directions he aimed for the starboard centre of the smoke where there was already a heavy concentration of bombs. George was in the thick of it – quite literally – as showers of bombs descended from the main force above him, and he was forced to take evasive action. A minute later, they were hit by flak:

"The bomb aimer said to me, 'They're firing at us you know!' and sure enough they were because one or two shells came through the wings and I could see at least one large hole about two feet from the astrodome."

The damage was in fact more critical than George had at first thought. Holes in his wings were the least of his worries. Petrol lines had been punctured, and the wiring for the fuel gauges severed so that the flight engineer had nothing on the clock. They didn't know how much fuel they had, how much had been lost, and whether they had enough to make it back to base. In the end it was touch and go:

"I knew we'd been hit, so I said, 'Well, the best thing is to land at the first airfield available' which was Thorney Island, a coastal command station, not far from Portsmouth. We landed without further mishap, but later it was discovered that we were losing fuel so quickly that we were lucky to have made it back to any base at all. The aircraft was categorised as 'AC', needing extensive repairs, and the next day an aircraft turned up to fly us back to Little Staughton. It was one way of joining the mile high club, being shot at in such a way, but nowhere near as much fun and in a completely different context!"

George took the excitement in his stride, but never lost his wariness towards low-level daylight raids that were now becoming increasingly the norm. On his very next operation to Troissy St Maxim his aircraft was again hit by flak. Three fuel tanks were holed, the port tyre burst, and the port outer prop feathered and put out of action. This, all on the same operation that one of the raid's leaders, Squadron Leader Ian Bazalgette, won a posthumous Victoria Cross.

> "The flak was concentrated defending the buzz bomb sites because they knew you were coming to attack them and it wasn't all light anti-aircraft fire it was 88mm heavy stuff."

Further obscure French towns and villages and equally obscure codewords began to appear on the target maps – St Leu d'Esserent, Mare De Magne, Tractable AP 28 – temporary homes and names for V1 launch sites or other 1944-style weapons of mass destruction including the V2 rocket, and the V3 long-range cannon being constructed at Marquise Mimoyecques. The nature of the attacks was changing. Large, single-target mass bomber raids had given way to smaller, multiple-target operations:

> "We were attacking buzz bomb sites all along the French and Belgian coast and as they were a much smaller target you didn't need as many aircraft. You had a system where you had a deputy master bomber who went in first and marked the target, as he thought. Behind him came the master – who came in and assessed whether he'd put them down in the right place. And when he'd done that he then started circling the target and in came the main force – who may only be 50 or 60 aircraft compared with 500 on somewhere like Berlin. And through that attack you would have backers-up – one every minute and it would all be over in 10 minutes. It sounds less dangerous, and indeed there was a ludicrous rule at one point that said the French trips should only count as a third of an operation. But remember we were low down because it was daylight, and the flak crews defending the buzz bomb sites knew their stuff."

An attack on the Opel motor factory in Rüsselsheim was launched on the night of August 12/13 resulting in the loss of 20 aircraft. This is reflected in George's log book entry that states simply: 'Very warm trip. Lots of chop.' A brief return to more common targets was announced for the second half of August, with a particular focus on port and harbour installations at Stettin (twice), Bremen and Kiel. Kiel was especially rough, the aircraft taking several hits, wounding the 20-year-old nav two – Charles Steele* – in his right leg below the knee.

---

* Charles Steele DFC returned to operations after a few weeks in hospital, and later went on to complete his tour of 49 operations with a Canadian pilot, Jimmy Brownlow.

George also remembers the Stettin raids very clearly:

> "The bombing on the first attack was very well
> concentrated and had developed well by the time we left
> the scene. Despite a thick haze, we could see flares falling
> all over the Stettiner Rafen. It was a very long trip, with a
> flight plan taking us close to the Swedish border. Swedish
> ack ack opened up on us as we approached the coast, stop-
> ped whilst we were over them, and then opened up again
> as we left. They were nowhere near us. It was all for show.
>
> "The second trip to Stettin was even longer than the
> first. My longest operation in fact, taking some eight hours
> and 50 minutes. Opposition was heavier than the previous
> trip, and a number of our crews were coned. Despite some
> confusion between the master bomber and the deputy
> master bomber, bombing was good apart from some slight
> scatter. The glow of the fires was visible for 110 miles after
> we left the target."

By this time, George and his crew had qualified through the ranks,
and were given a promotion to deputy master bomber to take out
the V2 rocket storage facilities and constructional works at
Agenville, their 34th operation. The attack was a shambles, one
main force squadron diarist (550 Squadron in North Killingholme)
recording that the raid 'was not considered a great success by the
crews that took part in it.' It was doubly bad for 550 Squadron that
afternoon as its 27-year-old Australian commanding officer Wing
Commander Alan Sisley failed to return.

George had occasion to make amends a few days later when he
took over the master bomber role over Le Havre, one of several
attacks on the target in the first two weeks of September:

> "We could hear the master bomber transmitting that the
> cloud base was at 6,000ft, and so descended and came in
> over the coast at 5,000ft (we daren't go any lower because
> the TIs were fused to explode at 3,000ft) and were
> immediately fired at by very accurate light flak. We saw the
> TIs through the cloud but then lost sight of them and so
> continued to orbit, calling the master bomber and telling
> him that we were unable to mark. We kept calling for
> about five minutes but could not contact him (the deputy
> had in fact given the order to abandon mission but not
> everyone received the message).
>
> "By this time we found ourselves in amongst the main
> force who had also started to come down low and were
> asking for instructions, so I told them to continue to orbit.
> We put our TIs to 'safe', and descended to 3,000ft below

the cloud base and for a short time could see the aiming
point. Two loads of red TIs were already on the ground, a
little off target, so I instructed the main force to
undershoot the big patch of red TIs by an estimated 200
yards. We got another good visual of the aiming point, and
ordered a 400 yard undershoot of the target."

George continued to transmit these instructions until forced to leave
the target area, still flying in cloud. His efforts had not been totally
in vain: 109 of the 333 aircraft taking part actually bombed the
target, albeit that two Lancasters were lost. Sadly, one of these was
from 582 Squadron. George, in fact, was not out of danger yet:

"Coming back from a raid, it was usual over the North Sea
to check for hang ups (i.e. bombs still stuck in the bomb
bay). No one wanted to land with a loose 500 or 1,000-
pounder sloshing about in the bomb bay if they could help
it. Returning from Le Havre, the check revealed nothing.
We landed back at Little Staughton, where the last thing
we would do as part of the routine before 'switching off'
was to open the bomb doors ready for the ground crew the
following morning. As I flicked the switch, the bomb doors
opened and we all heard – and felt – a 'thud' as a bomb
dropped free from the bomb bay and on to the tarmac. The
ground crew ran for cover and everyone froze."

Fortunately, it didn't go off. George Hall flew a further 17 trips with
582 Squadron, including another master bomber operation to the
islands of Walcheren which he had to abort. His last operation to
Ulm was also a disappointment, the attack being abandoned over
the target. On December 9 the ORB states the award of the DFC to
Flight Lieutenant Hall, and on the 28th he was granted the
permanent award of his Pathfinder badge. He was posted from the
unit on January 13, 1945.
    The citation for George's first DFC highlights his role in: 'playing
a leading part in attacks against many of the most heavily defended
targets in Germany. His courage and aerial skill were in keeping
with the finest traditions of the Royal Air Force, and reflect great
credit upon himself and his country.'
    A second DFC followed shortly after, citing: 'a high standard of
accuracy, frequently in the face of bitter opposition.'
    For some reason, he was also honoured by the Americans:

"They couldn't find me to give it to me because by that
time the war had ended and I had moved from instructing
at 91 Group to being seconded to BOAC. I have no idea
why I got one, no one ever told me, and no one else seemed
to have any idea either. We were all mystified."

ONE MORE FOR LUCK

The story of Flight Lieutenant Roy Pengilley DFC & Bar, pilot, 582 Squadron

Luck played an enormous part in Roy Pengilley's operational career. He was lucky to have found such an excellent crew, lucky to survive the mauling at Nuremberg before joining Pathfinders, and lucky later in his tour to miss the disastrous daylight on Cologne/ Gremberg because it was his fiancés 21st birthday, and the date chosen for their wedding. But his luck very nearly ran out on a cloudy summer's day over northern France.

Roy had planned to celebrate his own 21st birthday in style. Instead, he ended up in Ely hospital, fortunate to be alive, as the result of a daylight Oboe operation that so nearly went fatally wrong.

Born Bertram Ray Pengilley in the pleasant Oxfordshire town of Henley-on-Thames on July 22, 1923, Roy – as he has always been known – had wanted to fly from the moment he saw one of Alan Cobham's barnstorming Flying Circus take to the skies. It became almost an obsession with him, so much so that on leaving school at 14, he enrolled in night school to attain the necessary level of qualification, and at 18 joined the RAFVR as an air gunner.

> "I was told that it was pilots that they wanted, and that I could always become a gunner if I got washed out of flying school, so I decided to work a bit harder and apply again later."

His perseverance paid off, and it wasn't long before his Elementary Flying Training School instructors had passed him on to SFTS and ultimately 30 OTU at Hixon, flying Wellingtons. At Hixon he picked up the first of his crew – a navigator, bomb aimer, wireless operator and gunner – an exercise completed at a heavy conversion unit (HCU) with the addition of a flight engineer and second gunner.

Roy remembers well the process of 'crewing up'; hundreds of airmen crowded into a hangar and told to 'go find a crew'. Fortunately, Roy struck lucky:

"I had a wonderful crew, but it was just luck. How could it be anything else? How do you know just by looking at someone and thinking, 'he'll make a good navigator' that you will be right? What basis is that for whether he will make a good navigator or not? How can you possibly know? It was all luck."

For his navigator, Roy chose Don Anderson, a Canadian, who before the war had been a dentist in Toronto. As bomb aimer another Canadian, Bud Grange, a travelling salesman. The rest of the crew had equally eclectic peacetime occupations: the wireless operator, Dave Holden, was a builder's labourer; the flight engineer, Ted Dagger, a motor mechanic; the mid-upper gunner, 'Doc' Scott, a timpanist in a London orchestra; and the rear gunner, Tom Davies, a smelter. Despite, or perhaps even because of, their very different backgrounds, the crew worked for one another without question, knowing full well that their lives could, quite literally, depend on it.

Their first posting was to 625 Squadron, part of 1 Group, a relatively 'new' squadron formed in late 1943 flying Lancasters from Kelstern, and glorying in the somewhat melodramatic motto 'we avenge'. Here they took part in nine operations, including the massacre over Nuremberg, before being selected for Pathfinders, arriving at 582 Squadron, Little Staughton, after further navigation training in the second week of April 1944.

"Nuremberg was the worst trip. Whatever the casualty figure, you could always add another 10% to that number for aircraft that crashed on return or had wounded men on board. At Nuremberg it was nearer 20%."

Like others before him, his motivation for joining Pathfinders was wanting to be measured against the best, and a need to keep moving on. There was also a practical consideration. Casualties within 1 Group had been appalling, and Roy took the view that Pathfinders couldn't be any worse. The difference between the two groups, and the two squadrons, was instantly apparent as the novice crew found themselves immersed in a world of high-ranking, highly decorated corps d'élite:

"We had come from main force where a flight lieutenant and particularly a flight commander was a very exalted position. Most of us in main force were non-commissioned officers (NCOs); when we came to 8 Group, and at Little Staughton in particular, wing commanders were two-a-penny. I'm not decrying that. It was just noticeable that when you arrived at 8 Group, there was a vast change – not a social change – but a hierarchical change. Later, I became an officer too, but the only benefit I can remember is that the toast in the officer's mess was better!

"At 625 Squadron – and at Staughton – we were very much a 'journeyman' crew. On Pathfinders there were some real high flyers. The quality was very high, and the standard of navigation exceptional. The standard of the ground crews was also first class. I cannot recall any occasion when an aircraft broke down or failed. Given the circumstances, the quality of maintenance was exceptional."

Drafted into Dickie Walbourn's 'A' Flight, Roy's first operation at 582 Squadron was on May 11/12, a relatively short four-hour trip to the Louvain marshalling yards as a 'supporter', successfully planting his 18, 500-pound medium capacity bombs on the green TIs. Further operations followed to Duisberg (May 21/22), Aachen (May 24/25), and Rennes (May 27/28). Over Aachen both the H2S set and Fishpond, a fighter warning radar, were put out of action, and the aircraft hit by heavy flak. The bomb aimer's compartment was severely damaged and the fuselage gashed the whole length of the aircraft.

For D-Day, he 'loaned' his bomb aimer, 'Bud' Grange to Squadron Leader Arthur Raybould DSO DFM. He is still officially listed as 'Missing believed killed in action'. He was probably shot down over the Channel and is now commemorated on the Runnymede Memorial. In his place came Jimmy Humphrey who had previously been crewed with Wing Commander Patrick.

"Bud was a tremendous loss. I was always surprised when crews went missing without trace. It was fairly unusual. In many cases, even though it was dark you still had a good idea of what was going on around you and what might have happened. I am surprised there were as many as there were."

By July 6, following an attack on the constructional works at Wizernes, Roy's apprenticeship had been served, and he received a temporary award of his Pathfinder badge. Nine days later, it almost went spectacularly wrong.

Throughout the previous month and into July, the RAF had been called upon to bomb a series of targets related to the production, storage or launching of V1 flying bombs. Given the need for pinpoint accuracy, they increasingly relied upon their own new secret weapon, a precision device (PD) codenamed Oboe. Oboe was a blind bombing device that had first been used in December 1942 and perfected the following year. Used primarily at night, the device allowed for incredibly accurate bombing. Oboe-equipped

Mosquitoes would mark the target enabling the rest of the main force to attack. Tactics were also developed whereby Oboe specialists, often from a Mosquito squadron, would fly as a second pilot in an Oboe-equipped Lancaster (these were referred to as Heavy Oboe raids) and literally swap seats with the first pilot during the Oboe run and then swap back again for the return journey.

The powers-that-be at Headquarters Bomber Command saw in Oboe an opportunity not only to bomb accurately at night, but also during the day, especially when northern France was covered in 10/10ths cloud. The drawback to Oboe was that it necessitated the aircraft to fly straight and level for 10 minutes, at a set height, on a set course and at a set speed. This was essential or else the bomb aimer would lose the signal, and not be able to 'hear' the point at which the target had been reached. It was also essential because usually only one aircraft had the precision device, which meant that if the target was lost, then the whole raid would have to be aborted. This was difficult enough if the aircraft was unmolested by flak or fighters. But if the cloud cover broke, and the aircraft were exposed, it could prove fatal.

Training for Heavy Oboe raids in particular seems to have been very much 'on the job', and there were a number of failures as following aircraft – briefed to stick resolutely to the leader and drop their bombs when he dropped his – were thrown into confusion if the Oboe leader wandered off course. Further tactics were developed specifically for attacking the V1 sites in cloud. Oboe Mosquitoes or Lancasters with an Oboe specialist on-board would lead very small formations of bombers to their target. Then one of three things would happen: either the crews would release their bombs the moment they saw their leader's bombs go down; or, in the case of larger formations taking more time to arrive over the target, they would wait two seconds before bombing; alternatively, the leader would fire a smoke puff when over the target and the crews dropped their bombs as they drew level with it.

Nucourt, along with St Leu d'Esserent and Rilly La Montagne, was one of the larger flying bomb storage depots that Bomber Command was briefed to attack. It had been hit by 582 Squadron on July 10, and five days later, on the 15th, they were asked to attack it again.

Roy's name was not on the battle order. Squadron Leader John Weightman, however, was taken ill that morning and Roy was volunteered to take his place, one of 15 crews from 582 Squadron taking part. There were actually two attacks planned for Nucourt that day, one in the morning, and the other in the afternoon. In the morning, Wing Commander 'Slim' Somerville of 109 Squadron (also based at Little Staughton) and his deputy rode shotgun in a 156 Squadron Lancaster, whilst a Mosquito flew alongside in reserve should the Lancaster's Oboe set fail. This had now become standard practice. The attack achieved partial success.

In the afternoon, the plan was repeated. Wing Commander George Grant, commanding officer of 109 Squadron, flying a second Lancaster Oboe, led the 15 582 Squadron aircraft, and two pairs of Mosquitoes from 105 Squadron led six Lancasters from each of 156 and 35 Squadrons. Roy recalls:

> "Wretched Oboes. Our 8 Group was probably as good a quality as it gets, and yet the air force was asking us to do something that was little short of murder. We were predominantly a night-time blind-bombing force. So what were we doing in broad daylight, flying straight and level waiting to get shot down?"

Roy has every reason to remember Oboe with such bitterness. Coming into attack, he kept the aircraft 'M' Mother straight and level, at a steady speed of 150 knots at around 8,000ft. There was a blanket of cloud above and below, so thick that earlier in the flight he had actually lost sight of the formation he was supposed to be following, and so icy that his instruments actually froze and his aircraft began to descend involuntarily. As he broke cloud, he had no way of recovering formation. His navigator took a fix, and they decided to continue on and make their bombing run on Gee, even though they were now five or six minutes behind schedule. By now, any opportunity for Roy to take advantage of the work being done by the Oboe leader had gone out of the window, and instead he was on his own. Fortunately, the weather cleared sufficiently for Jimmy Humphrey, his bomb aimer, to drop his bombs, a straightforward payload of 16 500-pound general purpose munitions. Despite a faulty bombsight, the 500-pounders appeared to fall near to what Roy had taken to be the aiming point. Then the heavy flak opened up. In Roy's words:

> "I got bowled over."

The aircraft was hit several times, the Lancaster taking strikes to the port inner, the tailplane, and most worrying of all, the cockpit. The shrapnel slicing into the cockpit did not go all of the way through. Roy's left arm got in the way.

> "I didn't feel on top of the world at this point, Don Anderson, my navigator, was very quickly at my side and looked at the damage to my arm. He managed to find a nail file and began digging the bits of shrapnel out of my arm."

Roy's arm was patched up as best they could in the circumstances and they headed for home. A Lancaster is a heavy aircraft to fly; pilots often finished trips soaked in perspiration at the sheer physical effort involved. To fly a Lancaster with only one arm, even with the help of the flight engineer, required almost superhuman effort. The return leg, a flying time of a little over one hour and 20 minutes seemed like an eternity. It was with considerable relief that Roy spotted the familiar flashing beacon on the nearby hill side, blinking the initials 'LS' – Little Staughton. Home.

> "It was a lovely sight when I saw the airfield. With considerable effort I managed to line the Lancaster up to come straight in. It was then that I got a command on R/T from Dickie Walbourn, the flight commander, in Flying Control telling me to wait and go around again. It was the first and only time that I have disobeyed an order. I simply couldn't go around again. I had to get down. I am sure I caused quite a bit of consternation in the control tower as I came in for my shaky landing, but Walbourn was a decent chap and afterwards, when he knew what had happened to me, he was very good about it."

It was the end of Roy Pengilley's operational flying for almost seven weeks. While he was in hospital, his promotion to flight lieutenant came through, news that was given to him in a letter from the adjutant, 'Timber' Woods. The letter is dated August 10, 1944 and says:

> "Your rank is quite correct old boy and I offer my sincere congratulations thereon. I had hoped to do so to you in the flesh, but you will get in the way of flak! ...I enclose herewith particulars referring to (a) wound stripe. I've had them in my tray awaiting your collection, but you may just as well complete them and return them to me."

His recovery was slow but steady. For his 21st birthday on July 22 the nurses baked him a cake, and gradually he began to get his arm back to full working order. In the meantime, the Canadian Don Anderson and Aussie Jimmy Humphrey laid low on the station, until being 'obliged' to put in at least one trip with the new CO. It was not until early September that the crew was once again reunited, and operating again over the docks at Emden as a supporter, an attack that went off without incident.

After his excitement with Oboe, the remainder of Roy Pengilley's operational record was – comparatively – uneventful.

> "Because I had a very competent 'blind' crew we didn't take part in many Oboes. Thank God."

John Weightman, the man he had replaced for the attack on Nucourt, was himself lost on an Oboe trip shortly after. A happier event – his marriage to Mary on December 23, her 21st birthday – meant he was not operating on the day 582 Squadron flew another Oboe mission to Cologne/Gremberg with disastrous consequences. Again, luck had played its part in keeping Roy safe.

Having 'lost' seven weeks, a number of his crew, including the Canadians, finished their tours before Roy had attained his '45', and returned home. Some of them, Roy remembers, disappearing from the station quite literally a few hours after they landed from their final trip. The Dominions clearly wanted them back. In the end, Roy actually flew 59 operations straight off, the argument being that with the end of the war so close, it made little sense to lose such hard-won expertise.

> "Because of our expertise in Pathfinding, we carried on. I suppose it made sense. We had the training and the experience. It was silly to lose the expertise after 30, so they invited us to do 45 ops straight off. That's fine, – and if you added the 45 to the dozen or so you did somewhere else, then that would be your two tours. There was no rest period. Most at Staughton would have done between 50 and 60 trips. If you'd gone away for a six-month rest period, you would have come back too late to finish a second tour."

Apart from flak and fighters, operational flyers also suffered the very real danger of collisions:

> "If you think about a box, 20 miles long, one mile high, three miles wide, and put an enormous number of aircraft in it, all basically heading in the same direction, it's amazing that there weren't more collisions, especially when you realise that some navigators used to dog-leg the stream or fly a direct reciprocal course (effectively fly back into the stream from the opposite direction). You wouldn't do that today."

His last operation was to bomb the Hemmingstedt Oil Refinery on March 7/8, 1945, a raid that actually largely missed its target – an anti-climactic end to an otherwise highly productive tour. Before leaving the squadron, Roy Pengilley and the remainder of his crew had one last sad task to perform, acting as pallbearers for the funeral of one of their fellow pilots, Johnny Gould, lost in tragic circumstances with only two months of the war in Europe left to run. A happier task came by way of squadron 'tradition':

"There was a nice occasion when I finished my second tour at Staughton, that you became flight commander – in italics – for one day. It didn't mean that you actually became responsible for who was operating or anything like that, but rather some of the stranger requests our flight commanders had to deal with, like signing the chitty for the WAAF to get a new pair of bloomers, that sort of thing. It was a very nice gesture. Throughout my entire air force life I was always pleasantly surprised at the quality of the flight commanders."

On March 21, Roy was awarded his permanent Pathfinder badge, being posted from the squadron on April 26, 1945, almost exactly 12 months after he had joined. Of the quality of the Pathfinders, and particularly their navigational expertise, Roy is in no doubt. They were the best:

"Given that we were primarily flying in the dark, the standard of navigation was extraordinary. We could fly hundreds of miles over land and sea, and arrive at a point somewhere in Germany, exactly where we wanted to be, to a given time plus or minus 30 seconds. Even with all of the new technology available today, you would struggle to do that now."

Chapter Three

A Squadron at War

July – September 1944

Less than a week passed between the loss of Norman Tutt and his crew, and the next fatalities at 582 Squadron.

The battle for Normandy was by now in full swing; attacks on V1 weapons sites, railways and troop concentrations became the norm, and with specific raids called for in support of the advancing Allied armies, target finding, and ultimately bombing accuracy, became paramount. The Pathfinders had never been in such demand. The scale of the operations also began to change. Rather than the massive, carpet-bombing 1,000-bomber raids that had become customary as almost showpiece events, the emphasis was now on a larger number of smaller operations, sometimes only including two or three hundred aircraft but nearly always led by 8 Group's Pathfinders.

Canadian Pilot Officer Donald Manson and his crew flying Lancaster NE169 failed to return from an operation to attack a flying bomb site at Wizernes. With the moon shining brightly, both flak and fighters were particularly active over Calais and Dunkirk, and the aircraft of Dickie Walbourn took several hits, scaring the mid-upper gunner by blowing some of his canopy away. Four aircraft were lost out of an attacking force of 87: two from 635 Squadron, one from 15 Squadron, and one from 582 Squadron. Three of them, including the aircraft skippered by the 28-year-old Manson, were lost without trace.

For the first two weeks of July, the targets were almost exclusively flying bomb sites: Coqueraux; L'Hey; Nucourt; Gapennes; Thiverny; Rollez; Les Hauts Boissens; Ferme de Forestal. Gapennes was a Heavy Oboe trip in 10/10ths cloud with Wing Commander George Grant of 109 Squadron in charge of a 582 Squadron aircraft. It was a success. The squadron went there again two days later but was recalled.

On 20th, Forêt de Croc was the target for a daylight Oboe to be led by Squadron Leader John Weightman with a mixed 582

Squadron/109 Squadron crew. Taking off a little after 14.20, they had been promised heavy cloud over the target, hence the need for Oboe. When they arrived, however, although it was hazy the cloud was virtually non-existent. Despite the change in conditions, Weightman changed seats with the 109 Oboe specialist Squadron Leader James Foulsham DFC, AFC to enable Foulsham, and his navigator Graham Aungiers to control the run.

The attack came in, straight and level at around about 140 knots as heavy flak began bursting all around. With Weightman in front, flying as back-up was Flight Lieutenant Godfrey O'Donovan, briefed to take over lest something should go wrong. And it did. In O'Donovan's crew, Flight Sergeant Bill Bagshaw had his thumb on the bomb release as they approached the target. Suddenly a tremendous burst of flak lifted their aircraft upwards, forcing his thumb down on the release. With the remainder of the formation behind him, many of them also released their bombs, taking it to be their signal.

Meanwhile up ahead, Squadron Leader Weightman's aircraft had been hit (possibly by the same flak) and severely damaged, almost immediately catching fire. On his starboard was Squadron Leader Bob Wareing, who called Weightman up on R/T to tell him that fuel and flames were coming from his port wing trailing edge. It was too late. With an enormous flash and an even louder explosion, the aircraft disintegrated, crashing into the ground with considerable force and killing all on-board instantly. Although they did manage to release their bombs, the Oboe device was faulty, and the attack was a total failure, with nearly all aircraft involved reporting that their bombs had fallen well short of the target. The squadron had a right to distrust Oboe.

The loss of such an experienced pilot after so long on operations was a bitter blow to squadron morale, but the misery for July was by no means over.

On July 23/24, Flying Officer Ray Rember, an American from Cincinnati flying with the RCAF was lost with his entire crew attacking Kiel. It was also the night that Ted Swales nearly came unstuck. Running short of fuel, he diverted to the Handley Page manufacturing facility in Radlett, Hertfordshire, and attempted an emergency landing. Unfortunately all did not go quite according to plan, and Swales, and his flight engineer were both injured in the crash that resulted. The aircraft, Lancaster JB417, was written off.

On an attack on Stuttgart the following evening, 19-year-old air flight engineer Sergeant Philip Dicerbo was killed by cannon fire from a German nightfighter; two nights later, on July 28/29, Squadron Leader Coleman was shot down near Heimerdingen, and although he survived, the remainder of the crew was killed. Among the dead were Pilot Officer William Bunting who had won a DFM after completing 40 trips on Wellingtons with 150 Squadron, and

Flight Sergeant Reg Lewis, who at 39 was one of the oldest aircrew to lose his life.

The full complement of aircrew by the end of July stood at 119 officers and 136 men; there were in addition two non-flying officers, 233 airmen and eight WAAFs. Amongst the officer class, a new wing commander, Peter Cribb, arrived to take over command from Wing Commander Dunnicliffe.

Dunnicliffe had done an excellent job in the eyes of his peers in organising the squadron, so much so that he was awarded an immediate Distinguished Service Order (gazetted July 14) not only because he was an outstanding captain of his aircraft, but perhaps just as much, according to the citation, because he had shown 'a high degree of organising ability and great drive, and his untiring efforts have been reflected in the operational efficiency of the squadron he commands.'

There was a DSO also for his faithful navigator, Squadron Leader Ross Ingalls, his citation stating that his 'navigational ability has been of a high order throughout and [he] has played a good part in the successes obtained. He has at all times displayed a high degree of courage and determination and his example has impressed all.' Ingall's place as navigation leader was taken by Flight Lieutenant Horace Backhouse DFC from 35 Squadron.

Peter Cribb was no less an achiever, and perhaps more of a character, and an instant 'hit' with the men under his command.

Like Dunnicliffe, Cribb had been in action virtually from day one, attacking Oslo on the night of April 17, 1940 and various other targets during the disastrous Norwegian campaign. By June 1941 he had completed his first tour and after an obligatory six-month 'rest' returned to operations in early 1942. One of the first sorties of his second tour included taking part in the hunt for the German warships *Gneisenau*, *Scharnhorst* and *Prinz Eugen* in the infamous 'Channel Dash'. As a flight commander with 35 Squadron (then part of 4 Group) he was recommended for a DFC, his legendary squadron commander Jimmy Marks writing:

> "Squadron Leader Cribb has carried out 31 operational sorties, involving a total of 211 flying hours. As a flight commander he has constantly shown the utmost determination and devotion to duty regardless of the opposition. He has at all times set a magnificent example and has led his flight with outstanding enthusiasm and initiative."

Cribb was still part of 35 Squadron when it transferred to 8 Group in July to become one of the first Pathfinder squadrons. By November 1942 he had completed 53 operations, and added another German battleship, the *Tirpitz*, to his list of targets. He had also added the ribbon of a DSO to his tunic, the CO (now Wing Commander Basil Robinson) referring to his 'record of successful missions, many in number, of which it would be hard to find equal'. Bennett endorsed the recommendation with his own comments, specifically noting Cribb's 'thorough knowledge of air warfare'. High praise indeed from the great man.

Cribb's bravery in the air was matched by his eccentricities on the ground. In the air, he had proven his consistent bravery over a sustained period of operations. On the ground, he had been known to take pot-shots with his service revolver at the light bulb in his room, rather than use the switch.

Amongst the new pilots posted in to the squadron, as Wing Commanders Dunnicliffe and Patrick were posted out, was Squadron Leader John Clough. Clough was another fascinating personality. An old boy of the distinguished public school Sedbergh, Clough had originally joined the army before the outbreak of war, being commissioned second lieutenant in June 1939 in the 5th battalion, West Yorkshire Regiment, a territorial unit. A veteran of Dunkirk, he subsequently abandoned soldiering in favour of flying, and after training as a pilot joined 101 Squadron flying Wellington 1Cs from Bourne. His experience was a welcome addition to the squadron.

Further experience came in the shape of Squadron Leader Robert Clifford Alabaster. 'Alaby' Alabaster, a law clerk pre-war, was a volunteer reserve officer and observer of exceptional ability. He had won his first DFC in April 1941 whilst operating Whitleys at 51 Squadron, Dishforth. His talents soon came to the attention of Donald Bennett, who appointed him to his air staff as group navigation officer in January 1943, before a further posting to 97 Squadron where he added a second DFC for a specific act of courage:

"One night in July 1943 Wing Commander (sic) Alabaster was captain and navigator of an aircraft piloted by Flight Lieutenant Clarke detailed to attack Cologne. Some 50 miles from the target the bomber was attacked by an enemy fighter. Before it could be evaded the aircraft was repeatedly hit. One engine was damaged, other structural essentials almost shot away, while the rear gunner was wounded and his turret rendered unserviceable. The bomber became difficult to control but, despite this, course was re-set for the target which was attacked successfully. On the return flight shortly after crossing the enemy coast, the damaged engine caught fire and could not be extinguished but Flight Lieutenant Clarke flew on to the nearest airfield to effect a masterly landing. This pilot displayed outstanding skill and tenacity while Wing

Commander Alabaster's high navigational skill and excellent captaincy proved a valuable contribution to the success of the operation."

Unusually for a navigator, although not uniquely, Alabaster became a flight commander at 97 Squadron, adding the Distinguished Service Order to his list of decorations for his efficiency and inspirational leadership both in the air and on the ground. Wangling his way onto a pilot's course in the UK, rather than waste time in Canada, by the time he arrived at 582 Squadron he had flown more than 80 operations.

In August, the depressing run-rate of casualties continued. A great loss undoubtedly was that of Squadron Leader Bob Wareing DFC & Bar. He had been briefed with 15 other aircraft from the squadron to bomb a strongpoint in the Normandy battle area. His aircraft failed to return, although as it transpired not all of his crew was killed.

Another experienced bomber captain, Canadian Flight Lieutenant Elmer Trotter, was lost five nights later. Trotter had arrived at 582 Squadron via 156, 626 and 101 Squadrons, and had won the Distinguished Flying Medal in December 1943 on his fourth operational flight. Then a humble flight sergeant, Trotter's aircraft had been hit by fire from the ground just after releasing his bombs on Berlin. The Lancaster was thrown completely out of control and dived down towards the target. In the words of his citation:

> "Flight Sergeant Trotter ordered his crew to put on their parachutes, but displaying magnificent skill and coolness he was able to regain control of the bomber, to find that part of the starboard mainplane had been shot to pieces and that the aircraft had scarcely any aileron control. Other damage had also been sustained. Later, whilst endeavouring to gain height he was attacked by an enemy fighter. By skilful piloting, Flight Sergeant Trotter evaded his adversary but only after the bomber's port outer engine had been damaged. This airman then flew the severely damaged aircraft to base where he made a successful landing at the second attempt. In bringing his crew and aircraft back to this country under such harassing and difficult circumstances, Flight Sergeant Trotter displayed high courage and fortitude."

Trotter had been commissioned on February 8, and flown at least 13 operations with 156 before coming to Little Staughton. Taking off in the evening of August 12/13, the squadron, joined by its new commanding officer Peter Cribb in the role of master bomber, headed out to attack the Opel works at Rüsselsheim. A new method of Newhaven was being trialled that night: the blind illuminators went in first and dropped flares, closely followed by the visual markers; a second force of blind illuminators would then only drop their TIs if the visual markers failed to mark the target. This prevented too much illumination or too many flares burning on the ground at one time that tended to dazzle the bomb aimers in main force. In the event the attack only attained limited success, because the target was obscured by haze. The defences were also lively, and Trotter was intercepted by a nightfighter over the target and two of his engines set on fire. Trotter, his nav one Squadron Leader Bart Mathers and Flight Engineer Rawcliffe escaped by parachute and were captured, but the rest of the crew was killed.

For more than two glorious weeks the squadron avoided further loss of life. A mixture of attacks on the airfields at St Trond and Volkel, a long-haul to Stettin, the Ghent-Terneuzen canal, Bremen, and a further raid on Rüsselsheim were completed without loss, but not without incident. Over Kiel, Squadron Leader Philip 'Willie' Williams was forced to return early when his mid-upper gunner lost consciousness. Flight Lieutenant Graham Nixon had the frustration of making it all of the way to the dockyards, only to abort when his bombs hung up.

A greater mishap befell the crew of Squadron Leader 'Alaby' Alabaster attacking one of the 'tractable' targets. It was a 'simple' daylight in support of Canadian troops who had stalled north of Caen. With the target close to the UK, the crew had been briefed to make use of Gee for blind marking. This effectively involved 'sliding' down one co-ordinate from roughly north to south until crossing another co-ordinate, at which point the bombs and the TIs would be released some 6,000 yards in front of the Allied lines.

The co-ordinates had to be set up manually in flight by the navigator who would then give directions to the pilot to main-tain track on one co-ordinate until crossing the 'release' co-ordinate. The co-ordinates were delineated on the cathode ray tube (CRT) by two green lines about four inches long, sub-divided by ticks at decimals. Alaby's navigator, a Canadian, must have set up the wrong release point, for the TIs and the bombs fell amongst his own countrymen.*

---

* Alaby Alabaster writes: "Butch Harris was rightly aggrieved, having assured the generals of accurate support and took us off marking duties to be sent to a main force squadron. Bennett appealed against this but Harris was adamant, so Bennett compromised by letting us (the navigator and I) go on to Mosquitoes, within PFF but not on marking, on 128 Squadron at Wyton, I as a flight commander. November came and 608 needed a new CO so Bennett let me take over the squadron at Downham Market where I saw out the war." Alaby was awarded a Bar to his DSO in June 1945 having completed 100+ operations, going on to fly the first commercial flights of the Comet 1.

This in itself was bad enough, but the situation was compounded when the troops on the ground began firing off their own 'stop bombing' flares that happened to be the same colour (yellow) as the TIs already dropped. The result was that a large number of the main force took the mass of yellow to be the target, and released their bombs accordingly. Tragically, 13 Canadian soldiers were killed, and Alaby and his navigator were released for service on another squadron before the month was out.

A new target, the V3 very long-range multi-barrelled gun battery at Marquise Mimoyecques, appeared on the battle order for August 27, and nearly spelled the end for Wing Commander Bernard Nathan RAFO (later DSO and commanding officer of 142 Squadron from October 1944) who limped home with his aircraft riddled with flak. The next target was again the far-away city of Stettin on the Baltic where the squadron's luck finally ran out, with Australian Squadron Leader Al Farrington and crew failing to return. The men flying with him that night comprised the regular crew of the new CO, Peter Cribb, so the loss was doubly felt. Farrington had been with 582 Squadron for only a few weeks, although his experience went back many years, indeed as far back as the RAF's ill-fated campaign in Greece and earlier campaigns in Palestine, Syria and Egypt.

By the end of August, the Allied armies had at last broken through the German defences in Normandy and linked up with the friendly units that had recently landed, relatively unopposed, in southern France. Paris fell on August 24, and the Allies advanced into Belgium. The German frontier was almost in reach. Along the way, however, pockets of German resistance still held out, some of which had been by-passed and all of which now needed to be destroyed. One such pocket was in Le Havre, and on September 5 the squadron took part in the first of six raids in seven days with the purpose of bombing the defenders into submission.

Wing Commander Peter Cribb, taking Roy Pengilley's crew, acted as master and Brian McMillan deputy master bomber for the first attack that went well and without loss. Cribb and McMillan were again in charge the next day, reporting 'no wild bombing' from the 344 aircraft involved, and again there were no losses. For September 8, the squadron put up six crews – Nixon, Gipson, Peacock, Hall, Goddard and Norman Mingard arriving on target at 08.01. Flak came up to greet them thick and fast as they crossed the coast. Freddie Gipson had to take evasive action during his bombing run, upsetting the bombsight gyro, rendering it virtually useless. Squadron Leader Doug Peacock's Lancaster was shot at continuously and hit in the port wing. He began to lose control of his aircraft, so much so that he turned out to sea to jettison his bombs as well as a cache of target indicators that had begun to explode in the bomb bay. Mingard dropped his TIs only to see them land 'safe' and fail to ignite. His aircraft was also badly hit. George Hall took over the attack and marshalled the forces well. When they got back to Little Staughton, however, one of their band was missing: the 21-year-old Australian, Flight Lieutenant John Goddard, one of the 'originals' to join 582 Squadron in April. No one had seen him go down, but most likely Goddard's aircraft had been hit by flak and crashed in the target area. Two of the crew managed to make it out safely.

Mixed in with bombing German troop concentrations and supporting the Allied advance, Bomber Command was also called upon to attack Germany's synthetic oil production, the argument being quite simply that without oil, the German aircraft couldn't fly and their tanks couldn't run. The name Castrop-Rauxel therefore appeared on the target map three days later, on the night of September 11/12, in what was undoubtedly the most ferocious battle in which the squadron had been involved to date.

It was a comprehensive operation, calling for 379 aircraft – 205 Halifaxes, 154 Lancasters and 20 Mosquitoes – carrying out attacks on the Castrop-Rauxel, Kamen and Gelsenkirchen (Nordstem) synthetic oil plants. They were to be escorted by no fewer than 26 squadrons of fighters – 20 squadrons of Spitfires and three each of Mustangs and Tempests. In the event, no German fighters were encountered, but in the brilliant sunshine, the German anti-aircraft defences were at the very top of their game.

Wing Commander Dickie Walbourn, the master bomber, was hit by heavy flak in the port wing, starboard wing and port outer engine. Squadron Leader Philip Williams, flying to the stern of the master bomber, had his DR compass damaged by flak, and took hits to the tail plane with one hole in the starboard inner engine, eight holes in the bomb bay, two holes in the main plane between the starboard inner and outer, and five holes in the fuselage. George Hall was hit by heavy flak, causing two small holes in the fuselage, and one small hole in the bomb doors. Flight Lieutenant Graham Nixon was hit by heavy predicted flak in the petrol tank (starboard side) and had his pneumatic pressure line severed. Johnnie Clough was also hit, putting his starboard engine out of action.

Indeed not a single aircraft or crew from 582 Squadron came through unscathed or without incident, with some of the 'newer' arrivals to Little Staughton bearing the brunt of the attack. Flying Officer Bob Cairns' Lancaster suffered hits to its starboard wing whilst an American pilot, Pilot Officer Walt Reif, was hit by heavy flak in both wings, the fuselage, the mid-upper turret, and nose. For good measure his hydraulics were also pierced. Flying Officer Jimmy Brown received several small holes in the fuselage, tail plane and port wing. Wing Commander Bernard Nathan was similarly hit in the port wing, whilst Flight Lieutenant Peter Thomas ran in but suffered a hang up. He came in again on reciprocal course but again his bombs refused to drop. Flying Officer Morgan was heavily engaged by predicted heavy flak to such a degree that he had no opportunity of identifying the aiming point visually so he pottered off and bombed Dortmund (the approved secondary target) instead. Hit by heavy flak, his starboard outer radiator and mid-upper turret perspex were both damaged. Flight Lieutenant Owen Milne took flak in both wings and the fuselage.

Inevitably there were casualties. Flying Officer Smith, who had come to 582 via 156 and 625 Squadrons, took hits in the starboard wing, fuselage and bomb doors, injuring his navigator. He turned for home. 'Tiny' Shurlock, however, wasn't so lucky. Tiny, a massive South African, was not in his usual aircraft 'T' Tommy that day, but rather 'N' Nuts, the 'regular' aircraft of their flight commander. Coming in to attack, flak began to explode all around them, and one of the gunners, 'Taffy' Jacobs, who had been with Philip Patrick's crew, suggested they should weave. Tiny was having none of it as it would upset their bombing run. In the nose was the flight engineer, Warrant Officer Victor 'Davy' Davis DFM, waiting to bomb. He was on his 97th trip. Just then they took three direct hits, shattering the front of the aircraft, and fatally wounding Davis. The aircraft had also been fatally hit, its starboard outer engine literally blown off and the inner engine on fire, and the skipper gave the order to bale out. Somehow Tiny managed to keep the Lancaster stable enough for a few precious seconds to enable the rest of the crew to escape, before he too left through the hatch.

After the trauma of Castrop-Rauxel the squadron deserved better luck. Unfortunately they didn't get it.

Flight Lieutenant Graham Nixon and his crew, who had arrived in July, were lost on September 15/16 whilst attacking Kiel, shot down over the North Sea. They were one of only two Lancasters lost that night. Within the crew was the rear gunner, Pilot Officer John Norris, who already had a tour under his belt at 158 Squadron, and who had been awarded the DFM (December 1943) after taking part in several successful engagements with enemy nightfighters.

Flying Officer William Shirley and his crew were then lost on September 23/24, not on operations but in a flying accident. Shirley, a 22-year-old New Zealander, was engaged in a fighter affiliation exercise (i.e. to give both gunners and pilot an opportunity to practice against fighter attack), and the aircraft was reported to have lost control whilst executing a diving turn from 8,000 feet. Everyone perished, including LAC William Alston, a Londoner whose rank suggests that he had almost certainly only gone along for the ride.

Despite the very best efforts of the ground crews, accidents – through engine or critical airframe failure as well as pilot error – were part of squadron life, but fortunately few and far between. Some aircraft simply 'misbehaved', for reasons that were unclear at the time or after subsequent investigation. One pilot returned early from a trip claiming that he was unable to reach operational height, and that his controls were 'sluggish'. 'Fatty' Collings was unimpressed, and decided to fly the aircraft himself. Try as he might, he couldn't get the Lancaster to climb above 13,000ft, exonerating the pilot on one count. He then proceeded to throw the aircraft around the skies in a display of aerobatics that had the whole squadron standing in awe. Apart from looping the loop, he did just about everything that a fighter could do, and as he landed and stepped out of the aircraft, he received a spontaneous round of applause. It was clear there was nothing much wrong with the controls of this particular Lancaster!

There was at least one amusing incident to come from an attack on The Hague in September, involving two 582 Squadron Lancasters, one piloted by Philip Williams as deputy master bomber. Having successfully dropped his TIs, Williams descended several thousand feet and began slowly circling the target when there was a sudden shout from the New Zealander rear gunner that they were under attack from an enemy fighter. Williams threw the aircraft into a turning dive and headed out to sea and safety, whilst Jack MacLennan in the mid-upper turret searched everywhere for their aggressor. When they landed, Jack – who usually flew with Walt Reif – confronted his oppo as he hadn't seen anything. "That's because there was no f***ing fighter mate," the rear gunner told him. "If I hadn't had said something, we'd still be circling the f***ing target!"

The month ended with an attack on the oil plant at Sterkrade. Most failed to bomb the oil factory since the target was covered in cloud, and resorted instead to dropping their bombs in the town centre. All 582 Squadron aircraft returned safely.

TEENAGE PATHFINDER

The story of Warrant Officer Roy Last,
air gunner, 582 Squadron

By the time he completed his tour on Pathfinders, London evacuee Roy Last was still only 19 years of age, and had been wounded in action. It had been a baptism of fire for any young man, and a tour packed with incident, success and sadness, including the experience of seeing one of his crewmates killed on a trip to Stuttgart in July, an operation that could so nearly have accounted for them all.

The target was the Mercedes-Benz factory at Stuttgart. The night of July 24/25, 1944. Flight Sergeant Michael 'Paddy' Finlay in Lancaster PB136 taxied to the start of the runway and waited for the signal to go. Finlay, an Irishman from County Wicklow, appeared a little older than the rest of them. Indeed at 21 he seemed positively ancient to Roy Last, the teenager occupying the mid-upper turret. At Finlay's side was the flight engineer, Jock Dicerbo, his hands hovering above the throttle leavers, waiting to be given the command to move them 'through the gate' (i.e. maximum revs) for take-off. The rest of the crew was similarly occupied with their final checks: the Australian Alan Rogers, nav one; the nav two Graham Corran; Tom Thomson, the wireless operator; and Roy's partner in the rear turret, Freddie Jones. A 'green' from Flying Control, an 'ok' from the rear turret that nothing was behind, and they were rolling. It was 21.55.

> "The trip started badly, our 'Y' set (i.e. H2S) did not seem to be working as it should have been and the nav two was having problems getting the right bearings. The result was that we were south of the track and missed Stuttgart, having to go around again and join the stream which in the end made us about 20 minutes late over the target. Fortunately there were others still bombing. I know that because we nearly collided with one of them who came towards us on a reciprocal course!"

Over the target, Tom Thomson stood by the flare chute to make sure the photoflash went down with the bombs, without which they wouldn't get their essential aiming point photograph. Unfortunately the flare got stuck in the tube, only dropping when Tom reached inside to give it a furious shove. He returned to his wireless set and began listening in to broadcasts from base. In the rear turret, Freddie Jones thought he noticed something. Then he definitely saw something. It was a burst of tracer fire from a marauding Junkers Ju88, and they were aimed at him. At exactly the same time, another Ju88 attacked from the starboard low, and put in another burst.

> "It was all a blur. We had Ju88s attacking us from the front and from behind. I saw one come in from the starboard quarter. I kept him in my sights and had a go, but as a gunner you knew that actually your only hope was that he missed you. If he missed with his cannon, he would then come in range of our .303s, and you could fill him. At close range they were lethal."

As Roy fired, Freddie gave the command to his skipper to corkscrew – a violent form of evasive action. As he did so, the aircraft rose, and as it did Freddie fired and hit one of the German nightfighters in the belly. Immediately it broke away to the port quarter up, and dived away from sight.

> "In the corkscrew I was thrown out of my seat and out of my turret, finishing up in a heap at the bottom of the aircraft, all jumbled up with intercom leads, suit heating leads and oxygen hose."

It seemed like they had been mortally hit. Tom Thomson sat patiently on the main spar fully expecting to be told to abandon the aircraft that now seemed to be falling and tumbling in a most erratic fashion. The nav two, Graham Corran, grabbed his chute and made for the escape hatch in the nose, whilst the other navigator Alan Rogers made to follow. As Corran reached the nose, however, he found the flight engineer, Jock Dicerbo, slumped over the exit. He had been killed instantly by a cannon shell that had entered from the bottom of the bomb bay and hit Jock in the left hand side of his body.

> "At this stage I was still untangling myself, and Paddy told Tom to check that I was all right. Tom helped me back into the turret and then went forward with as many oxygen bottles as he could carry to go and give Paddy some help."

The aircraft was in a parlous state. Freddie suggested they made for Switzerland, and for a moment there was silence while the idea was contemplated before someone finally said: "No. Let's press on."

Paddy asked for something to help hold the control column back, and so Tom gave Alan his sheath knife to cut a length of the dinghy rope that was housed in its position near the rest bunk.

> "Paddy and Tom then tied the rope to the control column and then around Paddy's right-hand arm rest, but Paddy wasn't happy with that because he thought it might get in the way if he had to get out in a hurry. So they tied it around the back left-hand side of the seat instead with a couple of hitches around the arm-rest. For the next three and a half hours, Tom sat there holding on to that rope, watching the artificial horizon and praying that it wouldn't start to head down. After about 10 minutes, Tom began to run out of oxygen so they fixed some of the hoses in place and connected to them so it wouldn't be a problem."

On Paddy's instructions, Alan plotted a course for Normandy and then for the emergency field at Woodbridge. By now it was clear that the hydraulics had been damaged, and the emergency air that would be essential for the undercarriage, flaps, brakes etc. was also non-operational.

> "The skipper ordered us all into our crash positions, except Graham who had had pilot training before being remustered and so might be able to help. Graham took over the rope from Tom and on Paddy's instructions pulled and slackened the rope as we came in for a beautifully smooth belly landing without the help of flaps."

With the top of the escape hatches jettisoned, Tom fired off a red emergency Verey cartridge to indicate that there were wounded on board.

> "No one else was injured in the crash-landing, but Paddy and Graham looked like chimney sweeps from all the dirt and sand that had come in through the broken nose. As we jumped onto the wing, an ambulance, a fire engine and a truck arrived from Flying Control to help. We ran around the nose to pull Jock's body out, but it had gone, and was later found underneath the aircraft."

A survey of the aircraft revealed just how lucky they had been. The starboard elevator had been stripped of all but about five percent of its covering; a cannon shell had passed right through the stabiliser. The rear turret was damaged enough to make it immovable and several cannon shells had struck the bottom of it. Some splinters passed under the rear gunner, through the Elsan chemical toilet, through the 'Y' scanner, through the fairings of the mid-upper turret, and through the draught-proof doors behind the wireless op's position. Some came through the floor, severed the bomb aimer's oxygen tubes and punctured the pilot's windscreen.

> "Ground staff counted 117 holes from the rear entrance door to the rear turret. Luckily no motors or fuel tanks had been hit, but two of the parachutes had bullet holes in them. In the initial panic we thought more of us had been killed but that's because we couldn't hear anything on the intercom. The shell that killed Jock Dicerbo had come up through the floor."

Jock Dicerbo was the 19-year-old son of Italian parents Antonio and Pasqualina Dicerbo of Moffat, Dumfriesshire who had been interned on the Isle of Man when war broke out. Roy had first met him when they picked him up at 1657 Heavy Conversion Unit (HCU) at Stradwell. Up to that point, Roy's life had already been filled with incident. Born in Blackheath, at the height of the Blitz he had been evacuated to Ashford in Kent. With gas mask and identity label tied around his neck, he and two other boys were taken in by the head draughtsman of the Southern Railway Company, whose large house overlooked a local park, and had servants in the form of a cook and a maid:

> "He and his family were very kind to us. However, our education suffered as we had to share a school with the local children and were taught for only three hours a day. After six months we were moved to a purpose-built school set in lovely woodlands in Ewhurst, Surrey. A year or so later I was summoned to see the headmaster and he told me that my father had died. That was the end of my schooling as I had to go back to London and join my mother."

Roy opted to take a job in the city, working as an estate agent in Leadenhall Street. He helped with firewatch duties and joined the Air Training Corps:

> "We were taken to Biggin Hill quite often to crawl over the Spitfires – they were flown by Battle of Britain heroes like Sailor Malan and Bob Stanford Tuck, and of course we all wanted to be Spitfire pilots."

In the event, when it came to volunteering, Roy's training followed a familiar path: called up to ACRC St John's Wood (being billeted in London Zoo and being given his injections in the Long Room at

Lord's!) then on to ITW in Bridlington (for some of the best fish and chips in the world) and finally Air Gunnery School in Stormy Down, South Wales:

> "We trained on Ansons and my first flight ended in chaos. I had been given a bar of Fry's chocolate cream and having never seen anything like this in years gulped it down rather quickly before the flight. After half an hour of waiting to get into the turret for a tracer demo I felt rather sick. Someone opened the door for me and I was pretty well covered in Fry's chocolate cream!
>
> "We spent about a month at Stormy Down, firing at drogues (targets akin to an airborne wind-sock being towed behind an aircraft) and learning about Browning machine guns, and trying to hit moving targets in the air and on the ground at the clay pigeon range."

Passing out as a sergeant air gunner on October 25, 1943, Roy was sent to 26 OTU in Leighton Buzzard where he 'crewed up'.

> "Paddy was an exceptional pilot, and the nicest man you could ever meet. He never lost his temper, and never panicked. He always kept his nerve. As for the others, it was a great crew. Alan Rogers, our navigator, was a very posh Australian. Indeed he, Graham Corran (then the bomb aimer) and Tom were all Australians. Alan used to have his bed by the door in our billet, and whenever Graham got up to go to the loo in the night and couldn't find the door, he used to just piss on Alan's bed. They were all a bit mad; they would think nothing of shooting the lights out, singing Eskimo Nell while they did it. It knocked the corners off you very quickly."

Their training in Leighton Buzzard lasted a month; any longer and they might not have made it through:

> "There were a number of crashes at OTU. I remember one crew failing to return from a night cross-country, and we had a frightening experience ourselves one night over the North Sea. I was in the astrodome, waiting for my turn to fire off some rounds in the rear turret when we flew into a cumulonimbus cloud. After a few minutes we iced up and plummeted thousands of feet. I was floating in the fuselage with parachutes and navigation instruments flying by and I thought: 'this is it. I am going to die'. Fortunately Paddy managed to regain control as the ice broke off and we pulled up over the sea."

After an escape course at Methwold in Norfolk, the crew was posted to the Stirling-equipped Stradishall HCU where they met Jock. They completed the last part of their training at 1 Lancaster Finishing School before being posted to 101 Squadron, Ludford Magna. Roy's time at Ludford was short-lived. He flew his first operation to Aachen on May 27, 1944; his sixth was over the invasion front on June 5/6. At the end of June they were selected for Pathfinders, trained at Pathfinder NTU and posted to Little Staughton, arriving on July 8:

> "Our first op was to St Phillibert le Terre. We then went mostly on daylight raids, supporting the army, hitting flying bomb sites. It was fascinating flying over the convoys, going to the Normandy beaches the sky would be crowded with bombers going and returning from the war zone. Up until now, we had been very lucky – apart from the usual flak damage and seeing the odd fighter we kept moving and kept weaving and had little trouble. And then came Stuttgart."

Stuttgart was a tragedy, although they had the satisfaction at a subsequent interrogation of learning that they had definitely accounted for one of the nightfighters that had attacked them, and so the balance sheet was at least 'even'. Jock Dicerbo was replaced by Phil Brownlow, and the crew settled in to the routine of squadron operations. On August 29 they made the 10-hour trip to Stettin, flying over Sweden where the towns were lit up as though the war never existed.

> "They made a token display of firing at us, but the flak was thousands of feet below us," he says. "I often felt sick before we took off, but once I was in the turret, there was much to do. It was very cramped in the mid-upper, and very uncomfortable, with a seat that we clipped on that wasn't really designed for long journeys. It could get very tiring, especially when we went to places like Stettin, but then perhaps it wasn't quite as bad as being in the rear turret where you could quite literally freeze to death if you weren't careful."

For the attack on Le Havre on the 10th, 'Fatty' Collings was in the pilot's seat, and after returning from leave, they went again to northern France on the 24th.

The target was Calais, an afternoon attack. Wing Commander Brian McMillan was master bomber and gave the basement (i.e. the bottom of the cloud base) at 2,500ft. They needed to get below the thick, 10/10ths cloud that had formed over the town. The attack did not go well, with the majority of aircraft too low to get a good bombing run, and a number of bombs falling well east of the aiming point. Heavy flak was also causing a hazard, and McMillan's Lancaster was hit several times in the fuselage and wings, cutting his hydraulics. Flight Lieutenant Bill Spooner's aircraft, flying alongside, was also hit in the starboard outer. The third of the 582 Squadron aircraft assigned to the target, Lancaster JB422 'N' Nuts, was being flown by Paddy Finlay:

"We were deputy master bomber, and the master bomber, McMillan, called on us to find the cloud base. We broke cloud over the town at about 2,000ft, and were immediately raked from end to end by light flak. In the mid-upper turret, your thighs were exposed, and as the flak came up it not only hit one of the starboard engines, putting it u/s, but it also hit me in the leg. It hurt a lot, and there was a great deal of blood. Tom Thomas, our wireless op, managed to help me down from the turret and on to the rest bed, dress the wound and give me a shot of morphine. That seemed to do the trick."

Finlay recognised his gunner was in a bad way, and had lost a large amount of blood. Although out of pain, he was by no means out of danger. The aircraft too was in far from an ideal condition. Not only had the engine been hit, but also the hydraulics were u/s, the tanks had been punctured, and there were flak holes all over the fuselage. Their aerial had also been shot away, making communication difficult. Finlay opted to make for one of the first landfalls, and an emergency landing strip at Hawkinge.

"Paddy managed to somehow coax the battered bomber across the channel. I remember clearly the plane vibrating and being badly shaken, and the noise of the flak as it hit us like stones rattling on a window-pane. As we came in to land, and remembering that the Lancaster didn't have any hydraulics and therefore no flaps or brakes, we veered across the grass and headed for the control tower. The occupants promptly baled out, but in the end Paddy managed to bring the aircraft to a stop before hitting anything or doing any further damage.

"An ambulance was waiting and took me to the Kent and Canterbury Hospital where they removed the flak from my thigh (which I kept for many years afterwards). I was spoiled by the nurses and was almost sorry when I had to leave four weeks later to convalesce elsewhere."

Roy's wounds took almost two months to heal, and he returned to

Little Staughton towards the end of November 1944. He took part in the Cologne/Gremberg raid in December and flew with the 582 Squadron CO Peter Cribb as master bomber to Leuna on the 28th. His tour ended with a deputy master bomber trip to Nuremberg in January, after which he was posted back to NTU for a rest:

> "I flew almost every day in the rear turret, whilst the navigators trained in cross-country exercises and bombing runs. The commanding officer was the famous Group Captain Hamish Mahaddie, Bennett's 'horse thief' and chief recruiting officer and talented skipper in his own right. It was a happy unit – plenty of West End shows were put on and the mess had its own dance band led by Buddy Feathersonhaugh. I was still at NTU when the war in Europe ended. They asked if I would rejoin 582 Squadron as it was then being readied to go to the Far East as part of Tiger Force, but then along came the atom bomb and it was all over."

For many years after the war, Roy kept silent about his service in Bomber Command, made to feel as though he should be in some way ashamed of what the bomber boys did. Like many he suffered immediate demotion from warrant officer to sergeant (although he knows of sergeants who went down to LAC2s) and feels there was no excuse for such humiliation. Today, however, he is proud of his record, and proud of his skipper who went on to fly around 100 trips, and receive the DFC & Bar. He says:

> "There was great kudos in being a Pathfinder. We had the crack crews, and to wear your Pathfinder eagle was as good as any medal they could give you.
> "Just before I was called up in 1943, a mixed force of Fw190s and Me109s swept through South London, dropping bombs on Sandhurst Road School, Catford, killing 38 pupils and six teachers, and strafing kids cycling home for lunch. At that point I thought that perhaps I could see if I could kill a few Germans. In the event I probably helped to kill thousands."

THE LUCK OF THE IRISH

The story of Warrant Officer John Torrans, flight engineer, 582 Squadron

John 'Paddy' Torrans, from Belfast, arrived at 582 Squadron for his second tour, having survived his first with main force and a period instructing at HCU. His skipper, Squadron Leader Wareing, held the DFC and Bar, the first for an attack on some of the German Kriegsmarine's finest capital ships in Brest at a time when the RAF seemed fixed on doing the navy's jobs for them. Paddy was into the fray immediately with a couple of dicey ones. And then came Operation Totalise, and the breakout of the Allied forces from Caen.

Lancaster ND 817 'S' Sugar was one of a batch of 600 Mk III aircraft delivered between December 1943 and May 1944 with the Merlin 38 engines. Now at least two of those engines were on fire, and the pilot, Squadron Leader Bob Wareing DFC & Bar, was in danger of succumbing to the flames, with his legs, hands and face badly burned. Somehow, however, he managed to keep control of the aircraft just long enough for three or maybe four of his crew to make it out.

The strong point at Mare de Magne in northern France was the designated target, one of five on the Bomber Command 'hit list' for that evening, the night of August 7/8. It was a bright moonlit night, and the raid, part of Operation Totalise, was being led by Wing Commander Brian McMillan. Zero hour for Totalise was 23.00. Accuracy was the watchword. In order to dislodge the Germans, the Allied troops had actually pulled back over a mile from their positions to allow the bombers a clear run. The ground forces were briefed to help with the attack by shining searchlights and firing red starshells over the target area.

The first aircraft to bomb Mare de Magne did so at 23.36, from 5,500ft. McMillan instructed main force to maintain height and bomb the centre of the red TIs that had landed bang on the aiming point. He continued issuing instructions as the target became obscured by smoke, ordering them to adjust their aim for the port edge of the target indicators. As well as the 582 Squadron aircraft,

100 Lancasters from 3 Group and 60 Halifaxes from 4 Group were also in attendance and combining well.

Warrant Officer Ed Hawker was in the nose of 'S' Sugar, and pressed the bomb release as the red TIs came into his sight, sending his 1,000-pound and 500-pound medium capacity and general purpose bombs spiralling down. The attack was proceeding most satisfactorily. The bombing was well concentrated, and the master bomber seemed pleased with the night's efforts. With the all-important aiming point photograph taken and bomb doors up, Bob Wareing dipped the nose of the Lancaster slightly down and eased the throttles forward to gain speed and head for home, being given a course to steer towards Le Havre.

John Torrans, the flight engineer, was keeping a wary eye on the gauges and dials on his panel: the oil pressure, oil temperature and coolant temperature, one gauge for each engine clearly marked from left to right starting with port outer to its starboard equivalent. Any sign of a racing engine, or a slight rise in oil or coolant temperature, may be the first sign of a bigger problem, and he didn't want any of those. He also monitored the fuel content gauges: six tanks in all with a total capacity of 2,154 gallons. Enough to get you to Berlin and back.

Torrans was on his second tour. Indeed they all were, with the exception of the radar set operator, Australian Flight Lieutenant Bob King. The skipper was the most experienced. A volunteer reserve officer, he had received his first 'gong' as a pilot officer with 106 Squadron in April 1941. He had been detailed to carry out a low level attack on two enemy battle cruisers in the port of Brest. When making his attack, he had come down to 1,000 ft, but owing to the darkness, he found he was short of the target. He was also caught short by the German defences. Searchlights seemed to suddenly appear as if from nowhere, and the German flak gunners opened up with a fearsome barrage. Despite this, Wareing decided to go around again, flying over the target area for a full 40 minutes before finally being able to drop his bombs on at least one of the ships, and seeing one of the bombs explode close by. He received a second DFC on completing his tour in the December.

That said, Torrans was himself no novice. He had completed his first tour with 103 Squadron, and was then 'rested' as an instructor first at Sandtoft, and subsequently at Faldingworth, both heavy conversion units with Lancasters and Halifaxes. The crew had been busy since joining 582 Squadron in the April of 1944. Their first trip had been to Essen, and their first daylight to Les Bayons in France.

"I remember it well because that evening in the mess we were entertained by an ENSA party, and one of the artists was an Irish singer who a few years later won the World Flyweight Championship – Rinty Monaghan. This particular day (June 24) sticks out in the old memory bank because it was my 21st birthday."

As an experienced crew, they were quickly promoted through the Pathfinder ranks, and on June 30 found themselves as deputy master bomber for a daylight to Villers Bocage, the raid in which George Hall and his crew nearly caught a packet:

"There was cloud cover over the French coast up to about 18,000ft and our captain decided to get below it and establish the cloud base. We broke cloud at about 9,000ft and the captain decided to call the main force down to that height for their bombing run. This was on the instructions of the master bomber (Brian McMillan). The main force at that time appeared to have gone stone deaf or switched off their R/T; about 15 percent of them carried out these instructions and the remaining 85 percent stayed at around 20,000ft. With us at 9,000ft and main force at 20,000ft it was, as the Yanks would say, 'an ass-tightening sensation' to be on the bombing run with bombs, incendiaries etc. all falling around us. Fortunately none of them hit us, but it was a day to remember."

Another day to remember was the daylight Oboe in which Squadron Leader Weightman was killed:

"We were flying on his starboard at about 6,000ft over France when his aircraft was hit by anti-aircraft fire. Fuel and smoke started to emit from the port wing trailing edge. We immediately called him on R/T to inform him of this damage. There was a large flash and an explosion, and the aircraft just disintegrated and all that was left was a large black cloud. There were no survivors."

The trip to Mare de Magne, meanwhile, had been remarkable in the fact that nothing untoward had happened. And then the nightfighter struck:

"As we approached the coast near Le Havre, our gunners – Flight Sergeant Robert Campbell and Warrant Officer Wilf Gaughran – spotted the nightfighter and were passing evasive tactics to the captain. We corkscrewed to port and the mid-upper got a burst in at the fighter, then on instructions from the rear gunner to climb to starboard we were raked along the underneath of the aircraft by cannon fire. The rear gunner also got a burst in at the fighter who continued to fire at us.

"Our aircraft by then had caught fire inside the rear fuselage, and there was fire in the nose section and wings. The captain also appeared to be hit."

The aircraft was in a dreadful state, and decisions needed to be taken quickly. The navigator, Squadron Leader Alan Hill, gestured to John to clip on his chest-type parachute pack which he did and headed for the nose. He then opened the escape hatch and returned to his position:

"Squadron Leader Hill then made further signs at me to abandon the aircraft as the fires were completely out of control. I descended feet first out of the hatch, and on glancing upwards towards the aircraft that was trailing flames from both wings, the fighter that had attacked us was clearly illuminated and still firing at the aircraft. I think it was a Messerschmitt 109E, although I cannot be certain.

"My 'chute opened successfully but one of my flying boots disappeared, a usual occurrence until ankle straps were fitted. I also discovered that when fitting my parachute chest pack I had only hooked on one side (there were two clips to which the pack was meant to attach). I landed in a field not a mile away from where the aircraft had crashed and could see the glow of the flames and hear the ammunition exploding."

John had baled out in the area of Lillebonne, and as he landed felt a sharp pain in his right leg. It was only now that he realised he had been wounded in the thigh, and that his left leg was also burned. Knowing that the burning Lancaster would very quickly attract the unwelcome attention of any passing Wehrmacht, John removed his parachute, harness and Mae West life preserver and hid them as best he could in a ditch. Unable to walk, he spent the next few hours crawling as far away from the crash site as he could, until he collapsed, exhausted, into a haystack.

Although he didn't know it at the time, John was not the only one to make it out of the aircraft alive and in (comparatively) one piece. Alan Hill was also at that moment hiding in a ditch, waiting for salvation. He too had burns to his legs, and also a severely sprained ankle. He stuffed his parachute and associated safety gear under a hedge and began crawling in the direction of Le Havre, hoping to come across a farm.

John Torrans, meanwhile, emerged from his hiding place at around 10.30 on the morning of the 8th, just as Francis Marical, a local road mender, was on his way to work. When Marical reached his little hut, he decided to have a look around to see if some birds eggs, which he had noticed a few days earlier, had finally hatched. He found a 'flyer' of a rather different nature, coming face to face with the battered airman. John asked him if he spoke English, but the silence gave him his answer. Through the waving of hands, Marical encouraged John to follow him and hide in his hut, and then set off for help. He returned with a friend, along with some tomatoes and hard-boiled eggs, as well as a change of trousers, a shirt and some shoes. John was grateful, but even more grateful with the bicycle that had been brought. Although in some discomfort, John mounted the bike, whilst Marical and his friend hid his flying jacket and boots in the drains under the road. The three of them then set off for the home of Bernard Beauvais in nearby Oudalle.

Beauvais was an old hand at helping British airman on the run, and took John where he took all of the others, to some caves in the hillside that the Germans appeared to know nothing about. John waited to see what happened next, and was delighted when a little after two o'clock that afternoon another airman was brought to the cave – and he immediately recognised the familiar face of his navigator Alan Hill.

Hill's experience had been virtually identical to John's. Having lain hidden alongside the Le Havre coast road for quite a while, he at last managed to attract the attention of a man and a woman cycling by. He explained to them his predicament, was told to wait, and that they would return. They were good to their word, coming back with four or five others all on bicycles, and bidding Alan to change places with one of the riders. Despite his wounds, Alan cycled to a nearby café, and then only two of them continued on to a wooden shack near Le Havre. Here Alan was left, in the company of two evacuated 'mesdames', until eventually he was taken to the farm owned by Monsieur Beauvais and carried up to the caves.

Alan Hill was in a bad way, and a doctor was sent for from St Romain de Colbosc, Docteur Evins. John helped the good doctor in treating Alan's wounds, and also received medical attention himself. Within a short space of time, the local Resistance chief, Emile Schild, arrived, and arranged for their transportation onwards. A horse and cart took them to a farm where they awaited developments. They did not have long to wait:

> "We were told that British troops had entered St Romain about seven kilometres from the farm, and so we were taken by motorcycle to the village where we made contact with a reconnaissance unit. We stayed overnight with a doctor and were then taken to 49 Division HQ at Anquetierville on September 2, 1944. On September 3 we were flown in a couple of Austers to a landing strip north of Bayeux, and then by tank landing craft to Newhaven."

John and Alan had survived, and made it home, but up to that point they still had no idea what had happened to the rest of the crew. It was sometime before they would find out, and when they did there was a mix of bad and good news. The bad news was that four of the crew were dead: the two gunners, Campbell and Gaughran, had not made it out alive; neither had Ed Hawker, nor the wireless operator, Flying Officer Reg Blaydon. Blaydon, a 29-year old from Cambridgeshire, had won the DFM whilst serving with 9 Squadron in 1942. Unusually Blaydon had already been rescued once before by the Resistance, an earlier battle he had won; this time he had lost.

There was better news concerning the two other members of the crew: Flight Lieutenant Bob King and the skipper, Squadron Leader Bob Wareing. Both had survived, and both were now prisoners of war. Bob King had been picked up by the Germans almost immediately, but Bob Wareing had at first made it safely into the hands of the Resistance before being betrayed.

A local farmer had rushed to the crash scene as soon as he saw the bomber coming down. Wareing had managed to scramble out of the aircraft just before it crashed and parachute into the surrounding marshes. Somehow he had managed to crawl far enough to hide in a nearby barn where he had been discovered. He had terrible wounds to his legs, hands and face. The farmer ran for help, calling at the house of Mademoiselle Pillot, convinced that she would know what to do.

Mme Pillot spoke fluent English; because of this she was sometimes called upon to translate for the local Resistance. The farmer arrived out of breath, but between gasps told her what had happened, and that there was a badly injured airman in one of his barns. Mme Pillot acted instantly, and sent the farmer for the doctor – Evins – the same man who would treat Torrans and King. Mme Pillot was anxious. She knew that the Germans would be out searching, and if they were aware that Dr Evins had been called for, then it could easily be because they had found one of the aircrew. Two policemen had also arrived at the barn, and were taking a little too much interest. Although they might turn a blind eye, it couldn't be guaranteed. When she arrived at the farm, she found the pilot was indeed in a bad way, and in a state of shock. He was lucid enough, however, to ask her to remove his wedding ring which she did, and hid this and his identity papers, maps and watch in her dress.

Unfortunately Bob Wareing's time 'on the run' was short-lived as he was soon after betrayed. Along with Bob King, he would last out the war in a prisoner of war camp on the Baltic: Stalag Luft 1 in Barth. They were liberated on May 8, 1945.

ONE OF THE MANY

The story of Squadron Leader Al Farrington,
pilot, 582 Squadron

Allan Farrington came to 582 Squadron on July 27, 1944. He failed to return from operations to Stettin on the night of August 29/30, scarcely a month later. He was one of the thousands of Australians who went to England to fight in Bomber Command, and die for the cause. Al Farrington was by no means a novice, but rather a veteran of the bleak days of the RAF being outnumbered and outfought in the Middle East. Along with many of his contemporaries, Al Farrington was very much the professional soldier.

There was a book published in 1942 that can still occasionally be found called *Wings Over Olympus*. It is written by Tommy Wisdom, as a journalist's story of the Royal Air Force campaign in Libya and Greece. In the early pages, it follows the fortunes of a Blenheim bomber squadron, No. 211, and the men who flew in it. Several mentions are made of a 'thickset Australian, a chap with an infectious laugh and a great sense of humour, one of the "gay" flyers of the squadron.' His nickname, not surprisingly, was 'Dinkum', although friends and family called him 'Tup'. His real name was Allan Leonard Farrington.

Born in Young, New South Wales, a small country town famous for its cherries, Allan Farrington had always been fascinated with aircraft. Educated at Sydney Technical High School, his school text-books and scouting books are filled with doodles and drawings of war planes and soldiers, so it was no surprise when he volunteered for, and was accepted by, the Royal Australian Air Force on a short service commission. Training for cadets wishing to be officers in the 1930s was undertaken at Point Cook, in many ways the spiritual home to the RAAF. Point Cook, in Victoria, had been set up in 1914 as the central flying school for the Australian Flying Corps, and was the site seven years later when the RAAF and Australian Naval Air Service officially came into being.

An exchange scheme existed between the RAAF and the RAF whereby the first year's training at Point Cook would count as the first of a five or six year commission in the RAF. The individuals

concerned would be Australian members of the RAF, and it was with
the intention of joining such a scheme that Allan signed up in July
1936. He spent 11 months at Point Cook before being selected for
training in the UK, arriving in August 1937 having already been
awarded his wings. He was checked out again at 8 Flying Training
School (FTS) in Montrose flying Hawker Harts and Avro Tutors
where he was rated 'above average in armaments and navigation'.
and a 'safe, reliable, above average pilot'. 'Above average', it should
be noted, was exemplary by any other word.

Six weeks at 8 FTS was followed by a posting to 211 Squadron,
then based in Grantham, Lincolnshire. The squadron had originally
been formed on April 1, 1918, born out of 11 Squadron Royal
Naval Air Service. After service in the last few months of the Great
War it had been disbanded and reformed on June 24, 1937 as a day
bomber squadron at Mildenhall and then Grantham, flying Audaxes
and then Hind biplanes. Allan arrived just as the squadron was
preparing to leave for the Middle East, which it did on April 30,
1938, arriving at its new base in Helwan in the second week of May.

In a broadcast home as part of the *Calling Australia* series transmitted by the BBC during the war, Allan spoke of these earlier times:

> "It is four years since I left Sydney with 24 other RAAF
> officers trained at Point Cook. We were on transfer to the
> RAF and to England. Not long after my arrival here I was
> posted to Grantham to join 211 Squadron. I was to spend
> much of my service both at home and abroad, at peace and
> at war, with that grand squadron. I found the Empire well
> represented at 211. In it were 'Vicki' Boehm of South
> Australia, Doug Cameron of Victoria, and 'Pookie'
> Edwards with whom I went to school in Sydney. As well as
> these Australians there were Magill, a New Zealander, and
> Kearey and MacNab, South Africans. Their company
> made me feel at home.
>
> "But no sooner had we begun to settle down in England
> and we were off to Helwan in Egypt. Three months after
> our arrival in Helwan we were sent to Ramleh in Palestine.
> We were there during the Munich Crisis and in our
> Hawker Hind biplanes helped in the trouble that was then
> rife between the Arabs and the Jews, by air patrols and co-
> operating with the army and the police."

The next stage in Allan's journey was from Palestine to the Western
Desert, a journey that also saw a change in squadron aircraft. Out
went the dated Hawker Hinds in favour of the much more
contemporary Bristol Blenheim twin-engined monoplane, then one
of the fastest light bombers of its day. Blenheims put the squadron
much more on a war footing and just as well, because within a few

months rumours of war had given way to actual war itself, but it was not until Mussolini entered the arena in June 1940, that Allan was called upon to take an active part in the struggle:

"In those months of waiting, we found the desert and the inactivity most boring and irksome. The only flying we did was of a routine nature. While we read of the exploits of our fellows in England, our lot was limited to the monotony of humdrum training programmes. It is not to be wondered at that most of us were almost glad when Italy came in.

"From then on, 211 was well in the thick of it. We went over the enemy lines to bomb places like Tobruk, Bardia and other places made famous by the Libyan campaign. The Blenheim Wing made a name for itself in those days, and was brilliantly led by a Canadian, Air Commodore Raymond Collishaw, a 1914-18 air ace.

"Life in the desert was pleasant enough up to a point, so long as we found something to do. People don't realise what it's like to come back from a flight, after having been shot at by ack-ack and fighters, and to look out on to nothing but sand. Soon you find sand in your drinks, sand in your everything. Luckily we discovered ways and means to keep ourselves occupied and amused. We were on the shore of the Mediterranean so I built myself a surfboard with timber from the Royal Engineers, and spent my time off-duty riding the surf which occasionally rolled in. It took me back to days which now seem long ago when I used to bask on the sands of Manly Beach.

"The AIF were arriving in full force, but unfortunately were nearly all based in Palestine. Because of this I was unable to look up old friends from home, but occasionally I did manage to run across one or two. Some New Zealand Army men came to live near us in the desert and our squadron was well represented by officers Down Under so we frequently visited one another. Most of their names slip my memory at the moment, but the one I can remember best was Jim Wynyard, All-Black footballer in more peaceful days. I still see him going back to his unit on his motorcycle after one of our parties in-between raids.

"It was in the evenings that we found our chief relaxation from the heat and the flies of the day. Our mess was perched on a cliff-top overlooking the Mediterranean and we used to sit out in the evenings with our sundowners, talking of pre-war life and our exploits on the last leave in Cairo, and our plans for the next one, and many were the sing-songs we had.

"Life in the air force officers' mess was rather easier than that in the army as we did not have to move quarters so often as they. We of 211 particularly liked to think that ours was the best of all the RAAF messes in the desert. It became well-known and people on their way to more advanced positions would always drop in and be sure of a welcome."

Amongst those that were regular visitors to the mess were two Australian war correspondents, John Hetherington and 'Big Bill' Glennie, with whom Allan struck up an immediate rapport, and happily took them on a practice flight to show them what flying was all about. Their paths would cross many times.

Towards the end of 1940, Allan, by now a flight lieutenant, had been in the desert over a year with the squadron, and the strain of operations was beginning to tell. But his sense of fun was still largely intact. Whilst on leave in Cairo, he chanced upon an Australian officer in a bar and pretended to be English, his impersonation helped by an imitation monocle fixed firmly in one eye. As the Australian's boasts became greater, so too did Allan's impersonation become bolder with cries of 'by jove' and 'amazing' and other such expressions. He kept the joke going for as long as he dared before finally lapsing into his own Australian brogue, much to the hilarity of those around him.

Operations could also be amusing. On one flight, their CO, who happened to be the son of a distinguished British general, chastised his pilots for breaking formation, and warned them that the next man to step out of line would get a rocket. Returning from a raid the following day, Allan kept overtaking and then returning to the rear of his CO's aircraft, which had a duff engine. The CO was delighted indeed to find one of his flight so zealously covering his retreat and said so when he got back. Allan admitted that he had actually only stayed with his leader because he feared he would be torn off a strip if he broke formation!

Then Italy declared war on Greece, and the squadron found itself on the move again to defend a new border.

"We arrived at Tatoi near Athens in the pouring rain. After months of desert life on a ration of one gallon of water a day, this seemed absolute heaven. We wasted no time in getting our aid to those magnificent Greeks for the day after we arrived we were off on a raid to Garezzo in Albania. We then realised that this was not going to be altogether a picnic. After the ideal flying weather of Egypt, the mountainous, cloud-covered terrain of Greece was quite another proposition. Soon, however, we came to look on those clouds as our allies, for we were able to enjoy their friendly cover while taking avoiding action from Italian fighters, and I may add that we rarely attacked a major target such as Valona or Durazzo without encountering a dozen or so of these.

"Weeks passed into months in Greece and we flew on, maintaining a steady series of bombing attacks on Italian positions and in our spare time we hit the high spots of Athens. There is no need to say how hospitable were the Greeks. It is sufficient for me to point out that I spent some of the happiest days of my life there. It was there that I met my wife on the eve of 1941. She was an English girl, Alison Barbour, who was working in the British Legation there, and we were married three months later in the English church of St Paul's in Athens*. But that is another story.

"Next came the threat of the German invasion of Greece and 211 moved up to an advanced position on the west coast at Paramythia from whence we bombed the Italian lines not half an hour's flying away, sometimes as many as three times a day, day in, day out. Hurricane fighters came to join us and soon the air force had air superiority in quality though not in numbers. Daily the troops were pouring into Greece from Egypt. The Australians and the New Zealanders brought with them many old friends – Hetherington and Glennie, the Aussie war correspondents, Jim Wynyard the All-Black New Zealander and his gang – on their way to get a snap at Jerry. The next time I saw Jim he was back in Egypt recovering from a bullet wound in the mouth, and his only complaint was that his drinking was temporarily impaired."**

It was about this time that the Germans came and spoilt all of Allan's fun, although it was not without its adventure:

"There is no need to tell the story of the Greek show. We lost our superiority in the air. They had standing patrols of up to 50 aircraft over our aerodrome and we just had to get out. I got out on a Yugoslavian tri-motor Savoia of Italian manufacture which was on its way to Egypt. My wife left some days earlier by a small boat and had to leave her mother and aunt behind, nursing her invalid father. They are still there, interned. If they should hear my voice, I should like them to know that we are both well and thinking of them constantly.

---

* One of the guests was Richard Dimbleby, later to report on Pathfinder operations with 582 Squadron.
** Jim Wynyard was killed in North Africa in 1942.

"Back again in Egypt after months in Greece, I was posted from 211, those desert greyhounds with whom I had spent so many happy times. My time was up in Egypt, and I was sent back to England in August 1941. Our ship was once well-known on the England-Australia run, and we were made very comfortable and saw a lot of the world. If Dunn, the Australian third officer of the ship should be listening, I should like to send him my greetings.

"We arrived back in England without mishap, thanks to the grand work of the Royal Navy, my first time on English soil after three and a half years in the Middle East. Now I am settled down in the more peaceful atmosphere of training command, for the time being at any rate. But I often wonder how those chaps are whose paths ran parallel to mine, and I hope that one day, after we have won this war, some of us may be able to get together to talk it over."

Allan had been in combat for 18 months without respite, and in the Middle Eastern theatre for twice that period. As he intimates in his broadcast, he was exhausted, and in late 1941 he fell ill as a direct result of flying fatigue. His broadcast home to Australia was dated February 24, 1942. As was customary after completing a 'tour', he then undertook a period of 'rest', although the term does not have quite the connotations one might think. 'Rest' could mean serving on headquarters staff, it might mean an administrative job elsewhere, or it might mean – as it did in Allan's case – a period instructing. This was a crucial element of aircrew training. Tour-expired officers and NCOs were imported into OTUs to impart as much knowledge as they could to their fledgling students. It was probably the job they feared most. The 'chop rate' whilst training was alarming; in one class, more than 25% of the trainees were killed in accidents before making it to a frontline squadron.

His training as an instructor took place between December 1941 and March 1942 at 7 FIS Upavon by which time he was qualified to teach novice pilots on elementary and multi-engined training aircraft. Promoted squadron leader, he was given command of No. 2 (T) Squadron, part of No. 6 (P) AFU at Little Rissington. Little Rissington had originally been home to 6 Service Flying Training School (SFTS) in August 1938 flying Audaxes, Furies, Harts and Ansons, at much the same time as Allan was on his way to the desert. By April 1942, 6 SFTS had been re-designated No. 6 (P) AFU (Pilot-Advanced Flying Unit). Allan's role was to provide final training for pilots who had completed basic training in the commonwealth training schools, mostly flying the ever-reliable twin-engined Airspeed Oxfords. He, and the other instructors under his command, were responsible for honing the skills of their pupils before moving on to OTU. (During the war 5,444 pilots were trained by No. 6 FTS/(P) AFU at Little Rissington. Of these, 705 were awarded various gallantry awards; four received the Victoria Cross.)

In July 1942, Allan attended the Empire Central Flying School (ECFS) at Hullavington for two months in order to gain wider experience on instructional techniques, subsequently taking charge of a training squadron at 11 AFU, Shawbury where he stayed until August 1943. Three days after reporting to No. 2 Personnel Despatch Centre (PDC) on August 26, he arrived in Canada as a qualified flying instructor (QFI). Here he stayed for six months at 35 SFTS in North Battlesford, Saskatchewan before coming home in March 1944.

There is a little confusion in Allan's service record at this point, at least in terms of the specifics. He attended both 13 OTU (Bicester) and 12 OTU (Chipping Warden) in April and May for a Mosquito course and further training on the aircraft. The following month he found himself posted to Pathfinder NTU at Upwood for conversion onto four-engined aircraft. A return to operational flying, no doubt long-overdue, finally came at the end of July 1944, when he was told to report to 582 Squadron, Little Staughton.

A bout of chronic tonsillitis meant it was a full three weeks before Allan flew his first operation with 582 Squadron, and his first operation for almost three years, albeit that he had amassed many thousands of hours instructing – and survived. The target was the canal linking Ghent with Terneuzen, and the master bomber was Dickie Walbourn. Taking charge of Lancaster ND880 'A' Apple (subsequently lost in a crash landing on its way back from Wanne Eickel in October), Allan 'borrowed' his commanding officer's crew to accompany him on the raid. Such a practice was not unusual. With the CO, Peter Cribb, not able (and sometimes not allowed) to fly on operations as often as he liked, it meant his crew were often obliged to fly with others to complete their required quota of ops. Allan was flying in a 'supporter' role, reaching the target without incident and dropping 12 x 1,000 pounders on the target from less than 4,000ft. He arrived home safely shortly before three o'clock after a trip of two hours, 25 minutes.

He was in the same aircraft, and with the same crew, the following week when briefed to attack targets near Brest, and specifically the Karvinion light coastal battery and Pointe de St Mathieu. Again the raids passed without incident, but there was rather more excitement the next day (August 26/27) over Kiel, a large raid comprising some 372 Lancasters and 10 Mosquitoes. The Pathfinders' marking was severely hampered by smokescreens, and Allan – flying this time as an illuminator in PB123 'O' Oboe – did not see any flares going down until he dropped his own. Even with the smokescreen, the target was still well and truly plastered, with the Rathaus completely destroyed along with many other public buildings obliterated or severely damaged. Bomber Command most certainly didn't have things all its own way, however, losing 17 Lancasters including six Pathfinder crews.

Even after a comparatively short time back in the saddle, the strain of operations was beginning to tell. Family remarked that Allan had already lost his sparkling sense of fun, and he himself felt sure that with losses on the squadron so high, it was only a matter of time before his number finally came up. Contemporary photographs reveal the man as a shadow of his former self, no longer 'the thickset Australian with an infectious laugh' that Tommy Wisdom described with such obvious affection. For the evening of August 29/30, the target was Stettin on the Baltic involving more than 400 aircraft, including 16 from 582 Squadron with Brian McMillan in charge.

Allan was in a different aircraft again, this time PB202 'E' Easy. But at least he had some consistency with his crew. Joining him for the trip once again were: Flight Lieutenants Alfred Strout and Vincent Tyndale, nav one and nav two respectively; the flight engineer, Flying Officer George Bradley; wireless operator, Pilot Officer Henry Silverwood; and the two gunners, Flight Sergeant Douglas Stevens (who had recently married) in the mid-upper, and Flying Officer Charles Stewart in the rear. The men were all highly experienced: Bradley and Stewart both had the DFM from their service on 35 Squadron; and Henry Silverwood, a 24-year-old Yorkshireman had won his DFM whilst with 77 Squadron, surviving a tour (when many didn't) flying twin-engined Whitleys in 1940.*

Take-off was timed at 21.10. The aircraft carried mixed ordnance comprising 1,000-pounders and flares. The course in would take them over Sweden, and a similar track would be taken for the return leg. The gunners, Stevens and Stewart, were on the alert, quartering the night skies. The flight engineer, George Bradley, was also keeping a careful watch on the fuel gauges. The total flight time would be approximately 10 hours – right at the very limit of a Lancaster's endurance. Henry Silverwood listened out for any last minute recall. Unbeknownst to them all, they were also being watched, tracked by a radar of 8/Ln Rgt 222 Habicht based at Hjardemål.

The radar operators were experts at their game, and skillfully vectored a Junkers Ju88G-1 nightfighter on to the target. The nightfighter was piloted by a young feldwebel named Bruno Rupp of IV/NJG3 who already had 10 victories to his name. He was no novice. In his first four operations he shot down four aircraft – the only pilot in his squadron to achieve such a feat. During a major attack on Hamburg he accounted for three Lancasters in seven

---

* Silverwood's older brother, Geoffrey, had been killed on the night of January 30/31, 1944, shot down in a 100 Squadron Lancaster over Berlin.

minutes. Over Lodberg, with the familiar darkened shape of the Lancaster now in sight Rupp attacked at 3,600 metres, his cannon shells immediately finding their mark. The time was recorded at one minute past midnight.

Allan tried to turn away heading towards Kullen in Sweden. The aircraft turned again over Lyngby where it was also shot at by German flak. Sadly the stricken aircraft and crew were already doomed. It fell vertically, north of Førby Sø lake, clipping a dune as though the pilot was trying one last desperate attempt to bring the Lancaster down in one piece, but to no avail. The mighty bomber crashed and exploded with tremendous force; Rupp's 11th victim was confirmed, and the life of one of Australia's most stalwart servants was cruelly snuffed out.

During the next day, the Wehrmacht buried the crew not far from the crash site, erecting a simple wooden cross by the grave. Axel Rasmussen, a local man in charge of the planting and preservation of dunes, noted where the Germans buried the crew and informed the head of police in Thisted about what had happened. The following week, a team of three trucks and personnel of Nordjydske Udrykningskolonne in Sindal arrived to clean up the crash site after the Germans had removed the major parts of the wreckage including two engines. After the liberation of Denmark a fence was put around the gravesite to protect it, and on 3 February 1947 the remains of the crew were disinterred and re-buried at the nearby Nørre Vorupør Vestre cemetery.

At the end of *Calling Australia*, Al Farrington said:

> "It's grand to be talking to home again, particularly at this time when we are all right in the thick of it. No matter in what parts of the world they are, I know I speak for all Australians when I say that you are nearer to us in our thoughts than ever before. Wherever we are, we are in it together, we will see it through together."

Sadly, it was not to be.

MASTER NAVIGATOR

**The story of Flight Lieutenant Bill Heane DFC, MiD,
nav one, 582 Squadron**

Bill Heane from Preston had the very good fortune of being picked as navigator to one of the very best master bombers, Squadron Leader 'Min' Mingard. It was a partnership that lasted well, surviving six trips in the master bomber role, on three occasions being hit by flak and on two consecutive sorties to Le Havre in September very nearly coming to grief.

> "Our skipper, Squadron Leader 'Min' Mingard, used to say that if you're at the front of the queue you've got more chance of making it back. It worked. We flew 57 trips on Pathfinders on an extended tour, six as master bomber and one as deputy master bomber. And survived."

Ironically, Bill Heane might never have been a Pathfinder. He might never have actually been a navigator had he not frightened the living daylights out of one of his flying instructors so much in the United States that he had to be re-mustered. And even then the course of Bill's war service might have been very different:

> "I had joined up and been sent to the US as part of the Arnold Scheme to become a pilot. I spent six months in training before being re-mustered, and was then sent to Canada to train as a navigator, returning to England in February 1943. My next move was to an operational training unit flying Wimpeys and I was due to be sent to the Far East. We were all set – we'd had the jabs and everything – but at the last moment we were told we were staying and only the pilot and the air bomber went. That meant we were spare bods. From OTU we went to a heavy conversion unit near York with a view to joining 4 Group. It was here that we came across 'Min' Mingard who was looking for a crew and wanted to go to Pathfinders."

Norman Stanley Mingard, always referred to as 'Min' by his crew or more commonly 'Skipper' – primarily because no one seemed to know his Christian name or ever use it – was an extremely 'press-on' type. An experienced flyer, with more than 2,000 hours of blind flying under his belt, Mingard was something of an expert as Bill remembers:

> "One night, some US aircraft based at Kimbolton were having trouble getting down in the dark, and one had already crashed on the runway. The Americans had different frequencies for standard beam approaches (SBAs) – dashes on one side, dots on the other – where a constant noise would tell them they were on track. Min, with the help of the groundcrews, strapped an Aldis lamp to the back of an Oxford – a real Heath Robinson job – and guided them all safely to land.
>
> "Mingard was a good bit older than the rest of us. The oldest of us was 23. Min was 30, and a different generation. That's how it was. I was 21 (my birthday was April 12), and the youngest was 19."

The rest of the crew included Gordon Blake, nav two, and Arnold Bowyer, wireless operator. 'Blakey' had been born in Nairobi, whereas Arnold Bowyer, with whom Bill was particularly friendly, came from a family of butchers in South London. He had had polio as a child and walked with a limp. The two gunners were Fred Holl and Ken Moye who started out as mid-upper and rear gunners respectively, but later changed positions. Ken was the son of a gamekeeper which probably accounted for his excellent gunnery skills and equally superb night vision. The flight engineer was Ron Hughes. To begin with they were posted from Warboys Pathfinder NTU to 156 Squadron, but in the event they were sent directly to 582 Squadron, arriving as one of the first intake on April 1, 1944. The first trip to Noisy-Le-Sec on the 18th passed without incident; two days later, however, was a very different story.

The target was Cologne, never an easy trip. Four groups were taking part, 379 aircraft in all, including 13 Lancasters from 582. Among them was ND 438 'B' Baker, a Lancaster III being navigated by Flying Officer Bill Heane. The flight out was almost exactly two hours, and they arrived over the target to see the first red/yellow flares going down. Despite the cloud the radar navigator identified the target using his H2S set, and their load of six 2,000-pounders went down from 18,000ft, adding further damage to an already concentrated effort that would ultimately account for nearly 2,000 homes destroyed and a further 20,000 damaged. It was just after two in the morning. And then they were hit.

"We got well peppered by flak, Gordon Blake, navigator two, was sat at the H2S set. I was leaning over the chart as we were going in on our bombing run. Suddenly there was a great noise as shell splinters smashed into the side of the aircraft. We both shot to our feet, and turned to one another, our mouths open, but no screams coming out. 'They missed us Blakey,' I said. He just nodded."

Fortunately the damage was only superficial, save for some additional ventilation. There were four aircraft lost that night, including a Lancaster III from 100 Squadron that exploded over the Ruhr. It was probably this that Bill and the crew reported as a 'scarecrow' seen directly over the target shortly after they had bombed. Scarecrows were reported to be a special high-velocity explosive shell that the Germans had developed to bring down Allied bombers even with a near miss. It was only a long-time after the war that it was suggested that scarecrows did not really exist, and what crews were actually seeing was their own aircraft exploding.

For the next few days and weeks that followed, Bill Heane settled into the routine of Pathfinder operations, experiencing the hazards of searchlights over Düsseldorf, and the frustrations of an aborted attack on Essen all before the month of April was over. The following month, over the Louvain marshalling yards, they again received the unwelcome attention of German flak, but again without sustaining serious damage. They also had the unusual experience of hearing a faint voice on the R/T instructing them not to bomb, and return to base. It was a German spoof that went on for about 40 seconds and was repeated, going on for a further 15 seconds. The voice was heard for a third time but ceased when the master bomber came on air. The contemporary report at the time suggests that the message was given in very good English, apart from a slight twang!

In June there was some respite, with the crew stood down. Whilst Bill had little to do with his commanding officer, Wing Commander Dunnicliffe, he had nothing but the highest regard for the station commander, Group Captain 'Fatty' Collings. One story illustrates the point:

"In my opinion, the foundation of the spirit of 582 rested with Fatty Collings. He mixed with the lads, helped us out. In June we were stood down for a time. I had my father's car and Min had an Austin Seven with a streamlined boot and two seats. We all bundled off for a sortie. It was a scorching day, so we travelled up the A1 and decided to look for a watering hole. We found a pub and went inside to grab a beer and a sandwich, which we then ate, sitting on a high curb by the side of the road, our tunics off and our legs dangling over the edge.

Top: Philip Patrick and crew whilst at 7 Squadron, Oakington. Patrick assumed command of training.

Bottom: Godfrey O'Donovan (centre) described as the 'master' of master bombers.

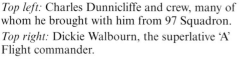

Top left: Charles Dunnicliffe and crew, many of whom he brought with him from 97 Squadron.

Top right: Dickie Walbourn, the superlative 'A' Flight commander.

Middle left: Les Hood the morning after his aircraft sustained severe damage over Düsseldorf, April 1944.

Bottom left: Bobby Chelu (centre back), Johnny Austin (middle row 2nd right) and Douggie Coole (front) died landing in the burning wreckage of their aircraft.

Bottom right: Les Hood (left), Jack Brandt, Jeff Morris and Bill Geeson with Mme Renault, in whose house they hid.

Top: A corner of a foreign field that is forever England.

Middle left: George Hall as a young volunteer reserve officer shortly after being awarded his wings.

Middle right: Members of the Hall crew pose on the wing of a clapped out Halifax at Faldingworth HCU.

Bottom: George Hall, Phil Tovey, Tommy Nichol, Lloyd Taggart, Len Stewart, Les Bellinger and Art Day at HCU.

Top left: George Hall DFC & Bar. Consummate Pathfinder and master bomber.

Top right: Roy Pengilley DFC & Bar. Roy arrived at 582 from 625 Squadron having flown nine operations.

Bottom: Roy Pengilley with members of both his air and ground crews. Together they made a winning combination.

Above left: Roy Pengilley and his crew which included a dentist, motor mechanic, builder, smelter, salesman and a timpanist.

Above right: Davy Davis and his skipper 'Tiny' Shurlock. Davis was killed on his 97th trip.

Left: Roy Last. Teenage Pathfinder wounded in action.

Below: Paddy Finlay (centre back) and crew including Roy Last (left). Lucky to make it home after an eventful trip to Stuttgart.

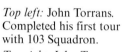

Top left: John Torrans. Completed his first tour with 103 Squadron.

Top right: John Torrans and Alan Hill, shot down and on the run in France.

Middle: The mangled remains of Allan Farrington's Lancaster.

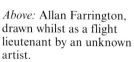

Above: Allan Farrington, drawn whilst as a flight lieutenant by an unknown artist.

Left: Allan Farrington and his young son John. Farrington's smile would quickly fade.

Right: Renowned for his sense of fun, Australian Allan Farrington (front right) in happier times.

Below: Henry Silverwood (in open sheepskin) survived a tour on Whitleys but did not survive the war.

Bottom left: Bill Heane. Portrait by an unknown artist, and a present for his mother.

Bottom right: Flight Sergeant Hughes shows off Norman Mingard's Lancaster, badly damaged over Le Havre.

Top left: Vera Jacobs. As flying controller she made sure everyone got up – and down – safely.

Top right: Vera Jacobs (centre) and friends in 'best blue'.

Middle: Three of 'Tiny' Shurlock's crew: the two navigators Gorman and Lenz, and wireless operator Hazelhurst (centre).

Bottom: They also serve. The maintenance section helped keep the aircraft in the air.

Top left: 'Taffy' Jacobs (left) and fellow gunner Reg Simmonds.

Top right: Haydn 'Taffy' Jacobs showing none of the ravages of his wartime captivity.

Middle: Russ Yeulett (left) survived the Cologne/Gremberg massacre – the only one to get out of his aircraft alive. Bill Lanning is centre.

Bottom left: Target Saarbrücken. A rare aiming point photograph courtesy of 'S' Sugar.

Bottom right: Target Scholven. Pathfinder flares can clearly be seen going down.

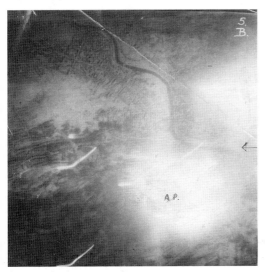

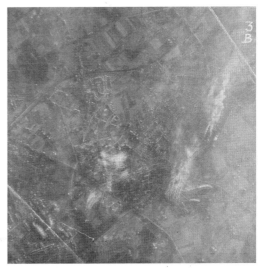

Top left: Bob Palmer VC. Specialist Oboe pilot from 109 Squadron killed displaying heroic endeavour beyond praise.

Top right: Owen Milne. Shared the flying with Bob Palmer VC on the daylight Oboe in which they both lost their lives.

Middle: Mid-upper gunner John Smith in residence.

Bottom: John Smith and friends at the Dorchester for one of the first post-war Pathfinder gatherings.

Top left: John Smith and crew whilst at 576 Squadron prior to joining Pathfinder force. Frank Dockar is far right.

Top right: John Smith DFM managed to get out of his burning aircraft just in time.

Middle: Bill Hough (centre back) and colleagues on a goodwill trip to Brazil with their interpreter Captain Umberto Aguiar.

Bottom left: Art Green. A talented pre-war pilot and popular skipper.

Bottom right: Hough, McKeown, Naylor, and Campbell with their skipper Art Green (2nd right).

Top left: Frank Lloyd and Des Lamb, larking around before take-off.

Top right: Ken Hewitt (far right) next to Dave Spier. Hewitt was murdered, Spier survived.

Middle: American Walt Reif and his crew, whose luck ran out on their second visit to Cologne. Bob Pearce (centre back) and Jack MacLennan (2nd right) survived.

Bottom: Bremen docks, March 1945. As seen through the CO's bombsight.

Top: The airfield at St Trond under attack by Walt Reif. Two explosions can be clearly seen.

Middle: Lancaster 'N' Nuts, the regular mount of Vivian Owen-Jones. L to R: Jack Offer, Johnny Gower, George Fenn, Ron Hughes, Fred Longcluse and Evan Thomas (kneeling).

Bottom: Owen-Jones (left) and crew the morning after a trip to Dessau in which their mid-upper gunner was killed.

Top left: 'Hal' Mettam and crew. Mettam was flying in loose formation with Johnnie Gould when the latter's aircraft exploded over Chesham.

Top right: Frank Lloyd at the controls of his Lancaster, most probably 'P' Peter.

Middle: The tranquillity of war. Frank Lloyd's aircraft at dispersal.

Bottom: David Mansell-Playdell (centre with pipe) baled out when ordered but subsequently wished he hadn't.

Top left: Ted Swales (4th from right), 582 Squadron's only VC. Once criticised by his CO for an early return, he vowed never to do so again and lost his life in the process. Dudley Archer is third from right.

Top right: Ted Stocker, believed to be the only flight engineer to be awarded the DSO and survivor of 108 trips.

Middle: The New Zealander Flight Lieutenant Nairn and his crew.

Bottom: Stafford Coulson as station commander at RAF Scampton, beneath a mighty Vulcan.

Top left: Group Captain Stafford Coulson. The last wartime squadron commander of 582.

Top right: Coulson showed the same paternal instincts to the men under his command.

Bottom: Brian McMillan (centre), 'B' Flight commander and crew. McMillan survived the war only to disappear in the Bermuda Triangle.

"At that moment, an RAF staff car came into sight with pennants flying, and then suddenly stopped. A rather officious flight lieutenant – obviously an aide to whoever was inside – came over to us, ticked us off and took our names for being improperly dressed and behaving in a manner unbefitting of our rank. When we got back to base, Mingard was summoned to see Collings. It turned out that the passenger was none other than Air Vice-Marshal The Honourable Sir Ralph Cochrane, AOC 5 Group who was not the biggest fan of the 8 Group Pathfinders. He wanted us put on a charge; Fatty just told us to be more careful next time and find a pub further away from the main roads!"

By the end of July, the crew had served their apprenticeship as Pathfinders and been promoted through the ranks. Bill received the temporary award of his Pathfinder badge on July 4. In August they went to Stettin. Twice:

"Stettin was our longest trip – nine and a half hours. We flew across the Baltic and across Sweden, even though it was neutral and we weren't supposed to. After Sweden it was then a five-minute leg across to Stettin and out again. We saw a nightfighter over Denmark on the return trip but he didn't see us. Min used to say: 'If you see another aircraft first then don't shoot at him unless he is going to attack you. Don't give our position away.' It worked. To my best knowledge, we never fired a single shot in 57 trips."

On August 31, they were ready for their first sortie in charge, as the master bomber for an attack on the V2 rocket storage facilities at Agenville. All did not go according to plan. On the way in there were two long layers of cumulonimbus cloud moving from east to west which contained the potentially lethal perils of both electric storms and icing. The brave – or the foolish – flew right through it, whereas the more circumspect edged around the worst of it to keep up with the main stream. Worse was to follow over the target that was obscured by 10/10ths cloud:

"We ordered all aircraft to descend, transmitting the height to bomb at 12,000ft. Some of the main force came down, but of course others didn't. We then transmitted for them to come down to 8,500ft, and then 6,000ft but by now, as they broke cloud, a great number of them had already overshot the target and so had to go around again. Flak was quite heavy, and as the main force came in again the intensity and accuracy of the flak increased."

The raid was not a success. Indeed probably the best that could be said about it was that all 582 Squadron aircraft returned safely. That night, 601 aircraft bombed various V2 sites; six Lancasters were lost, four of them over Agenville. Amongst those lost was an aircraft flown by an Australian pilot from 166 Squadron, Two, including the skipper, managed to evade; three were captured and made prisoner; and two were killed. One of those captured was Flying Officer Donald Pleasance, later one of the country's most familiar stage and screen actors.

Agenville may have been a failure, but was quickly forgotten. There was no time to dwell on what had been, only to look forward to what was coming, and in the first two weeks of September, Bomber Command only had one target in mind: Le Havre.

In the advance through France, Belgium and Holland, the Allies had left behind them various pockets of resistance that now required mopping up. The Germans had in effect created fortresses that on the dramatic orders of the Führer were to hold out to the death. The Allies, however, had no wish to lose their own troops for no significant gain, and turned to Bomber Command to deal with the most important that had been singled out for special attention. One of these was Le Havre, whose garrison under the command of Oberst Eberhard Wildermuth comprised more than 11,000 men, 115 guns of all calibres, and enough rations to hold out for 90 days. As it transpired, Bomber Command dealt with this potentially tough nut in the space of seven days, with seven daylight attacks involving 1,863 aircraft dropping 9,500 tons of bombs. The first of these raids was on the 5th, and was a complete success. But it was only the start. The next day they attacked again, and again the bombing was concentrated and well on target. The attack on the 8th had to be abandoned as Le Havre was covered in a thick veil of white and grey, but not before several of the squadron aircraft had been hit, and Fight Lieutenant Goddard shot down. Lancaster NE140 'F' Freddie also found itself in trouble.

Bill had navigated the aircraft to the target in a little over an hour from take-off and they began circling the target, struggling to identify the aiming point. Orbiting to the left, they came in at 2,500ft and were immediately hit by flak:

> "This was our worst trip," Bill says. "We were a backer-up and there was 10/10ths cloud. Min flew in low, and went down lower and lower to try and get down beneath the cloud base. We got down to below 2,000ft, conscious that the high ground to the east of Le Havre is up to about 1,300/1,400ft! We came out of the cloud and the light flak opened up.

"We took 40 hits to the port inner engine nacelle, and all the engine casings fell away. Min quickly popped back into the cloud. We tried to mark, but because we were at such a low altitude our TIs fell 'safe' and did not explode. If you think about it, we were down to 2,000ft and the gunners were perched on top of the hills less than 500 feet away. They couldn't miss."

The gunners didn't miss. As well as taking hits in the bomb bay, the aircraft was lucky not to have suffered severe structural damage:

"It was only after we'd got back – having flown home all the way at 3,500ft until reaching the English coast on three engines – that the full damage to the aircraft was clear. The diheydral on the wing had disappeared, and we had taken so many hits to the main spar that the weight of the engines had made the wings droop."

On September 9, the crew was selected as master bomber, with the call-sign 'strawberry'. Arriving over Le Havre shortly before 08.00, Mingard began calling his deputies – Hockey two and Hockey three – but only Hockey two replied. He ordered the main force to orbit over the sea and await further instructions, and then proceeded with his run over the target. The weather was foul, and thick cumulus cloud blanketed the skies. Originally at 8,000ft, Mingard went lower, to 5,000ft, and called his deputy again to ask whether he had found 'basement'. Receiving a reply in the negative, he decided to go down and look for himself before giving the signal to abandon mission.

Their luck changed on the 10th, when again the Mingard crew was detailed to lead. The attack was an operation of epic proportions: there were no fewer than eight aiming points, each with its own master bomber, and with the whole attack 'controlled' by the 582 Squadron CO, Group Captain Peter Cribb, in a new role as 'longstop'. His mission was to oversee each attack in turn, dropping yellow flares to cancel any misplaced TIs or wild bombing. Every aiming point was given a codename after a make of car, Mingard's target being Alvis IV. It was a solid attack, with Mingard giving a running commentary for main force from when he arrived at 17.34 to when he left 20 minutes later, continually urging them on and not to stray to port or overshoot. When the TIs began to dim, he called for more markers to be dropped until at last calling for the attack to be abandoned. And then once again they were hit:

"This time we took cannon shells in the bomb bay and we still had a full load of TIs. They tore a hole in the bomb doors that you could fall through. We tried to jettison our load over the sea but couldn't get the bomb doors open. In the end we had to take them home."

Again they made it back, and there was a treat in store:

"We landed back late and no one was in the mess. There wasn't the usual eggs and bacon, but there were the carcasses of all these ducks, so we picked what meat was left off the bones with plenty of bread and butter and had a real feast!"

For a time at Little Staughton, Bill was in the same hut as Ted Swales:

"I didn't know him well, but you couldn't miss him with his big build and his khaki uniform. We didn't tend to integrate crews much. You might get to know someone in the mess, but that was about it. Our hut was on the edge of the airfield. I remember the other side of the fence were some pigs and they had three litters whilst we were there. We used to help look after them. We did well for food."

Bill Heane flew two more trips with his skipper as master bomber in September: once to Osnabrück, and once to Boulogne. Both were in daylight. The attack on Osnabrück went particularly well, so much so that on seeing a stick of bombs falling directly alongside the railway line, Mingard was heard to comment: "That's a good one." It was only a small raid, comprising mainly Halifaxes, but it was extremely effective. The attack on Boulogne was considerably larger, in fact more than seven times the size with more than 750 aircraft. It was a 'softening up' attack in preparation for a troop assault, and given that the garrison surrendered soon afterwards, appeared to have the desired effect, but the crew had to work for it.

"The skipper again had difficulty with his R/T, and the first wave of 17 aircraft were so accurate in their bombing that they actually obliterated the TIs. Main force was told to wait whilst the target was re-marked, but orbited so far out to sea, that when they were called in to bomb, they took too long to reach the target and the TIs had gone out."

Despite telling them to bomb 200 yards to port of the TIs, almost without exception they disobeyed. Frustrated, and not a little annoyed by main force's incalcitrance, Mingard called off the attack, but even then the last few stragglers went in and did their own thing. To add one final insult to injury, their aircraft, PB512 'J' Juliet, had the ignominy of being hit by a 37mm cannon shell in the port tail plane, but they made it home without further incident. Bill took such incidents in his stride:

> "As navigator, I was stuck behind the curtain, and only used to go through to the cockpit as we went over the target. During the bomb run I would stick my head in the astrodome. It was then that I used to eat my orange that we used to be issued with as part of our rations."

Bill flew once with the CO on October 2/3 to Düsseldorf, and his final trip as master bomber was to Homberg on October 25 – a raid they had to abort because of cloud. The last trip of his tour was on December 13, an early evening sortie to the Happy Valley, and the Krupps steel factories at Essen. It was not a happy trip for Flying Officer Kinman, who failed to return.

With his tour over, and now a flight lieutenant, Bill Heane was awarded the DFC on January 17, 1945. His skipper, 'Min' Mingard received both the DFC and DSO. Bill added a Mentioned in Despatches after the war for his experimental work on Lincolns, 'endurance testing', an experience he describes as being "probably more dicey than flying Lancs".

He particularly remembers them not being allowed to fly over water in case any bits of the aircraft fell off!

THE FLYING CONTROLLER

The story of ACW Vera Jacobs, flying controller, 582 Squadron

Aircraftwoman Vera Jacobs admits to having had no idea about flying or signals before she joined the WAAF, but in the event ended up doing one of the most important and responsible jobs of any at Little Staughton: Flying Control. Getting a full squadron into the air, and down again, needed a calm disposition; it was not for the easily intimidated. It meant being alert to everything, even the smash and grab raids to steal their teas and biscuits.

The world fell apart for Vera Jacobs on September 11, 1944. At least it did once her shift in Flying Control was over.

Vera was engaged to a pilot officer air gunner Haydn Jacobs, known universally as 'Taffy' because of his Welsh roots. Haydn had come to 582 Squadron from 7 Squadron as part of Wing Commander Philip Patrick's crew, although he had reluctantly teamed up with a new skipper on 'Fatty' Collings' advice when Philip had been posted. Earlier that day, Haydn had asked Vera if she would be his wife, and of course she had accepted:

> "There were quite a few romances on the station at that time. I was friends with Jan January who drove the crew bus, and she and I were trying to get a flight in one of the aircraft. Haydn happened to be on the bus at the time and that is how we met. On September 11 we became engaged and that evening he was sent on operations to Castrop-Rauxel with his skipper, 'Tiny' Shurlock. I was on duty in Flying Control, landing the aircraft. All of them had got back except Haydn, so we knew something had happened. I couldn't do anything about it immediately. I had to carry on and finish the shift."

Vera had been posted to Little Staughton (as part of headquarters staff) on April 1, one of the handful of WAAFs on the station at that time. The Royal Air Force was not a natural calling. Brought up in a sleepy Derbyshire village, she had left school with a view to training as a milliner. But then the war came along and everything changed. She cannot remember why she chose the RAF, but doesn't think it was the uniform. Having answered a call for volunteers she found herself doing the obligatory period of 'square bashing' and parades before moving on to a signals course at RAF Cranwell.

> "My knowledge of signals at that point was zero, although I always reckoned I was good with my hands. I might have been working on teleprinters in the hub of things but I recall being given an IQ test and doing rather well, and from that it was suggested that I would specialise in Flying Control. I was given further instruction, including a spell at OTU in Lichfield for a short time, learning procedures, but a great deal of what I did was learned as we went along."

On arrival at Little Staughton, Vera found herself billeted in Nissen huts on the edge of the field. As with the men's accommodation, it was all rather primitive:

> "Our hut was very basic, with just a single stove in the middle that was meant to keep us warm. There were only a few of us girls, but all who worked in the signals section along with those in the met shared a hut. It was very sociable. There were the usual dances and music groups to keep us entertained, and lots of sport and activities. The local families took us under their wing, and I remember one farmer in particular I used to go to the market with to sell cattle.
> "Given that for most of us this was the first time we had been away from home, I think we all coped rather well. Everyone was 'together'; if you had a problem, you tended to share it and help one another along. Even though many of us were from totally different walks of life, service life – and doing our bit for the war – seemed to bring the best out of us."

Being in Flying Control meant sharing a 24-hour watch. It was not just when 582 Squadron was operating; it also meant being on duty when its sister squadron, 109 (who shared Little Staughton) was in the air. Even when neither squadron was flying, there was always the possibility of landing an aircraft in trouble, or coping with similar emergencies.

> "Part of our duties included listening out for 'Darkie' calls. The 'Darkie' system was a position fixing procedure using radio transmission so that the pilot of an aircraft who was

lost could speak to us when over England and we could tell him where he was."

Using the system, the pilot would be given either his approximate position, or courses to steer and distances from ground station to ground station until eventually he rediscovered his own airfield. It was primarily intended for those pilots in distress, and with the pace of raids over Germany on the increase, pilots in distress were a common occurrence.

Whilst a male corporal was in charge of day-to-day activities within Flying Control, the officer commanding (flying) – often one of the flight commanders – was always on duty for aircraft taking off or landing. Group Captain Collings, the station commander, was also a frequent visitor, and although formidable, managed to impart a calm assurance in a crisis.

> "We worked to set procedures and were not to waver from those procedures unless there was very good reason. Everything that we did or said was recorded in a log book – names of captains of aircraft, aircraft numbers and details – nothing was omitted. We kept status cards on each runway, and a blackboard indicated who was flying. I shall never forget seeing those names rubbed out after the Cologne/Gremberg trip.
>
> "Our main duties of course were making sure that all of the aircraft got off the ground safely, and were landed safely, as well as controlling air traffic in our immediate vicinity. Before take-off, some of the pilots would have little rituals; they would say certain things. When they came back to land, they just wanted to get down as soon as they could.
>
> "The Mosquitoes of course tended to be back first. Not only were they much faster than the Lancasters, but they also had longer-range R/T. Even if a Lancaster was in front of them, they could call Flying Control sooner and we would give them their slot to land. Our call-sign was 'Breadboard'. If there were several aircraft over the airfield at the same time, we would stack them until it was their turn to land. Once they were in the circuit, they would be given permission to land and once clear of the runway, we would allow the next aircraft in and so on. Obviously anyone in difficulty or with wounded on board was given priority.
>
> "There was always an OC (Flying) on duty and he would handle anything out of the ordinary or out of our depth. Because he had operational experience, he was better placed and more experienced to make judgements

and take difficult decisions, and tell us what to do. Collings was particularly good at this. He was very sizeable and had definite presence. He might come across as a bit of bully but actually he had a kind heart. He was a very human 'groupie' and you always felt that he would back you up 100%.

"One night the commanding officer, Wing Commander Dunnicliffe was in Flying Control. He wanted to change the procedure whilst we were in the middle of landing some aircraft and he very nearly caused a catastrophe. We knew the procedures better; they were there to be followed."

Flying Control was not without its creature comforts:

"We had a 'gubbins' room where we used to make tea and coffee. Every so often one of the aircrew would come along and try and pinch it, and we would send them packing. We shared the tower with the Meteorological section, and shared very well."

It took more than a cup of tea to stop Vera from worrying the night Haydn went missing, even though she had complete faith in his pilot, 'Tiny' Shurlock. Tiny had come to 582 Squadron having completed 12 operations in the Middle East, but with very little experience of four-engined flying. He had not gone through the usual OTU, HCU or main force channels. He was therefore crewless, but not for long. Amongst one of his first recruits was Haydn Jacobs, who had been booked to go on a pilot's course but volunteered to remain on the station, having by that time met Vera and preferring to stay put. The rest of the crew comprised the flight engineer Warrant Officer Davy Davis DFM, navigator Flying Officers Ken Lenz and Jack Gorman, wireless operator Warrant Officer Bill Hazlehurst, and mid-upper gunner Flight Lieutenant Reg Simmonds. Most of them were on their third or even fourth tours. Reg Simmonds, for example, had survived two tours on Blenheims in the Middle East in 1941/42. 'Davy' Davis was close to his ton of operations.

Their initiation with Tiny did not go very well. Tail wheels through the hedge on take-off, undercarriage checks after landings and so forth. Vera remembers Tiny's legendary inability to land:

"We often used to go outside, even if we were off duty, to see the aircraft coming in to land. Tiny always used to smack his aircraft down on the runway. There was one occasion when he was on the R/T asking permission to land. He was cleared for landing, and a few moments later said he was down, suggesting it was a perfect landing. We asked him to repeat his position as we couldn't see him and he said that he was just clearing the runway. Still we couldn't see him. Then it transpired he had actually landed at nearby Thurleigh airfield, a US base that had the same QDM as Little Staughton. It was always amusing that the time he made a perfect landing, nobody was there to see it!"

After some initial misgivings, the crew soon grew to trust their new skipper and completed 19 trips together before being briefed for the Castrop-Rauxel raid. Haydn Jacobs, writing an account of the raid in 1994 described what happened:

"On the run in to the target we were predicted, the flak was very hostile and Davy was in the nose ready to drop visually if necessary with Jack Gorman and Ken Lenz bombing on the 'box'. I warned Tiny to weave but he told me in his quiet but authoritative voice that he was on the run in and that he would not weave until the bombs were away. Alas we had three direct hits, one on the nose severely wounding Davy (he died in Jack's arms), the starboard outer was blown off and the inner on fire. Tiny ordered us to bale out. Jack and Davy went together, Bill Hazlehurst left through the rear door but Reg Simmonds was stuck upside down in his turret. I managed to release him and push him out. I went forward to help Ken Lenz toggle the bomb load off but to no avail. How Tiny managed to keep 'N' Nuts under control I will never know but he managed to hold her while Ken and I jumped. The last I saw of the aircraft it was inverted and going down well on fire. I thought Tiny would never get away with it but he did. After many harrowing experiences, with the exception of Bill Hazlehurst we all arrived at Stalag Luft I."

Of course Vera knew Haydn was missing, but not that he was safe. It was one occasion when she would have dearly loved to have seen Tiny arriving home for one of his infamous landings:

"It was some months after that we found out they were OK. Haydn's name was mentioned in a broadcast from Germany by Lord Haw Haw (aka William Joyce, hanged after the war as a traitor) so we knew they were safe before we actually received official notification on December 6. Haydn was put in solitary and was given a rough time. He said afterwards that the Germans seemed to know everything about our squadron, the commanding officer, and the crews, but Haydn kept quiet."

Meanwhile, life for Vera had to carry on. Incident followed incident, almost to the point that nothing was unusual. Aircraft crash-landed with full bomb loads on board; others came to grief on the surrounding electricity pylons; aircraft skidded off the runway in bad weather. And it was not just British aircraft that caused hearts to momentarily stop beating. A German intruder in the circuit may have wreaked havoc had it not been for Fatty Collings' calm intervention. Everyone also remembers the day they had an unexpected visit from a B17 Flying Fortress.

The Fortress had taken off from nearby Kimbolton and aborted almost immediately, the starboard outer having packed up. Finding the nearest airfield to land, the Fortress came straight in, but its undercarriage collapsed and the aircraft skidded off the runway, finishing less than 50 yards from Little Staughton's bomb dump. Given that the Fortress still had its own bombs on board at that time, the results might have been disastrous. Fortunately, nothing exploded. Eventually it was repaired at Little Staughton except for the starboard outer engine that was removed but not replaced. A skeleton crew arrived and to everyone's astonishment decided to take off on the short runway on three engines. Most of the station turned out to watch, and there was general astonishment that the American pilot got away with it, clearing the wire fence at the end of the runway by inches, no more.

Vera continued on the squadron until the war's end. Haydn and Tiny returned from Germany, both spending time in hospital in Cosford and St Athan, recuperating. Remarkably, Tiny had been diagnosed with advanced TB, and had flown all of his 31 operational sorties with the condition. He would spend the next four years in care, having seven operations and emerging in the summer of 1948 minus one lung and a number of ribs. Haydn's recovery was more rapid, and he was well enough to marry Vera on August 4, 1945. Vera left Little Staughton the following month.

DOUBLE JEOPARDY

The story of Flight Sergeant Tom MacLachlan DFM, air gunner, 582 Squadron

Tommy MacLachlan flew the majority of his tour with two skippers, both of whom he admired greatly. He was on compassionate leave the night that the first, 'Sam' Little, was shot down and killed over the centre of Aachen. He was on operations on September 17 when his new pilot, 'Joe' Street, almost came to grief on a relatively 'simple' trip in daylight to Boulogne. And in-between he also played his part in an operation that set something of a Bomber Command record.

Whilst Bill Heane was navigating his skipper 'Min' Mingard successfully to Boulogne, Flight Sergeant Tommy MacLachlan was in the mid-upper turret of PB119 'H' How, protecting his skipper Flying Officer Joe Street from fighter attack. Tommy had come to 582 Squadron from 'C' Flight of 156 Squadron, but with another crew. He had been 'teamed' with Flight Lieutenant Stuart 'Sam' Little DFC, a 30-year-old Canadian, and they had flown at least 17 sorties together at 156 before arriving at Little Staughton. Included in their record up to that point had been no fewer than seven trips to 'The Big City', Berlin, as well as Stuttgart (twice), Frankfurt (twice), and long hauls to Leipzig and Stettin. Good fortune, albeit for unfortunate reasons, dictated that he had not been flying the night that Sam Little and his crew were lost:

> "I started operational flying in October 1943 until May 24, 1944 when we were briefed to bomb Aachen. Not long after briefing I was granted compassionate leave to go home to see my father who had not long to live. I had intended to leave for home immediately after we landed from the raid but Bernard Webb, the mid-upper gunner in Joe Street's crew told me to go straight away and that he would take my place. I owe him my life for he perished with the rest of the crew when they were shot down in the centre of Aachen."

The loss of his much-admired skipper and the rest of the crew came as a profound shock. Along with Little and Webb, the other casualties included the two navigators, Flight Lieutenant John Flynn, a 25-year-old Canadian and Pilot Officer Gwynfor Jones, a 22-year-old Welshman from Glamorgan, as well as the flight engineer, Sergeant Wilf Truman, 26, wireless operator Flight Sergeant Alfred Oram, 22, and a 19-year-old gunner, Flight Sergeant Neville Rawlinson. All are buried in the Rheinberg war cemetery.

From that moment, Tommy became a regular in the Street crew, sharing their adventures. And there had been many, but none as dramatic as the ordeal they were about to face attacking Boulogne on what should have been a relative 'milk run'. The navigators, Franklin and Tommy McComb had had an easy job finding the target, and had visually identified the aiming point by the loop in the river and nearby houses:

"On the first run up to the target we did not have the correct bombing position so we orbited and came in to attack at 2,300ft. Every gun in the German army suddenly seemed to open up on us as we were on the point of releasing our target indicators and bombs. We were hit in the bomb bay by 88mm flak and our TIs exploded. The aircraft was engulfed in green flares. The aircraft was hit many times and a hole approximately 6ft x 5ft was blown in the tailplane and the aircraft immediately plunged into a dive. At the same time there was a scream of pain and thinking the pilot had been mortally wounded, I scrambled out of my mid-upper turret, fighting against the 'G' force and clipped on my parachute.

"By this time the aircraft had levelled out, and I was able to open the rear exit door. When I looked down I saw that we were only at about 500/600ft and at the same time I saw the wireless operator coming down the fuselage signalling at me not to jump. The scream had come from the rear gunner (Pilot Officer Minogue) who had been hit many times in the back by flak. The wireless operator and I managed to get him out of his turret and up to the rest-bed in the fuselage. We made him as comfortable as we could and injected morphia to relieve the pain. The navigator one (Franklin) had also received minor shrapnel wounds to both legs so we bandaged them and as all of the hydraulic lines had been cut we headed for the nearest airfield across the Channel which was Tangmere, where we crash-landed.

"The rear gunner, who was Canadian, was taken away by ambulance and we never saw him again. (I believe he was returned to Canada but up to the time of my leaving

> the squadron I never knew whether he survived or not.)
> The crew was picked up by another Lancaster (flown by
> Wing Commander Walbourn) and returned to the
> squadron the following day."

The damage to the Lancaster was considerable: it had been hit in the
tail unit and the bomb bays, all pipe-lines had been severed, and the
R/T and D/R compass rendered u/s. It was repaired, however, and
after serving time on an HCU was finally scrapped in September
1947.

Boulogne was by no means Tommy's only near brush with death,
and certainly not the only time he was in an aircraft hit by flak: over
Wizernes on June 28, in his first daylight operation, his Lancaster's
port inner oil tank was holed and the hydraulics damaged; he
witnessed 'Splinter' Spierenberg being shot down on the 29th on a
night of intense fighter activity, and also the Lancaster of Squadron
Leader John Weightman over Forêt du Croc on July 20:

> "The leading aircraft [Weightman] was only a hundred
> yards from our port side. Within seconds the port inner
> engine began to smoke and as the mid-upper gunner
> (George Macarthur) waved to me the Lancaster's port
> wing broke off and the aircraft went straight down and I
> saw it crash in a wood. The wing seemed to take forever
> before it spiralled down to land some distance away. None
> of the crew was able to bale out."

As well as being shot at by the Germans, Tommy also had the
unpleasant experience of being shot at by his own side coming back
from Stuttgart:

> "On the outward journey the rear turret oxygen supply
> pipe snapped forcing the operation to be aborted. When
> returning over the Channel and about to cross the coast
> near Dover we got mixed up with a group of flying bombs
> (V1s) and our anti-aircraft defences opened up on them –
> and us! We turned out to sea again and crossed the coast
> at another point."

Joe Street was off duty on September 10, the result of a slight
accident on a motorcycle. It meant Tommy had the pleasure of flying
with the squadron CO, Group Captain Peter Cribb on an operation
he describes simply as an 'epic'. The plan was ambitious: eight
separate coastal batteries represented by eight separate aiming
points, all of which were named after cars: Buick I and II, Alvis I to
IV, and Bentley I and II. Because of the close proximity of the
Canadian troops, as well as having an individual master bomber for

each target (Mingard was master bomber of Alvis IV), a 'long stop' was added to control the entire attack.

Flying Lancaster PB141 'C' Charlie, take-off was just after three in the afternoon. Along with most of the regular Street crew, Cribb was also flying with a third, highly experienced navigator, Squadron Leader Dudley Archer, who guided them onto their first target – Buick I – by 16.11. Incredibly, the next two and a half hours were spent moving from one target to the next. At Buick II, Cribb advised the master bomber to abandon the mission as main force was tending to overshoot, and one of the red TIs had landed 600 yards adrift of the aiming point; on Alvis IV he stepped in to assist 'Min' Mingard, and on Bentley II, where again the main force was ignoring accurate markers and bombing TIs 400 yards away, he put a line of yellow markers down to indicate the point beyond which the bombs must not be dropped. They left for home, having considered six of the attacks to be quite good, with the aiming point well covered, one attack to be slightly less good with the bombing scattered, and the eighth attack to be a considerable overshoot, with some of the bombs missing the aiming point by more than a mile.

"The attacks were scheduled at 20 minute intervals and we were master bomber on all of them. The duties of the master bomber were to instruct the Pathfinder crews where to drop their target indicators and correct any errors in bombing by the main force. This was done by transmitting on a pre-arranged wave length to the bomber stream. Flying at only 2,000ft, we had a perfect view of the raids and of the advancing Canadian troops. It was like watching a film, seeing the German troops running from cover to fire their 88mm shells at us, and then run back when more bombs began to fall.

"On this trip instead of target indicators and bombs we carried yellow markers to drop on top of and cancel out any TIs that fell too close to the Canadians. We had the distinction of creating a record for this operation, being over the target for a total of two hours and 50 minutes. This was the first time I had visual contact with the Germans and it was fascinating to see their vehicles dash about the harbour area and around the perimeter of the town."

After the epic that Tommy describes, the remainder of his tour must have seemed like an anti-climax, but it was still not without its heart-stopping moments. Like, for example, the time they saw a German fighter, as clear as day because it was a moonlit night, but somehow it didn't see them. Or the time they were attacked by a German jet fighter on their way back from Cologne. It was going so fast, that by the time it had attacked, missed and overshot, Tommy had not even managed to bring his guns to bear, and could not believe the speed with which the aircraft was travelling.

(That night, October 31/November 1, they had a very special passenger on board; the war correspondent Richard Dimbleby to witness an attack by almost 500 bombers in which nearly 100 Germans were killed.)

Tommy remembers well his time in 582 Squadron:

"It was an unforgettable experience of comradeship, excitement, laughter and fear all rolled into one. Each day when you woke the first thought that came into your head was 'will I be flying tonight?'. After leaving our hut, the crew would go to their different messes for breakfast that, compared to civilian rations, was usually very good. The crews would then assemble in the crew room and it was there that we would find out if operations were 'on'. We would then go out to the Lancaster and each crew member would check their respective equipment before taking off on a night flying test (NFT). This enabled us to make sure that everything was in working order but unfortunately it also alerted the German radar systems that operations were scheduled for that night because of the increased wireless activity.

"In the afternoon (assuming this was a night operation), we would attend briefing and find out what the 'target for tonight' would be. By this time, Little Staughton would be 'closed down', i.e. no outside phone calls, no leaving the airfield, and the armourers would go from aircraft to aircraft loading the different types of target indicators and bombs. At the same time, the petrol bowsers were busy putting the high-octane fuel into the petrol tanks. I distinctly remember that the fuel load for a Berlin raid was 2,154 gallons and for a Ruhr raid 1,200 gallons.

"Before take-off, the meal was always the same, comprising eggs and chips. I believe there was a medical reason for this which is probably true. The waiting between then and take-off was the worst time of all because although everyone was frightened and hoping that for some reason the raid might be called off, no one had the courage to admit it! It was always a relief when the time came to start up the engines and we taxied round the perimeter track to the end of the runway ready for take-off.

"Once we were airborne all thoughts of a negative kind were eliminated and the adrenalin started pumping through one's body. Crossing the enemy coast was an experience that never failed to excite, with the combination of anti-aircraft fire (flak) and searchlights. Invariably on the way to the target one could see bombers being shot down by the nightfighters and combats taking place between the fighters and the bombers but the superior cannon fire of the former gave very little chance to the .303 ammunition of the latter.

"Over the target was an experience that anyone who has witnessed it will never forget. Searchlights, flak, flares and target indicators all combined to turn night into a huge, colourful, beautiful but frightening event. When a shell burst close to the aircraft, the powerful smell of the explosive filled the oxygen masks of the crew and the plane would rock as if it were taking part in some aerial dance in a noisy symphony concert! The worst part of the raid was the 10/12 seconds straight and level run that the aircraft had to make after the release of the 'cookie' (4,000-pound HE bomb). This was necessary because the photo flash was timed to enable the camera to record where the bombs fell in relation to the aiming point.

"After leaving the target area, the relief among the crew was always the same, and one began to believe that, after all, we were going to make it back home.

"When we landed and had been to de-briefing, we had another meal and made our way back to our billet but the anti-climax of a peaceful morning after the nervous tension of the past few hours made sleep – although it would have been welcome – almost impossible.

"The camaraderie of the personnel on an operational bomber squadron not only existed among the aircrew but with the groundcrews also. The aircrew trusted the work of the riggers, mechanics, fitters and armourers implicitly and the work and hours they put into making the aircraft as safe as possible will always be remembered by the aircrew with the utmost respect and affection.

"In our spare time most of the aircrews stayed together, whether having a night in the mess or going out of the camp. One of our favourite evenings was to go in Joe Street's car to a little pub in the middle of nowhere called the Tally Ho. Life was strange in those days, a mixture of every experience you can imagine. Some crews arrived on the squadron and before you got to know them they were missing. Their replacements would come and the same thing happened. In those days the casualty rate was very high and the average amount of operational trips was seven or eight. Other crews, like my first and with Joe Street, were fortunate enough to survive not one but two tours of operations."

Tommy's last flight with Joe Street was to Leuna on December 6, which they had to abort when the starboard inner stopped dead and they couldn't make the necessary height. The bombs had to be jettisoned into the sea. He was awarded a Distinguished Flying Medal on November 10, 1944, and permanently awarded his Pathfinder badge at the end of his tour.

It was not the end for the remainder of the Street crew however. On the 12th they went to Essen, and three days later, Ludwigshafen where they arrived more than three and a half minutes late over the target – in Pathfinder terms, unforgivable! On the fatal mission to Cologne/Gremberg, Joe Street led one of the three formations and luckily made it back in one piece. He was posted from 582 Squadron on January 13, 1945.

Chapter Four

A Squadron at War

October – December 1944

October started gently with a series of training flights, the usual mixture of cross-countries, fighter affiliation exercises and air-to-air firing practice.

On October 3, the squadron returned to operations, putting up four aircraft to mark the sea wall at Westkapelle, the most western point of the island of Walcheren. Walcheren held the key to the effective use of the port of Antwerp, which in turn held the key to the Allies' success in northern Europe. Antwerp could handle more than 40,000 tons per day of urgently needed supplies, assuming the cargo vessels could negotiate the heavy coastal batteries on Walcheren that threatened to sink them. The navy called in the RAF, and the RAF called in the Pathfinders.

The plan was for an attack by eight waves of bombers, with 30 aircraft to each wave. Initial marking was by Mosquitoes, with the crews of Group Captain Peter Cribb, Wing Commander Dickie Walbourn, Flight Lieutenant Godfrey O'Donovan, and Squadron Leader Bill Spooner – possibly the four most expert of all experts on 582 Squadron at that time – in charge of the show. Cribb was master bomber.

The attack started well, the first TIs going down at 12.57 (zero minus three). A succession of 1,000 and 4,000 pounders hit the target over the course of a two-hour period, causing a breach 100-yards across, and the seawater came flooding in. Eight Lancasters of 617 Squadron, the Dambusters, had been on stand-by with their massive 12,000-pound Tallboy bombs, but the Pathfinders – with whom there was an intense rivalry – had tremendous pleasure in telling them that their 'special' weapons would not be needed. It was a sweet victory in more ways than one. It was especially sweet for O'Donovan who was later awarded the Distinguished Service Order for his part in the raid, the citation saying that: 'he displayed the highest standard of courage and pressed home his attack with great skill and precision. O'Donovan has completed a very large number of sorties, involving attacks on a wide range of targets including such heavily defended areas as Berlin, Stuttgart, Stettin and Kiel.'

The next night attack (October 5) was a full squadron effort to Saarbrücken, to support the US Third Army by cutting communication and supply lines coming through the town. Harris must have been feeling well disposed towards his American Allies, or else obliged, because he committed no fewer than 550 bombers to the task, 16 from 582. All took off and returned safely, with most reporting that the bombing appeared accurate and well concentrated, and seeing a number of large and small explosions. Wing Commander Brian McMillan, one of three primary visual markers, stated that fires could still be seen 90 miles from the target, fires from nearly 7,000 houses in the process of being destroyed or seriously damaged.

Whereas the attack on the 5th had been an all-squadron affair, on the 6th the squadron's resources were split between two targets: Dortmund and Scholven. The seven crews despatched to Scholven were the first away shortly before 15.00. All went well, with the exception of Flying Officer Jack Kinman (NE 130 'L' Lucy) who had to abort as a result of a total loss of coolant causing his engines to overheat, and Flying Officer Jimmy Brown (PB179 'J' Juliet) whose navigator two was hit by flak and slightly wounded. All got home safely. The seven sent to Dortmund took off two hours later as part of a much larger operation that was remarkable in that more than half of the total effort came from the Canadian 6 Group. The raid heralded what was to become known as the 'Second Battle of the Ruhr', and resulted in serious damage to the industrial and transportation heart of the city. Only Squadron Leader 'Willie' Williams in PB538 'B' Baker experienced any difficulties, the pilot being unable to focus on his blind flying instruments, forcing him to return early.

The planners' obsession with Germany's oil producing capacity had led to the attack on the facility at Scholven and also prompted an attack on Wanne Eickel on the 12th. Once again it was Flying Officer Jimmy Brown who grabbed the headlines, bringing his crippled Lancaster back to the emergency field at Manston, and just getting clear before the aircraft burst into flames. It also signalled the 100th operation for one of the squadron stalwarts, Flight Lieutenant Ted Stocker, who received an immediate DSO for his support to the master bomber.

Operation Hurricane was intended to demonstrate to the Germans, if they hadn't got the point already, that the Allies could exert their total superiority over the Fatherland at any time they wished. To do so, Harris would mount two major raids in 24 hours, punctuated by a major assault by the American Eighth Air Force. The target chosen was Duisberg, 582 Squadron's contribution comprising 31 aircraft over Bomber Command's two raids.

Squadron Leader Mingard was in charge of the first attack, and had no difficulty in finding the docks to the south-east of the aiming point and the curve in the railway leading to the marshalling yards. The attack went well. Later that evening, 16 more aircraft took to the air and similarly enjoyed the party. Only Squadron Leader Douglas Peacock spoiled things, having to abort with an overheating starboard generator.

October continued with further attacks on Wilhelmshafen (15th), Stuttgart (19th), Essen (23rd) and Homburg (25th). In each case, all aircraft took off and returned. On October 28, squadron strength was again split between two targets: Walcheren and Cologne.

The Walcheren crews were the first away, leaving Little Staughton shortly after 10.25. Squadron Leader Clough, the former army officer, was in charge, instructing main force to come down below the cloud base (5,000ft) and bomb. Cloud continued to hamper the attack, as aircraft approached singly, rather than in any numbers, although the bombs that did fall appeared to be well concentrated. The last aircraft landed safely back at base at 12.50.

Wing Commander McMillan was in charge of the Cologne attack, in daylight, comprising two waves both controlled Musical Parramattas. The planners seemed to have a sixth sense that the Oboe results would be low, because the reserves, flying in formation, were instructed to drop their bomb markers on the primaries' release signal. Backing up was particularly impressive, and most of the squadron dropped their ordnance. McMillan controlled the first phase as a Parramatta until the TIs were totally obscured by smoke and later crews were instructed to bomb the centre of the smoke. McMillan circled the target area, sustaining flak damage to the port inner engine, cutting the electrical power and condemning the rest of the crew to a slow, lonely and cold flight home. He won a richly-deserved DSO for his efforts, the citation making mention of the considerable flak and his commanding officer describing him as '...an intrepid pilot [who] remained over the target for many minutes to press home a most determined and successful attack. This officer is a highly efficient flight commander, whose sterling qualities have impressed us all.' He was taken off operations with immediate effect.

There was also reward for one of the rising squadron stars, Flight Lieutenant Hugh Hemsworth, a Royal Australian Air Force pilot. In his own report after the raid, he recounts that his aircraft was hotly engaged by heavy flak, and as such he could see little of the attack. His peers, however, had seen enough to recommend him for a Bar to his DFC, singling out not just his bravery in maintaining a straight and level bombing run on this attack, but also his skill, courage, and response to the individual responsibilities that had been entrusted to him on the squadron.

Interestingly, and not in any way to demean the efforts of Hugh

Hemsworth, the aircraft of Flying Officer Walt Reif was similarly engaged by heavy flak and Reif returned home – just – with some 300 holes in his aircraft and his two starboard engines out of action. His brilliant piece of airmanship went officially unrecognised, save from the crew he brought back.

It was back to Walcheren the next day, with Squadron Leader Clough again in charge. The attack was a success, but one Lancaster was missing, a 582 Squadron aircraft flown by Flying Officer Lawrence Croft. Croft, a Kiwi, had taken off in PB630 'A' Apple at 11.45; by 14.10, with the last of the squadron aircraft safely returned, Croft was overdue. No one had seen or heard from him since take-off. His loss was especially tragic since that day he was flying with eight, rather than seven, in his crew, including Flight Lieutenant Eric Dawson DFC, an experienced navigator. It was the squadron's first loss for more than a month.

October ended with yet another raid on Cologne, a major attack with more than 900 bombers. No aircraft were lost. The month also saw the departure of two of the squadron's founding members, the 'A' Flight commander Wing Commander Dickie Walbourn (posted out October 12) and the signals leader Flight Lieutenant Charles Chetham.

November started where October left off: with an attack on Cologne. That night, the squadron had a very special passenger amongst their ranks – the war correspondent Richard Dimbleby. In his broadcast the following day he described how the attack developed:

"Last night I flew for the first time with the Pathfinders, the force whose job it is to ensure the accuracy and concentration of the attack by marking the exact aiming point with coloured indicators – red, green and yellow flares. The main force of bombers aims at the centre of the cluster of flares and thus gets its whole load of bombs into the exact ground area chosen as the target. This job of pathfinding, which is done by picked crews, demands a particular skill in navigation and, perhaps, a very high degree of determination, for the Pathfinder cannot let himself be deflected from his precise course as he approaches his target.

"Last night our job (Dimbleby was flying with Joe Street and crew) was to replenish the flares already dropped by the Pathfinders ahead. The first cluster went down as we were approaching, red and green lights hanging from their parachutes, just on top of the white cloud bank that hid Cologne. This was 'sky-marking'; the bombs of the main force, now streaming in above and below us, jet black in the brilliant light of the full moon, had to pass down by the flares. They vanished into the cloud and soon the underside of it was lit by a suffused white glow, the light of the incendiaries burning on the ground and the baffled searchlights. The flares seemed to be motionless, but round them and just under as we drove steadily over in a dead level straight line, the German flak was winking and flashing. Once a great gush of flame and smoke showed the bursting of a 'scarecrow', the oddity designed by the Germans to simulate a heavy bomber being shot down, and so to put any of our less experienced pilots off their stroke. There were fighters around too. A minute or two before we had seen the yellow glow of one of the new jet-propelled variety climbing at great speed above us and to starboard.

"We circled around the flares, watching the light under the cloud going pink with the reflection of fire and, silhouetted against it, the Lancasters and Halifaxes making off in the all-revealing light of the moon. Then we too turned for home."

With Cologne, the first week marked a return to some of Harris' favourite targets in and around the Ruhr: Düsseldorf (2nd/3rd), Bochum (4th/5th), Gelsenkirchen (6th). Over Bochum, heavy flak and nightfighters took their toll, shooting down no fewer than 23 Halifaxes (including five from one squadron) and five Lancasters. Flight Lieutenant Hemsworth, who had recently been notified of his second DFC, was particularly lucky to make it back in one piece. Pilot Officer Don Croney navigated his skipper to the target, ignoring the heavy flak that began bursting all around them. As their bombing run began, their Lancaster PB652 'S' Sugar was hit by accurate and concentrated anti-aircraft fire, wounding the Australian wireless operator, Pilot Officer Gordon Hunt, in the face and leg. Croney immediately went to the assistance of his injured friend, patching him up as best he could and administering morphia. Hunt insisted on returning to his station, despite continuous pain and in considerable distress. Hemsworth got them home without further damage, and both Hunt and Croney were awarded DFCs for their fortitude.

On the afternoon of November 11, 10 aircraft were detailed for operations and nine successfully attacked Dortmund. On their way into debriefing, each returning pilot was asked by the intelligence officer whether he had seen Flying Officer Mellor. It transpired that whilst every other member of Mellor's crew had gone out to dispersal, Mellor himself had gone missing. His body was found the following day, some distance from the airfield, in a potato field, his service revolver by his side. The 21-year-old Abel Mellor had taken his own life. He had been at 582 Squadron almost exactly four weeks. It was the only squadron casualty that month.

The second half of November saw some unusual names appear on the target maps. Jülich, for example, was the objective for November 16 in support of the American First and Ninth Armies, with the commanding officer leading the way. For once, main force (mainly Halifaxes) arrived early and behaved well, bombing accurately and where directed. Other targets for the month included Munster (18th), Koblenz (20th), Wesel, Worms, Castrop-Rauxel and Aschaffenberg (all on 21st), and Neuss (27th). It concluded with an attack on Duisberg.

It was a busy and exciting time for the squadron, both in the air and on the ground. One of the more light-hearted incidents involved the CO and station commander who were most displeased to let an escaped Luftwaffe prisoner of war slip through their fingers. The airman had escaped from nearby Colmworth POW camp, probably with the madcap idea of stowing away or stealing an RAF aircraft. He was spotted lurking near the bomb dump, and the duty NCO promptly organised a search party, drawing a Sten gun (unloaded) from the armoury. The poor escapee was quickly found in the corner of a toilet block – an ignominious end – and marched off to the guard house. The police, however, deemed it a 'civil' matter, and the prisoner was taken away before the group captain or wing commander had time to interrogate him.

November was a busy month for postings. Among those leaving the squadron was the splendid 'B' Flight commander, Brian McMillan, and Harold Siddons, the engineer leader who had baled out of the aircraft flown by 'Splinter' Spierenberg in June and returned to Little Staughton to finish his tour. Four new pilots were posted in: Flight Lieutenant Botha, Flight Lieutenant Nairn, Flying Officer McVerry, and Pilot Officer Gould. Of them all, the most experienced by far was Flight Lieutenant Bernhorst Botha. Botha had originally trained as an air gunner and by June 1944, with 50 Squadron, was awarded his first DFC whilst on his third tour of operations. He followed this soon after with the award of a DSO, the citation crediting him with helping to maintain the high standard of morale in his squadron, and having completed a very large number of sorties, both as an air gunner and a pilot.

A similarly experienced navigator also arrived on the squadron, Squadron Leader Dudley Archer DFC, DFM. Archer had won his DFM as a sergeant navigator with 102 Squadron in 1941 and had since been commissioned.

December did not start well, and ended in catastrophe.

Squadron Leader Frederick Grillage, who had come to 582 Squadron as gunnery leader, had opted to fly with Flight Lieutenant Art Green on a trip to Heimbach as Green's own regular gunner had shot himself by accident the previous day. It was bad luck for Grillage that German Me262 jet fighters happened to be in the vicinity of Heimbach that afternoon, and even with his experience he was not able to save the Lancaster from being shot down. Happily the majority of the crew got out and got home. Unhappily, Grillage was killed in his turret. As was the tradition, he received the permanent award of his Pathfinder badge. Posthumously.

Further casualties were taken on the night of December 12/13 with the loss of Flying Officer Jack Kinman and his crew. Kinman, 22, had been one of 15 pilots briefed to attack Essen, the last time they would do so at night. Out of an attacking force of 540 aircraft, six were lost, one each from 12, 103, 150, 460, 635 and 582 Squadrons. All were hit by flak whilst on their bombing runs, Kinman's Lancaster PB554 'M' Mother exploding in mid-air. Along with Kinman, two DFM recipients, Flight Sergeant Albert Plimmer, ex-101 Squadron and Flying Officer Patrick Hughes were also killed.

On December 17/18 the squadron took part in Bomber Command's first and only raid on Ulm, home of two large lorry factories, Magirius-Deutz and Kassbohrer, as well as being a military barracks. The attack lasted 25 minutes, during which time nearly 1,500 tons of bombs were dropped, starting in the centre and then creeping back to the west. About one square kilometre of the city was engulfed by flame, with many of the crews reporting explosions in the target area and the effectiveness of the incendiaries. Not everyone was having a good time of it. Flight Lieutenant George Hall's Lancaster NE139 'T' Tommy was hit, forcing him to abort.

The weather closed in, and so too, in the Ardennes, did the Germans as the Battle of the Bulge got underway. The squadron was summoned for an early briefing on the morning of the 21st and again on the 22nd with a view to attacking the marshalling yards at Cologne/Gremberg. On both occasions the attacks were cancelled at the eleventh hour. They were briefed a third time on the morning of the 23rd, and this time they went.

It was an unusual attack, with a heavy bomber squadron operating in daylight. Three waves of bombers were to take part, the first two comprising aircraft from 582 Squadron, and a third made up of 10 aircraft from 35 Squadron, based at nearby Graveley. Each lead Lancaster would have a specialist Oboe pilot and navigator (taken from neighbouring Mosquito squadrons) on the same aircraft as the 'regular' pilot and navigators, and a further Oboe Mosquito would also fly in reserve. Flight Lieutenant Owen Milne was to lead the first formation, playing host to Squadron Leader Bob Palmer DFC and Flight Lieutenant George Russell DFC from Little Staughton's 109 Squadron as the specialist Oboe crew. The second formation, although mainly comprising 582 Squadron crew, was to be led by a 35 Squadron pilot with specialists from 105 Squadron. The third formation was an all-35 Squadron show, again in the company of 105.

Take-off was a haphazard affair; the aircraft were lined up in a staggered formation on the runway and took off at intervals of 15-30 seconds. Outside was thick fog, but they had been promised better conditions along the way. The target itself, a major rail junction through which German re-inforcements were being rushed to support their new advance, would be covered in 10/10ths cloud, hence the need for Oboe, even in daylight.

The raid went wrong from the start. Two Lancasters from 35 Squadron collided on the way out, killing all on-board. On the approach to the target, rather than thick cloud, they found themselves in brilliant sunshine. Someone had blundered. Despite the change in conditions, there was confusion amongst the crews as to whether to break formation and bomb individually, or carry on in formation and bomb on their leader as they had been briefed. Palmer swapped seats with Milne, and his navigator listened to the Oboe signal for the release point. Heavy, predicted flak was being thrown their way. The German defences were having a field day. An Oboe attack meant flying straight and level at a constant speed and height for the better part of 10 minutes. The German gunners, therefore, had 10 minutes of target practice where they simply couldn't miss. And they didn't. All of the first formation was hit. And then just when they thought things couldn't get any worse, they did. A squadron of German fighters from JG26 appeared on the scene. It was a slaughter.

Palmer, courageously, flew on, believing that if he broke formation, the whole attack would have to be abandoned. He paid for such courage with his life. Lancaster PB371 'V' Victor was the first to fall, Flight Sergeant Russ Yeulett, the rear gunner, the only one to make it out alive. Four more Lancasters from 582 Squadron would also be lost: PB120 'P' Peter, flown by the American, Walt Reif, his two air gunners survived; ND899 'J' Johnny, Flight Lieutenant Peter Thomas' aircraft, all were killed; Lancaster PB141 'F' Freddie, piloted by Flight Lieutenant Reg Hockley, where they all baled out safely;* and PB558 'A' Apple, skippered by Flying Officer Robert Terpening, whose crew also all made it out in one piece. Other pilots fought heroic engagements, and were lucky to survive, notably Wing Commander John Clough, now a flight commander I/C 'B' Flight whose gunners had seen off several fighters, and Ted Swales, who had recently been promoted captain, and who corkscrewed in the battle area for no less than 15 minutes to escape danger. On all of the returning aircraft there were the scars of battle: dented fuselages, shattered cockpits, feathered props.

In all, in 582 Squadron alone, there were 27 men killed or at that moment unaccounted for, bringing the total for the month to 36. Whilst others would later return, for some it had been their final journey. Palmer was awarded the Victoria Cross.

---

* The flight engineer, Ken Hewitt, however, was subsequently murdered. See *Heroic Endeavour*, Grub Street, 2006.

December was a black month for the squadron. The very next day, Christmas Eve, some of those who had survived the horrors of the Gremberg attack were asked to go to Cologne again. Six aircraft took off, but because of bad weather were forced to land away from base – a miserable start to Christmas. One further raid on München Gladbach by 11 aircraft (one had to abort) was followed by the third and final trip to Cologne on the 31st, with all aircraft landing safely.

And so the winter of 1944 drew to a close. New crews were posted in to replace those lost, including those of Flying Officers Allen, Interiano, Underwood, Coombes, and Miller. The weekly strength at 23.59 on December 31 stood at 240 aircrew (officers and NCOs), 240 groundcrew (including two officers), and seven WAAFs. Total tonnage of bombs dropped since the squadron was formed was 6,512 tons and 17 pounds.

JOHNNY'S WAR

The story of Flight Sergeant John Smith DFM, air gunner, 582 Squadron

By October 12, 1944, John Smith had every reason to hate oil, or to be more precise, attacks on Germany's oil production and storage facilities. He had been to Castrop-Rauxel in September and been lucky to make it home. Wanne Eickel was next on the list.

There were 10 major oil installations servicing the German war machine: Nordstern, Scholven, Wesseling, Homburg, Sterkrade, Castrop-Rauxel, Bottrop, Dortmund, and Leuna. The tenth, Wanne Eickel, was the target for October 12, 1944.

The attack, comprising 111 Halifaxes and 26 Lancasters from 6 and 8 Group, went very well. Group Captain Peter Cribb, master bomber, was easily able to identify the canal, docks and marshalling yards as well as the distinctive triangle formed by the railway tracks that led to the aiming point. Marking with reds and greens was excellent, forming a ring around the aiming point, but they were quickly obliterated with smoke. A direct hit on an oil storage tank early in the raid started a fire, and the thick black, oily smoke began to obscure the target. Main force crews began bombing the smoke, following it as it drifted out to the north-east.

In Lancaster ND880 'A' Apple, Flying Officer Jimmy Brown was at the controls, his flight engineer, Sergeant Ray James close by. The two navigators, Sergeants Frank Dockar and Dave Reid were side-by-side, having successfully brought the heavy bomber to the start of the bombing run. The wireless operator, Flight Sergeant Alec Gostling had taken his place in the astrodome, and the two gunners, Sergeant Paddy Rayner and mid-upper Sergeant John Smith were on the alert for fighters. In the bomb bay were 10 American 1,000-pounders and four 500-pound general purpose bombs.

Flak bursts could be clearly seen, apparently harmless black puffs of smoke but with deadly intentions. Jimmy Brown seemed to pick out a flak-free corridor as he committed to his run, maintaining a constant speed of around 155 mph. To his port, John Smith had the perfect view from his mid-upper turret of a Halifax hit by flak and going down.* Then they too received a direct hit:

"It happened very suddenly. Three engines were hit simultaneously and immediately stopped, forcing the aircraft into a dive. Only the port outer was still going. The skipper was wrestling with the controls and our flight engineer doing everything he could to get the engines re-started. Somehow between them they managed to get the starboard inner going again, or at least wind-milling on half power. By then we had fallen from 17,000ft to about 2,000ft before we righted ourselves and regained some semblance of control. From nowhere, three Spitfires seemed to appear on our wingtips and that was very re-assuring.

"Jimmy, in consultation with Frank and Dave, opted for the shortest sea crossing possible and headed for Manston. Two engines were now working fine and he managed to gain a little height, probably up to about 4-5,000ft. It was touch and go as we approached the coast of England. Jimmy came on intercom and gave us the option of baling out. I think we all thought about it as there was a moment's silence before Frank replied that with the wind we would all be blown back out to sea. That seemed to decide us, and the skipper ordered us to take up crash positions.

"I got down from my turret and lay on the floor at the rear of the aircraft, hugging Paddy, our rear gunner. Jimmy brought the Lancaster in and I remember as we landed it lurched violently and then spun around in a full circle such that it was facing the wrong way. Then there was silence, except for the sound – and indeed the smell – of dripping petrol. By this time, ambulances and fire engines were racing across the grass towards us, and we clambered out as fast as we could and made towards them. The firemen started spreading their foam all over the aircraft, but the undercarriage was on fire, and pretty soon the whole aircraft was ablaze. Then there was a terrific 'boomph' and the whole thing went up. That was the end of ND880.

"Later, after we had been picked up and flown back to Little Staughton, I was wandering back to my billet but had lost my cap in the fire. Fatty Collings saw me

---

* This was almost certainly a Halifax Mk VII of 432 Squadron based in East Moor flown by a Canadian Pilot Officer Britton. The aircraft was one of only two Halifaxes lost on the operation, being hit by flak over the target, killing one of the crew (Flying Officer Todd, a veteran of 34 trips) and injuring the skipper and one other. Although John saw the aircraft hit, actually it made it home, or at least to the emergency landing ground at Woodbridge.

'improperly dressed' and was about to reprimand me when he asked me whether I was one of Brown's lot. I said that I was, and that I had left my cap in the aircraft. He simply smiled and told me to 'carry on'."

Wanne Eickel had been John's 17th trip, his seventh since joining 582 Squadron. Before the war he had been training as an artist, but had always been mad keen on flying. Volunteering for aircrew, he was too short for PNB (pilot navigator and bomb aimer) training which left engineer, wireless op/air gunner or just air gunner. The first two sounded too difficult, so air gunner it would have to be. From St John's Wood he went to Bridlington (ITW) and then on to Bishopscourt in Northern Ireland and finally 83 OTU at Peplow where he crewed up.

"Jimmy Brown was from a big brewing family in Sheffield and we used to think (unfairly no doubt) that he flew at his best when he'd had a couple. He was a good pilot, but he couldn't land the thing for toffee. He used to sit there, trying to force the aircraft onto the deck, all the time swearing. On one occasion the landing was so bad that Paddy hit his head and was knocked unconscious!"

Paddy and John had been together since ACRC, and had gone all through training together. All of the crew were sergeants, and immediately gelled. Most were about the same age, with the exception of Dave Reid, the air bomber (and later radar navigator/navigator two) who at 30 was very old indeed.

"I think in many ways Dave held us together. He'd done everything. He'd been a trucker, a lumberjack. You name it, he'd done it. He taught me how to play baseball, and I'd practice for hours trying to catch the ball in a glove, like he showed me. Being Canadian he used to get parcels from home, wrapped in hessian and string. He would always share it out – Camels for the smokers, Hershey chocolate bars and jars of cooked chicken. At one time Dave and Jimmy bought an Austin 7 and used to go to the pub and come back raring. He would then open up a jar and come round popping bits of chicken into our mouths!"

In April 1944, whilst still at OTU, they flew two Bullseyes – both of which counted as operations, after which John went off for further gunnery instruction at 1481 Gunnery School until moving on to 1667 HCU Sandtoft (where they picked up their flight engineer, Ray James) and 1 Lancaster Finishing School (LFS). John's introduction to the Lancaster he describes as 'hairy':

"An instructor took us up to show us what a Lancaster was capable of. You would see all of the new boys lining up waiting for their turn as the Lancaster came by. Then the doors would open and the crew would almost literally fall out. It reeked of vomit. The pilot would do everything in that aeroplane except turn it inside out.

"The only consolation I could see was that the turrets on a Lancaster were much better than the turrets on a Halifax. The Halifax used a Boulton Paul turret that was electro-hydraulically operated, and although it was very clever, I found it very cramped and virtually uncontrollable. The Lancasters had a Frazer Nash (Parnall FN50) turret that was hydraulically operated, smoother and much easier to control, and had considerably more room to move."

The crew's initial operational posting was to 576 Squadron, arriving in July 1944. They flew their first trip (their third operation counting the first two Bullseyes three months previously) on July 23 to Kiel. All went well. Very early in their tour, however, they became accustomed to attracting fighter attack. Over Stuttgart on the 24th they were attacked by a Focke Wulf Fw190; the next night, over Stuttgart, they were attacked by a Junkers Ju88. John also became accustomed to long, bottom-numbing flights over the sea.

"Even with a roomier turret, it was still uncomfortable on long trips. I sat on a seat that was clipped to the side, and was a bit like sitting on a swing. I had a step that I would have to pull down to get me into the turret, but the others when they passed would push it back up again so that I had no foothold to get down again."

John cannot remember precisely how it happened, but the decision to move to Pathfinders was taken very quickly and unilaterally by his skipper. Group Captain Hamish Mahaddie, Bennett's chief recruiting officer, persuaded Jimmy that he was up to the challenge, and the next thing they knew they'd all volunteered. Comfortably passing through Pathfinder NTU, they arrived at 582 Squadron in August, with their first Pathfinder trip to Stettin (August 29/30) in a supporter role. It was whenever oil was mentioned as the target, however, that trouble seemed particularly to head John's way.

The first of the oil raids was against Castrop-Rauxel:

"It was a real stinker. The nav said 10 minutes to go and I looked out and all I could see was a thick layer of flak and I thought we would never get through it. We were hit several times (the aircraft received several small holes in

the fuselage, tail plane and port wing) and I could hear it
rattling around like peas in a tin. I was always fascinated
by flak; I used to call them the little flak men, because the
shell bursts used to form shapes like little men."

Fortunately, they got home in one piece. Two weeks later, however,
they were briefed for another oil-related target – the synthetic oil
plant at Scholven, the squadron contributing seven Lancasters. One
of these was PB179 'J' Juliet:

"It was our flight commander's aircraft and brand new.
The flight sergeant in charge of the aircraft told us that we
had better take care of it or else."

None of the Pathfinders had any difficulty in identifying the target:
it had a distinctive 'shape', and the chimneys and the factory were
easily discernible. The attack started well: the first red TIs went
down about 50/100 yards north of the aiming point. Pretty soon, a
number of fires had begun to develop, and the master bomber
amended his instructions as new yellow TIs went down. The
Australian, Flight Lieutenant Hugh Hemsworth and Flight
Lieutenant George Hall were acting as markers, but the other five
crews had the same load of 18 500-pound general purpose bombs.
One of their number, Flying Officer Jack Kinman, was forced to
abandon the trip owing to a total loss of coolant which resulted in
the starboard inner being feathered and the starboard outer
seriously overheating. The German defences were now very much
alive, and the volume of flak began to increase. Two Pathfinder
aircraft from 7 Squadron were shot down, and another Lancaster
from 635 Squadron (flown by Flight Lieutenant Alex Thorn, later
president of the Pathfinder Association) was also hit. Then,
Lancaster PB179 was struck:

"Dave Reid, who had been lying in the bomb aimer's
position, was immediately hit and wounded. It wasn't
instantly apparent. He came on intercom and simply said
that he had been hit in the back. Fortunately he wasn't too
badly hurt, and although our aircraft had something like
300 holes in it, nothing vital had been struck. We landed
back at Staughton at 18.29, and as we taxied back to
dispersal, Chiefy came out, saw us and nearly had a fit. We
looked like a colander!"

John managed to avoid another oil target until the end of November
when they went back to Castrop-Rauxel and in early December
when they visited Merseberg Leuna (and were attacked by a Messerschmitt Me210). In between, John got to satisfy his ambition of

flying in the rear turret, an opportunity brought about by flying as a spare bod with two different skippers:

> "Paddy would never relinquish his rear turret. I think he liked the idea of wearing the pilot's parachute (at this time it was common practice for rear gunners in Pathfinders to wear seat-type 'chutes rather than the standard clip on chest 'chutes) which meant if we were in trouble, all he would have to do is traverse his turret and drop out. He also liked a smoke. The skipper always knew when Paddy was smoking as he could smell it. He would ask who was smoking, and the next thing I would see was a shower of sparks as Paddy flicked his cigarette out of the turret.
>
> "To Cologne on October 31 I got to fly with Reg Hockley, and got to go in the rear turret. Two nights later I flew with Owen-Jones (Squadron Leader Vivian Owen-Jones) to Düsseldorf. Owen-Jones was a flight commander and throughout the flight I kept calling him 'skipper'. When we landed, the others in the crew were mortified by my lack of respect. Being a squadron leader they all called him 'sir'."

By the turn of the New Year, the crew had completed their first 30 operations, not that it particularly mattered, having signed up for a tour of 45. They had, however, been 'promoted' to visual centrers. It was still a milestone. And they nearly hadn't made it. On December 15, they came close to losing their lives, and ended up losing their flight engineer:

> "We were on our way to Ludwigshafen. I was facing the front and could see sparks coming out of the port outer engine and so called Ray to have a look. I was pretty certain it was about to catch fire, and Ray obviously thought so too, but instead of feathering the port outer, he managed somehow to feather the starboard outer. This meant we were effectively down to two engines. In trying to rectify his mistake, he then feathered the starboard inner! By this point the skipper had lost patience and decided to take over (all of the critical pilot and flight engineer's instruments were replicated). He re-started the healthy engines and feathered the overheating port outer, which meant in the end we flew home on three.
>
> "It was the end of Ray unfortunately. He'd done around 30 trips but collapsed and had to report to the MO. He was subsequently taken off flying."

The rest of the tour was completed with a number of 'guest' flight engineers, among them Ted Stocker, at various times the squadron's engineer leader.

On the night of January 16/17 there was more excitement over Magdeberg:

> "We shot down an ME410 confirmed. We were leaving the target and the nightfighter had come up behind us. He can't have seen us but we could easily see him, because he was silhouetted against the glow of the burning city. To begin with I thought it might be a Mosquito (The ME410 and the Mosquito were both twin-engined fighters of similar sizes and from certain angles looked very alike) but then I could see that it was German. I don't actually remember whether I fired myself but I know that Paddy let him have it and it was confirmed by a Halifax from 6 Group who saw the entire action."

In total, John flew more than 50 operations, ticking off two more of the oil-based targets, Rauxel Tor and Sterkrade, unusually without incident, and being promoted again to primary visual marker, probably the most difficult of all Pathfinder roles. He also flew one trip to Dülmen as deputy master bomber, and took part in the successful raid against the pocket battleship, *Admiral Scheer*, with an aiming point photograph directly alongside the giant vessel. He was also flying the night that Ted Swales was lost coming back from Pforzheim:

> "The master bomber always broadcast in plain language so we could hear Ted's aircraft being attacked, and him calling for his deputy to take over. Then we could hear that the attack was over as he called the deputy and resumed control of the commentary. We knew he had been in trouble though and when we all got back, a large group of us hung around waiting for his return. After a little while we decided he wasn't coming back, and were surprised when most of his crew did."

One amusing incident John especially remembers encapsulates the high standards of professionalism – and respect – that existed within his crew:

> "We were on our way out to a target, I think it was to Leipzig, in beautiful weather and clear blue skies without a cloud or another aircraft in sight, when the skipper asks Frank (nav one) if we're on the right course. Frank answers in the affirmative. A few moments go by, and Jimmy starts asking us each in turn whether we can see any other

aircraft. None of us can. The skipper again asks Frank if he is certain we are on course. Even though Frank says yes, Jimmy decides that he is going to fly a dog-leg. At that point, Frank gathers together all of his charts and his equipment and stuffs them into his navigator's bag, marches into the cockpit and dumps them on Jimmy's lap, telling him that if he is so good, he can navigate himself! As it happened, we were precisely on course, and minutes after this occurred, aircraft began appearing all around us."

Another incident was not quite so amusing:

"I have seen a rear turret sliced off an aircraft by a cookie (4,000-pound bomb) dropped from above, and one night I thought the same was going to happen to us. We were on our bombing run, and as I looked up, directly above us was another Lancaster with its bomb bay doors wide open. I could see it as clear as day. I couldn't shout out a warning as we had to stay straight and level, but I can tell you that for those few seconds I wasn't looking for any fighters, I was looking to see if the bomber was going to drop his bombs on us."

At the end of his tour, John went on leave, and was disappointed on his return to discover that most of his crew had been broken up and gone their separate ways. He was awarded the DFM on April 17, 1945, and then flew a couple of Exodus trips (returning POWs) with an American Flight Lieutenant Oswald Interiano before being posted out on May 11, 1945. Paddy and John, still inseparable, were sent to 227 Squadron, training as part of Squadron Leader Swann's crew for Tiger Force. Latterly he moved to 35 Squadron, and then onward again when the requirement for air gunners became obsolete, commanding at one point the laundry and shoe repairs section at EAAS Manby.

His last flight in a Lancaster came on September 26, 2000, flying as a guest of the Battle of Britain Memorial Flight. It was pure co-incidence, but the Lancaster's route took them over the spot in Essex where Flying Officer William Shirley of 582 Squadron had crashed and been killed, and a memorial was being unveiled to his memory.

LUCKY THIRTEEN

The story of Flying Officer Bill Hough, wireless operator, 582 Squadron

Bill Hough might have known something would go wrong on his 13th trip. Having joined 582 Squadron from main force, a third of the way through his first tour, he had flown only one further operation before he was briefed for an attack on Heimbach on December 3, 1944. It sounded a relatively 'soft' target, especially as it was only 25 miles behind enemy lines. But then Bill hadn't bargained on losing his mid-upper gunner to a freak accident the day before the operation, or coming face-to-face with not just one but two German jets.

There are many people who believe in pre-destination. What happened before the raid on the Heimbach Dam in early December 1944 would suggest they might have a point. Bad weather had prevented any flying for a couple of days and on the afternoon of December 2, Warrant Officer Johnny Campbell, 'Mac' McKeown and Bill Hough were occupying themselves in their billet in different ways. Mac had decided to clean his pistol and in the process pressed the muzzle into the palm of his hand and pulled the trigger:

> "I don't think he was playing Russian roulette, but there was one up the spout and the bullet went clean through the palm of his hand, ricocheted off the floor and out through the wall of the hut. The hand started to swell immediately and Campbell and I rushed him down to get the MO where he received treatment and was put to bed. There would be no flying for him for a while! We checked in the mess and our crew was down for flying the next day with a 5am call; obviously there was a daylight on."

The next morning when Bill arrived at briefing, he saw that Mac's replacement was to be none other than Squadron Leader Freddie Grillage, the squadron's gunnery leader. It would be unusual to fly with a 'stranger' in the crew, however necessary. Until that time, they had flown 12 operations without significant incident.

When Bill had left grammar school in 1940, he had first found a job working for Imperial Chemical Industries, better known as ICI. As soon as he was old enough he volunteered for aircrew, and was accepted for training as a wireless operator/air gunner. His training followed the standard pattern: ACRC St John's Wood; ITW Bridgnorth; Yatesbury for his radio training; Castle Kennedy for gunnery training, and then on to 6 AFU and 18 OTU Worksop where he was crewed up:

> "The crew initially comprised four Canadians: the skipper, Art Green, navigator 'Willie' Mood, bomb aimer Ed Dalik, and mid-upper gunner 'Major' Campbell. We then moved on to HCU Lindholme where we picked up our flight engineer, Dennis Naylor, a Yorkshireman from Sheffield, and another gunner, Canadian 'Mac' McKeown. From HCU we were told we were being posted to a Lancaster squadron, 576, and so took our turn at the Lancaster Finishing School at Hemswell before setting off for Elsham Wolds."

No. 576 Squadron was part of 1 Group. It had been 'born' in November 1943 out of 'C' Flight of 103 Squadron, and commenced operations on December 2. By the time Bill and his crew arrived in August 1944 (the month after Jimmy Brown and his crew had arrived), the squadron had already carved out a reputation as one of the top-performing main force squadrons in the group, and was now under the command of Wing Commander Boyd Sellick. They were soon making their own contribution to the squadron's success, completing 10 operations from Elsham Wolds and one further trip from Fiskerton (576 moved to the FIDO-equipped airfield in October 1944) before volunteering for Pathfinders. The skipper, Art Green, had joined the RCAF pre-war, and held the AFC. Both he and the navigator Willie Mood had clearly caught the eye of the selectors, the former for his skill as an aviator and the latter for the consistency of his performance, and the accuracy of his navigation.

Having successfully completed Pathfinder NTU, they were posted to 582 Squadron in November 1944. After the customary local flying and training exercises, they flew their first operation with the squadron to Duisberg on the night of November 30/December 1 as a supporter. It went well. On the 3rd, with the gunnery leader drafted in as their spare bod, they were briefed to attack the Eifel town of Heimbach:

> "The target was to be Heimbach on the River Roer, about 20 miles inside Germany from its border with Belgium, and only about 25 miles or so ahead of the front line at the time. This was to be very much a 582 show with 16 of our

aircraft marking, including the master bomber, Squadron
Leader Mingard, and his deputy, Lieutenant Swales. There
was to be additional marking by 109 Squadron and a main
force of about 150 Lancasters. The met forecast was not
too good with some thundershowers in the area and about
6/10ths cloud cover."

Art Green was the first to taxi his aircraft, Lancaster PB 629 'J'
Johnny, to the end of the runway, and the first away. The time was
shortly before 08.05. The load was a mix of 1,000-pound bombs
and TIs. The flight out was uneventful. The navigator one, Willie
Mood, plotted the route that took them out across the French coast
at Dunkirk with about a 160-mile run to the target. Most of their
time in the air would be spent over Allied lines, and their time-on-
target (TOT) was estimated at 09.45. The cloud was much thicker
and heavier than they had been forecast, and pretty soon they found
themselves above 10/10ths cloud, although horizontal visibility was
good.
   Other aircraft were in sight and they seemed to be on the
starboard edge of the stream. Tension mounted as Art skirted
Brussels and Willie Mood told him that they had about 80 miles –
30 minutes – to run. He could not say where the front line was
exactly, as it seemed to move by the hour. A quarter of an hour
elapsed. Forty miles to go. And then it happened:

   "Johnny Campbell burst in on the intercom and shouted:
   'unidentified aircraft starboard quarter level (14,000ft)
   range three miles'. I fancied myself at aircraft recognition
   and immediately stood up under the astrodome. The
   aircraft was closing very quickly and I identified it, almost
   immediately, as a Messerschmitt Me262."

The Me262 was just coming into service as Germany's first
operational jet fighter, and was a potential war winner that might
have restored the Luftwaffe's command of the skies over Germany
had it been delivered (and flown) in sufficient numbers. Aircraft
began rolling off the production line in July 1944, and was an
instant hit with the pilots that flew it. It was extremely
manoeuvrable, exceedingly fast (it had a top speed of more than
500mph) and its four 30mm Mk108 cannon in the nose packed a
fearful punch. As Bill and his crew were just about to find out:

   "Before I could regain my seat, Johnny again burst in:
   'another enemy aircraft dead astern – up corkscrew
   starb....!' His words were lost in an almighty clatter and
   bang, the second aircraft firing its four cannon from a
   range of about 500 yards, the rear gunner firing back and

hits being registered on our port wings and engines.

"The first aircraft went underneath us and the second flew over the top at a tremendous speed (this was our first encounter with a jet of any kind and their speed certainly showed up against the Lanc's 170mph or so). Black smoke, presumably from the fuel tanks, poured from the wing and the port outer was quickly enveloped in flames. Fire extinguishers were operated up front and we went into a shallow dive but the fire only seemed to intensify, although the aircraft was still being held steady."

By this time it was becoming obvious to the skipper that the aircraft had been mortally hit. With no option left to him, he gave the order to abandon aircraft, instructing the two gunners and the wireless operator to use the rear exit:

"One moves pretty quickly in these circumstances and I grabbed the parachute pack and made my way to the rear exit. As I passed the mid-upper gunner (Grillage) I gave him a bang on the legs with my hand in case he had not got the message. Johnny Campbell had the turret centred and was just climbing out as I reached the exit. He indicated that I should go first and while I clipped on my parachute he opened the exit door and immediately there was a tremendous roar from the slipstream air. As I stood in the doorway preparing to dive out, suddenly my 'chute burst open and the canopy was deployed outside of the aircraft, billowing above the fuselage with the lines bearing on the rear edge of the door. I seemed to be snagged against the fuselage side, unable to move.

"I do not know to this day what happened. I can only suppose that either the 'chute handle caught on something or the force of the slipstream somehow sucked on the pack and pulled out the 'chute. Anyhow, at this time no one was theorising and Johnny Campbell quickly sized up the situation, got hold of me bodily and with some assistance from the billowing canopy pushed me out the door. Once free I was pulled by the 'chute over the top of the tailplane, banging my head on the top of the exit as I went out, hitting my ankle on the front edge of the tailplane and then between the fins, free of the aircraft."

Bill's first sensation was a feeling of peace and quiet after the trauma of the past few minutes, away from the noise of the screaming engines and howling slipstream. His immediate relief, however, almost turned to panic as he realised he had another problem:

"My harness had not been as tight as it should have been – I think it was common practice to slacken them off a little whilst sitting for hours – and instead of being tight up in the crotch it had slipped along the right leg towards the knee so that I was in imminent danger of parting company from the 'chute. So I held on grimly to the lines with both hands and began to enjoy the ride down. 'J' Johnny had disappeared from sight but one Me262 did pass close enough to be recognised.

"As I neared the ground, still hanging on tightly, I could see that I was going to land in a field on the outskirts of a village and could see people making towards me. I didn't make a copybook landing due to the harness and a fairly strong breeze, but I was OK and the villagers soon grabbed hold of the canopy and held on to me. After some 15 minutes or so two Americans appeared in a jeep and took me off to a hospital nearby. I learned later that I had landed near to Tongres and the hospital was at Hasselt."

Bill was kept in hospital for four days, and spent a further night staying with his American hosts at a nearby chateau. He was not aware of the fate of his other crewmates, neither was he aware that he had been posted as 'missing' and his family informed. On December 9 he was again taken by jeep to Brussels, and hitched a lift on a departing Dakota that took him to Northolt and then onwards to Down Ampney.

"From Down Ampney I made my own way towards base, by train, arriving in the square at St Neots late in the afternoon. I still had on the clothes, including flying boots but excluding helmet and parachute harness, that I set out in six days earlier. A telephone call to Little Staughton secured me transport and I finally arrived back at base somewhat behind schedule."

There was mixed news when he got back to the squadron. Art Green, Ed Dalik, Willie Mood and Johnny Campbell had all made it back safe and well. Dennis Naylor had also baled out safely, but in the event was not to return to the squadron. Squadron Leader Grillage would also not return. Grillage, a 36-year-old married man from Woking in Surrey had been posted to 582 Squadron only two weeks earlier, but now he was dead, killed in the exchange of fire with the German jets. Ironically, the raid on Heimbach had been a fiasco. The Pathfinders arrived over Heimbach at 09.43 to find the target covered in cloud. Mingard instructed main force to orbit and wait, and meanwhile went down to have a look, taking some hits to his aircraft from light flak for his pains. Neither he nor his deputy was able to mark, and so at 09.51 he gave the signal to abandon mission. Fortunately no further aircraft was lost. The next day a force including a single Lancaster from 582 (flown by Flight Lieutenant Owen Milne) and Mosquitoes from 109 Squadron returned to the target to have another go. Milne was forced to abort.

Bill Hough and the crew, minus their flight engineer, returned to operations on January 28 with an unremarkable trip to Stuttgart. Over the next eight weeks they were on operations almost constantly, making up for lost time: Ludwigshafen, Wiesbaden (where they saw an ammunition dump explode), Bottrop, Goch (where the trip had to be abandoned as they ran in for their third attempt at bombing), Mainz, Mannheim, Cologne (with the cathedral clearly visible), Chemnitz, Dessau, Kassel (where they experienced heavy flak), Essen, Hagen and Hanau. In comparative terms, they continued their tour unmolested.

They flew their 34th and final trip on April 18, a daylight to Heligoland. Within hours of landing after their final operation, the crew almost immediately dispersed, the Canadians on the first ship home. Bill's association with Bomber Command wasn't quite done, however. In the summer of 1945 he was selected as part of a 582 Squadron crew to accompany Air Chief Marshal Sir Arthur Harris on a goodwill tour of Brazil in their specially adapted (and painted) Lancasters:

"We had survived the war in Europe. VE Day was behind us; we'd done a couple of food drops to Holland, picked up quite a lot of POWs from Italy and Germany, made a couple of Cooks Tours down the Rhine Valley – what was to happen to us now? There was talk of a posting to the Far East but this thankfully did not materialise. Then the Canadians and Australians started to be re-patriated leaving me without the crew with whom I had spent the last year or so. So here I was in June 1945 doing the odd flight test or cross-country with assorted crews – a far cry from the headier days of a few months before.

"Then towards the middle of July there were indications that something special was about to happen, various people were sounded out – the requirements were that you had to be an officer, have completed a tour of ops, had a suit of civvies and, later, that you had to have been part of 1 Group. I was selected from the shortlist (other 582 Squadron aircrew included 'Jock' Cairns and Ted Stocker) and there then followed a hectic week of preparations during which time we had various vaccinations, drew a lot of special kit, including some tropical, and had a couple of days leave to pick up civvies. There was considerable speculation and we got our first clue when Squadron

Leader Cairns had to visit Bomber Command HQ. At the
CO's conference on the day I returned from leave all was
revealed: we were to accompany the great man himself to
Brazil."

In seven weeks, three Lancasters took Harris on a tour of seven
countries: Morocco, Gambia, Brazil, British Guiana, The Bahamas,
Canada and Iceland, a total flying time of more than 77 hours and
a distance of approximately 17,000 miles. It was a grand exit in
what Bill describes as 'a once in a lifetime journey'.

TWO OF A KIND

The stories of Sergeant Bob Pearce and
Sergeant David Spier, air gunner and navigator one,
582 Squadron

The war for Bob Pearce and David Spier came to an end on a beautiful winter's day over Cologne on December 23, 1944. Indeed to both men, Cologne had been somewhat of a nemesis. Although not ordinarily in the same crew, they had shared a difficult trip to Cologne in October when their Lancaster returned seriously damaged by flak and the pair were on the battle order with their respective skippers for the fateful trip to the Cologne/Gremberg marshalling yards when both would be shot down.

The flak over Cologne on October 28 was the worst Bob Pearce had ever encountered. Flak so thick you could get out and walk on it. With every breath he could smell and almost taste acrid cordite as it filtered through his oxygen tube and into his mask. At briefing earlier that day, they had been told that the German defence network was crumbling. Not from where Bob was sitting, uncomfortably perched in the rear turret of Lancaster PB625 'J' Johnny being flown by his American skipper Walt Reif.

They'd taken off shortly before 14.00hrs, one of 10 aircraft from 582 Squadron being led by their flight commander, Brian McMillan. It was their 20th trip, and they'd been promoted recently from a supporter to a backer-up. This was reflected in their bomb load, a mix of red TIs, two American 1,000-pound bombs, and a 4,000-pound HC Minol. They were also carrying a mix of crew. The 'regular' navigating team had been replaced by the combination of Flight Sergeants David Spier and Tony Smith, whose more usual skipper was Flight Lieutenant Reg Hockley DFM.

Bob remembers the operation well:

> "The bomb aimer was finding it hard to see the target with all the flak and suggested to Walt that he found some clear sky. Walt obliged and then instantly regretted it as every gun battery in the Ruhr seemed to open up on us. You knew the flak was close because you could actually hear the explosions and then they found their range. We took a

direct hit in the starboard outer engine, closely followed by the inner, setting it on fire. At much the same time, my buddy Jack (Flight Sergeant Jack MacLennan) in the mid-upper turret was hit."

With two engines dead, and the starboard wing and main body seriously damaged, Reif believed they were finished, and pushed the aircraft into a steep dive away from the target. The aircraft fell from 17,000ft to 4,000ft before the pilot was able to level out just long enough for them to drop their bombs, but also long enough to sustain further flak damage. Jack MacLennan's turret was hit and knocked out, leaving a gaping hole. The sudden rush of air convinced him that he had fallen out, and for a moment he panicked. Remarkably, and despite his flying suit being cut to shreds, he had not been hit again. Relief turned to euphoria, and just in time he realised he was suffering from oxygen starvation and discovered that his oxygen lead had been severed. He unclipped his seat and stepped down into the main fuselage to plug in to the spare outlet. He also reconnected his intercom to inform his skipper he was still alive!

Miraculously, the Lancaster was still flying, but the skipper was fighting the aircraft all the way. Over base, Reif called Flying Control on R/T and was instructed to put the Lancaster on automatic and bale out. As calmly as he could he told them that it would be difficult to put the aeroplane on instruments as he didn't seem to have any instruments left. He gave the crew the option of baling out but they declined. Reif tried to lower the undercarriage but one wheel refused to lock, and they were obliged to crank it down by hand.

David Spier recalls the event clearly:

"We had a terrible trip. Reif managed to get back over base by using the two good engines and full opposite rudder, but the snag was landing. The problem was that when the undercarriage touched down, we would slew out of control. Goodness alone knows what could happen. The whole of the station, fire engines, ambulance, and the COs from both 582 and 109 Squadrons all turned out to watch 'J' for Johnny limp home. We took up crash positions and prayed. In the event, the aeroplane touched down, swung violently to the left, narrowly missed one of the larger hangars and a petrol bowser, finishing up on the grass within yards of the main control tower. We made an emergency exit to enthusiastic applause from the onlookers."

The official damage assessment told the full story: two starboard engines out of action; 66 holes in the port wing; 153 hits in the body; mid-upper turret a complete write-off including a bent gun; damage to rudder and flaps; oil lines to undercarriage severed; rear turret u/s; navigational equipment u/s; and most instruments u/s. The Lancaster was a sorry sight as it was pushed into the hangar for repairs.

This was the only time that Bob Pearce and David Spier ever flew together, but both were to share in the horrors of the attack two months later with their respective skippers that spelled the end of their operational careers. Up to that point, beyond the squadron ties, their lives had followed rather different paths.

Bob Pearce was a 19-year-old Canadian who had been born and raised in Toronto. His father had been in the Canadian Army in the First World War and it seemed the right thing that Bob would follow in his footsteps and 'do his bit'. The army accepted him at 17, and he endured seven months in Debert, Nova Scotia before being accepted into the Royal Canadian Air Force 12 days before his 18th birthday. Initial training followed and after lack of success in his attempts to become a pilot, he was remustered:

> "I'd met Jack (MacLennan) at ITS (Initial Training School) as he was on the same pilot's course and we flunked it together. My maths was very poor and so they advised me not to take the navigator's course, and I didn't really fancy being a wireless op spending my time with 'dit and da'. So I asked them what was the quickest way of getting into the war and they told me gunnery. So soon after I reported to No. 9 Bombing and Gunnery School at Mont Jolie, Quebec."

Having qualified, he was told he would be transferred overseas, and arrived in England early in the New Year of 1944. At 28 OTU (Castle Donington) he found a crew: the skipper, Walt Reif, was an American of German extraction. A solidly built man, Reif had physical presence and they immediately clicked. Amongst other jobs, the 29-year old had been a crop-spraying pilot before the war, and had thousands of hours under his belt. With Reif was the navigator, Ken Austin, another Canadian of similar age to Walt who had been a schoolteacher before the war. Pete Uzelman, the air bomber, was also Canadian, and also of German descent. He smoked incessantly. The wireless operator was a young Salford lad, George Owen, and the second gunner, his buddy from ITS, Jack MacLennan.

Further training for Bob followed with gunnery flights at Wymeswold and Ingham, on Wellington ICs and Wellington Xs, before a move on to HCU at Blyton (where they picked up a flight engineer, John Paterson) and finally Hemswell (1 Lancaster Finishing School). His first operational posting was to 101 Squadron at Ludford Magna, from where Bob flew eight operations between June 4 and July 19, before his skipper volunteered them for Pathfinders:

"We knew that the Pathfinders were the elite and the commanding officer of our squadron (Wing Commander Bob Alexander DFC) asked us if we wanted to volunteer. Pete didn't want to go, but he also didn't want to break up the crew. He was always very level-headed. Perhaps we should have listened to him?"

Completing NTU Warboys by August 3, 1944, the next day he arrived at Little Staughton. His thoughts were never far from home.

"I regularly received letters from my family and friends back home in Canada. They sent me parcels including sardines, baby food (!), and cartons of cigarettes. I replied to all my letters but had to restrict my writing to trivia because military policy forbad me to write about operations. My fondest memories from the war are the times I spent, and the friendships I made, with the members of my crew. They were my constant companions. We spent long weekends in London and on longer leaves travelled to Edinburgh where the Scottish people treated us Canadian boys like their own sons."

David Spier, on the other hand, was 10 years older than Bob when he reported to ACRC St John's Wood for the first stage of his air force training. A university graduate from Manchester, David was a pharmacist with his own practice, and married. He shared at least something with Bob in that he wanted to be a pilot, and shared Bob's lack of success. Unlike Bob, however, David was accepted for navigator training, being sent to 48 Air School in East London, South Africa, where he learned basic navigation (dead reckoning and map reading), astro navigation, photography, reconnaissance, meteorology and signals. From 48 AS he went to 47 AS at Queenstown to complete his training before boarding a ship to return him to the UK via the Suez canal.

In early July 1944, David reported to an advanced flying unit at Halfpenny Green near Wolverhampton to accustom him to local conditions and local geographies and his training at last came to an end.

"The course finished and I received an order to see the flight commander who informed me that my navigational skill was of sufficiently high standard for him to recommend me to the Pathfinder force – the cream of squadrons of Bomber Command where every flying member was a volunteer and whether pilot, navigator, gunner or radio operator was selected on the basis of competence. I asked for time to consider and he recommended that I visit intelligence and consider the statistics of losses. I learned that the loss rate in PFF was less than in the main force. I talked the proposal over with Tony Smith – who had been a friend since we had first met at ACRC – and decided that I would not go without him; we were determined to stay together.

"The CO agreed, at the same time informing me that because of the installation of more up-to-date technical navigation equipment (i.e. H2S) PFF crews required two navigators. We could have no idea of the near fatal decision we had made. We had crossed our Rubicon and our lives took on an abrupt change of course. Early September 1944 we were posted to Pathfinder force NTU at Warboys. Tony and I alternated our respective duties on 10 successive daylight and night-time cross-country flights and concluded after 40 flying hours that I should do the navigating while he would operate the equipment and feed me the vital information. We made a good team. During the last week in September we were posted to 582 Squadron."

By the time David Spier and Tony Smith joined Bob Pearce and Walt Reif for the first daylight to Cologne, they had all already had their fair share of scrapes. One attack on Calais, David's first, especially sticks in his mind:

"We could clearly see the German soldiers on the battlements with rifles pointing our way and the recognised 'whoof whoof' bark of anti-aircraft batteries which explained only too clearly the rattle of hits on the outer shell of our Lancaster. One jagged piece of shrapnel landed on my navigation table. Not thinking, I asked Tony to take it off. It was almost red hot. We bombed on the third run and returned to base. Our hydraulics had been damaged and we had 39 holes in the aircraft. That was my first operational experience."

On October 23, David and Tony were assigned to a 'permanent' crew skippered by a rosy-cheeked mechanical engineer from Birmingham who looked five years younger than his actual age of 24 and had already completed his first tour – Flight Lieutenant Reg Hockley. With Reg was the wireless operator, Flying Officer Peter 'Pip' Parrott, a 23-year-old bank clerk from Woking who was also a second tour man; Pilot Officer Ken Hewitt, a slim fair-haired school-leaver of 19 was the flight engineer; and the two gunners Flight Lieutenant Vic Jehan, a civil servant from the Channel Islands in quieter times and Flight Sergeant Roy Shirley, a 19-year-old

Londoner who worked in newspapers. By comparison, David and Tony, by now both 31, must have seemed like old men.

It was a very foggy morning, the morning of December 23, 1944. The crews of Walt Reif and Reg Hockley went out to their respective dispersals to prepare for the attack on the marshalling yards at Cologne/Gremberg to support the US fight-back in the Ardennes. The duty flying officer dictated the order of take-off, with 'A' Flight – including both Reif and Hockley, taking off from the southern approach to the main runway. Both aircraft got away safely, and both dutifully followed the lead aircraft, skippered by 'Jock' Milne, as it approached the target. It was soon obvious that something was wrong. The lead formation was being heavily engaged by flak. Rather than thick cloud, there was brilliant sunshine that meant the order should have been given to break formation and bomb independently. But seemingly no such order came, and the crews played 'follow my leader' as the flak intensified and enemy fighters appeared on the scene, as David Spier recalls:

"The flight to the target was uneventful, the weather clear, no flak or enemy fighters. Our bombing height was 18,000ft. It was our fourth trip to Cologne. As Lancasters were very vulnerable to enemy fighters in daylight we were to have protection from RAF Mustangs. Tony and I had flown 20 operations together and never worn our chest-type parachutes as we were supposed to. They were very inconvenient to wear and work in; we always stowed them at the back of our seats. My reason being that the 'chute would protect the small of my back from any piece of shrapnel that may penetrate that area. I was very sensitive about my kidneys.

"It was now midday, our ETA spot on, Cologne clearly visible ahead on this beautiful, sunny, cloudless winter day. The target was beginning to come up. For no reason I have ever been able to understand, I turned to Tony sitting next to me, pointed to the 'chutes behind us and in sign language transmitted my intention to clip mine on. He nodded and did likewise. We turned onto our bombing course. Ken, the bomb aimer, was lying flat in the nose calling directions to the aiming point. We pressed on. Flak from the anti-aircraft defences was now very intense, and was rattling around the aeroplane while we dropped our bombs on the target. I gave Reg the course to fly out of the target. A perfect day for a visual attack. Unfortunately a perfect day also for enemy fighters.

"The course out of the target was 275 but 'F' Freddie would not respond to the rudder; the hydraulic system had been badly damaged by flak, and the aircraft was virtually out of control. Worse was yet to come. We were attacked by two enemy fighters coming unseen from under the nose of the crippled bomber. A burst of heavy machine gun fire hit the aeroplane, setting the port wing on fire and with the petrol tanks liable to blow at any moment, Reg gave the order to abandon aircraft.

"Ken, our flight engineer/bomb aimer went down into the nose, opened the escape hatch and left. Tony and I followed. He sat on the edge of the hole looking down from three and a half miles up in the sky, deliberating. I put my foot in the small of his back and pushed. There really is no time to get thoughtful about what one should or should not do when the port wing of an aeroplane is ablaze and likely to blow us all to Kingdom come! Tony exited. I sat on the edge and launched myself into space.

"I had read somewhere that when parachuting, count to 10 before pulling the rip cord. This I did, and added two more for good measure, and yanked the toggle. Nothing happened. Panic! Luckily I could get my hands on my 'chute and tore it open, losing two nails in the process, and up it went with a bang. There I was, suspended in the extremely cold winter air and what a sight. Planes going down in flames, the sky dotted with life preserving parachutes."

One parachute he could see was that of Bob Pearce who had experienced a similarly dramatic end to the raid, as Bob recounts:

"We were hit by flak and then attacked by fighters from the front, head on. It was clear that we had been hit, and hit badly. Walt gave instructions to bale out. I could hear his voice on the intercom, and it was very weak. I knew that he had been injured. I was in the rear turret and tried to open the doors to escape but they wouldn't budge. I turned the turret against the beam and thought that if I stood on the edge and leaned out, and then pulled the ripcord on my 'chute, that the slipstream would pull me out.

"By the time I did get out, the aircraft was engulfed by fire, and it had spread very quickly: the tail, fuselage and wings were all aflame. Jack (MacLennan) had already gone, and I could hear Ken on the intercom saying that he couldn't find his 'chute. It was the last voice I heard. After all of the noise, the thing I remember most about baling out was the sudden quiet. It seemed I was all alone in the sky. It was very windy, and as I was going down I thought that I could hear rifle fire, but in fact it was just the wind causing the parachute lines to 'crack'."

Both men made it to earth safely, and shared similar experiences upon landing. David Spier:

> "In a matter of minutes I was surrounded by members of the Volksturm (equivalent to the British Home Guard) complete with bayoneted rifles and a bloody great Alsatian dog yapping and nipping at my calves. They allowed me to disentangle myself from my parachute, ordered me to put my hands up in the air and commenced to search me. I just could not believe this was happening to me. My captors prodded a little with their bayonets but nothing serious. They deprived me of my watch (they missed the second one I was wearing further up my arm), silk escape maps, anything else I may have had in my pockets and hustled me into the back of a waiting car. There in the back was Vic Jehan, our rear gunner. He made a gesture that I understood to mean be quiet."

Bob Pearce met with much the same suspicion:

> "I was floating down, heading towards a Red Cross train, then the wind blew me in the direction of some high tension wires. I ended up in the backyard of a house, and suddenly there were lots of kids pointing Lugers at me. I didn't know what they wanted, but then realised it was my parachute so got up and unbuckled it. I knew the German people hated the English and was afraid. Wehrmacht soldiers arrived in time, surrounded me, and kept the local townsfolk away. In a nearby house I was searched before being moved off to the local police station. Early that evening I was transported to the local Luftwaffe aerodrome and locked up in one of two cells crowded with other men from the squadron. In the neighbouring cell I heard a familiar voice: Jack."

For Bob, there was only bad news. Apart from Jack, his fellow gunner, none of the others had made it out alive. Walt Reif, George Owen, Ken Austin, Pete Uzelman and John Paterson were all dead.

For David, there was better news. All of his crew had made it out in one piece, although not all of them conventionally. Vic Jehan was safe, as was Reg Hockley. So too Tony Smith, albeit that he had been beaten up rather badly. Pip Parrott and Roy Shirley had not made it out of the bomber, but had somehow, miraculously, survived the fall, trapped in the fuselage. It would be one of those stories that no one would believe in the future, but was absolute fact. Ken Hewitt was also alive, but sadly not for long. Soon after landing he was shot dead by a Nazi official.

For Bob and David, their war was over. Initially it was interrogation at Dulag Luft before being sent on to permanent camps, in Bob's case, Stalag Luft I in Barth; for David it meant Stalag Luft VII, Bankau.

Chapter Five

A Squadron at War

January – April 1945

New Year 1945, the sixth year of war, and the squadron welcomed its third and what was to prove its final wartime commanding officer. The ever-popular Peter Cribb was elevated to station commander, his record of 88 trips being recognised with a richly-deserved Bar to his DSO. The citation made note of the 'distinction and gallantry' with which he had led the squadron over a long and sustained period.

The squadron couldn't have wished for a better replacement CO than Wing Commander Stafford Coulson. Coulson was a pre-war regular who with his full moustache looked every inch the RAF 'type'. Like Cribb he had previously been a flight commander with 35 Squadron. Like Cribb also he had an impressive record of operations behind him, and was determined to put his own 'stamp' on the squadron.

January started with an early evening attack on the Eving coking plant in Dortmund, with the five squadron aircraft loaded with heavy explosives, primarily the 4,000-pound 'cookies'. A single aircraft flown by Flying Officer Gordon Baker (a 23-year-old Canadian who later went on to win the DFC and complete 42 trips) was also sent to bomb Witten. All returned safely. The very next day, the 2nd, 12 aircraft were sent to Nuremberg and two to Ludwigshafen, the latter target being specifically IG Farbenindustrie AG. Again all went well, despite some wayward TIs seen at least two miles from the aiming point and evident creep-back from main force, with the only real glitch being the early return of the Canadian Flying Officer George Harvey through distributor failure.

Further raids were laid on for the 5th (Hanover), 6th (Hanau), 13th (Saarbrücken), 14th (Merseberg Leuna and Grevenbroich), and 16th (Magdeberg and Zeitz).

During the attack on Merseberg Leuna, there was excitement for Flying Officer Frank Lloyd when he was hit from above by 'friendly' bombs and immediately gave the order to bale out. The navigator,

Squadron Leader David Mansell-Playdell was quick out of the gate but no sooner had he gone than Lloyd regained control of the Lancaster and ordered the remainder of the crew to stand fast. Through incredible skill he managed to nurse the bomber back on only two engines to crash land at Manston. He was awarded an immediate DFC.

That same night the talented RNZAF pilot Flight Lieutenant Nairn was the only one of three Lancaster skippers and crews taking part in an attack on railway yards at Grevenbroich, which was primarily a 6 Group affair involving Halifaxes. He marked the target with green TIs, dropping 12, 500-pounders at the same time. He reported the bombing to be well concentrated and returned safely to base.

There was perhaps even more excitement, though with ultimately tragic results, for another New Zealander, Flying Officer Patrick McVerry and his crew on the trip to Zeitz, near Leipzig. The target was the Braunkohle-Benzin synthetic oil plant. The squadron put up seven aircraft, including Lancaster NE130 'T' Tommy flown by McVerry.

Take-off was at 18.35hrs and went without a hitch. Not long into the flight, however, the flight engineer began reporting trouble with not one but two of the engines. McVerry was determined not to turn back and reduced revs on the troublesome engines to prevent them from overheating and packing up for good. With great skill, McVerry managed to coax the best out of his aircraft and still managed to reach the target on time with the rest of his colleagues, at about 22.00hrs. Further trouble came on their bombing run as searchlights began to probe the skies, looking for victims. They found Lancaster NE130, and almost immediately the flak began to burst all around them. Somehow the pilot managed to ignore what was going on outside and kept the aircraft straight and level, successfully dropping his bombs on target. Then the gunners shouted a warning, but too late as they were raked by machine gun and cannon fire from an enemy nightfighter. Shells slammed into the wings, causing serious damage to the control surfaces, and particularly the elevators, forcing the aircraft into a steep dive.

With all of his might on the control column, McVerry succeeded in levelling out and began taking stock of their situation. He had lost the nightfighter, but he had also lost almost all control of the aircraft, and was continually fighting with it to keep it in the air. He called his navigator, Flying Officer Warwick Thorby, and decided to plot the shortest route to friendly territory. Whilst McVerry and Thorby conferred, his Australian wireless operator, Flight Sergeant James Carroll and mid-upper gunner Sergeant Trevor Myatt, had made their way to the rear of the Lancaster in response to cries for help from the rear gunner, Sergeant Nick McNamara, an Irishman, who lay wounded and trapped in the rear turret. In total darkness, and lacking sufficient oxygen (all of the supply bottles had been damaged) they fought to free their injured friend, all the time being thrown around by the involuntary meanderings of the crippled bomber. The effort proved too much for Carroll, who passed out, quickly to be revived with fresh oxygen supplies from the navigator. At last they managed to reach Allied lines and prepared to bale out. Thorby, Carroll and Myatt checked the parachute of the rear gunner, and pushed him out of the emergency exit first, pulling his ripcord as he fell. The rest followed suit and shortly afterwards the bomber at last fell away to its death.

Not surprisingly, there were immediate awards for gallantry for the four concerned: a DFC for McVerry and Thorby, and DFMs for Carroll and Myatt. Sadly, the 21-year-old rear gunner was not so lucky, and succumbed to his wounds.

Fortunately, McNamara's death was the only fatality the squadron suffered that month. On the 20th, Flying Officer Keely, an Australian, crash-landed at Oakington whilst on a training flight, destroying the aircraft in the process but otherwise emerging unscathed. The weather closed in for most of the last few days of January and there was no flying. The month ended with 12 aircraft detailed for operations against Stuttgart. All took off and returned, many without bombing because of foul weather over the target.

February started in spectacular fashion. The day after 16 aircraft returned safely from an unsatisfactory trip to Ludwigshafen, a further 15 had been briefed to attack Wiesbaden, led by Wing Commander Coulson. The Lancasters were being fuelled, ready for a take off time shortly after 21.00hrs when it happened. Flight Lieutenant Boland, a Canadian pilot attached to 109 Squadron, was coming in to land, and somehow missed the runway altogether. Realising his mistake too late, he frantically pushed the throttles fully forward to execute an emergency climb. Unfortunately that had the effect of flooding the port engine which promptly seized. The aircraft clipped the wing of one of the waiting Lancasters before coming to an unceremonious halt on the grass verges. Then it caught fire.

Now there was real danger. The damaged Lancaster and the others close by were bombed up ready to go. In hitting the Lancaster's wing, the Mosquito had severed the bomber's fuel lines, still attached to an attendant petrol bowser. A very cool and very brave member of the groundcrew clambered into the cab of the bowser and moved it to the rear of the Lancaster. Here he attached a line and dragged the Lancaster away from the burning Mosquito. The navigator in the Mosquito had been thrown clear on impact but the pilot suffered severe burns before the rescue crews could get to him. The Mossie continued to burn for a full 30 minutes, but the accident was not allowed to hamper 582's efforts for the night. Of the 15 detailed for ops, all but three managed to make it away safely, although a number might have wondered later whether it had all been worthwhile: Flying Officer 'Windy' Gale in NE140 'O' Oboe was forced to abandon the operation two hours after take-off with a faulty starboard outer engine, and Wing Commander Johnnie Clough was obliged to divert to Manston with only three engines and a coolant leak that meant he had no brakes. Flight Lieutenant Butts, a Canadian with five other Canadians in his crew, also lost his starboard inner over Reading on the way out to the target but successfully bombed and made it back on three. Several crews also reported difficulties with their H2S and Gee sets, although overall the bombing appeared to be on target.

Bottrop was the target for the night of February 3/4 with all crews reporting a successful trip with the exception of one of the newer pilots, Flying Officer 'Hal' Mettam (ex-153 Squadron) of the RAAF who was unable to get his aircraft (Lancaster NE140 'O' Oboe again) above 8,000ft. He landed at Manston. A poor attack on Bonn followed the next night, spoiled by 10/10ths cloud, and an even more unproductive effort was made over Goch on February 7/8 when the master bomber stopped the attack after less than half of the bombers had dropped their loads. He had given the 'basement' at 5,000ft and early bombing was accurate but soon smoke had obscured the target. No fewer than seven of the 582 Squadron aircraft involved were forced to abandon their mission. Several could not hear the master bomber's instructions; others could not get down to the correct bombing height as they ran in for the second, third or even fourth attacks; one had a faulty bomb release. Captain Ted Swales could hear clearly what was being said, but did not think much of main force's efforts to comply. Other pilots reported similar reluctance from main force on what might have otherwise been an even more successful attack.

Operation Thunderclap was the codename for the plan devised by the air ministry with the signal objective of bringing about the final collapse of the German war machine and civil administration. It manifested itself in a series of operations focused on a number of major German cities: Berlin, Leipzig and Chemnitz. A further target was also included, Dresden, that would be attacked by the full might of both Bomber Command and the Americans. The Pathfinders were not called upon for the first attack on the city, which was an entirely 5 Group affair. It achieved only moderate success. The second raid, three hours later, was an all-Lancaster attack by aircraft from 1, 3, 6 and 8 Groups, involving 10 aircraft from 582 Squadron obeying the instruction of the master bomber and deputy master bomber, Squadron Leader Charles de Wesselow and Wing Commander Hugh 'Speed' Le Good. Many aircraft retained their TIs, unable to identify accurately the aiming point, although after the master bomber called for 'blind marking' a single group of TIs was adjudged to be accurate and de Wesselow instructed main force to bomb these with a two second overshoot. The water mains were hit early in the attack, and the city burned fiercely with fearful results. All the 582 Squadron aircraft returned safely, with only two crews – those of Flying Officer Robert Terpening (who had survived the Cologne/Gremberg raid despite being shot down) and Flying Officer Kelly – reporting problems with their H2S sets. Six aircraft were also sent to Bohlen and returned.

The very next evening, Operation Thunderclap continued with a raid on Chemnitz in which 16 Squadron aircraft took off and two were forced to abort. Captain Ted Swales was master bomber, with Paddy Finlay his deputy. Swales saw nothing of the main force after leaving Reading and brought all of his own bombs back. Cloud was a big problem, and most of the bombs that were dropped fell harmlessly in open countryside. The number of cows killed is not recorded.

The raid very nearly spelled the end for Flying Officer George Harvey. Shortly after dropping his bombs, the flight engineer, Bill Lanning, noticed his skipper, a diminutive figure, sweating profusely, his head lolling from side to side. Lanning, with sufficient knowledge of how to keep a Lancaster straight and level, suggested he took over to give his pilot a rest. Harvey took some persuading, but at last relented, and Lanning took the controls. A few moments passed and there was a sudden shout on the intercom from the rear gunner telling them to 'get their f***ing arse off the deck' or something very similar. Harvey began to fight Lanning for the controls as though he'd suddenly lost leave of his senses. At much the same time, however, Lanning recognised just how low they had fallen, and realised what must have happened. A check on the oxygen confirmed a piece of shrapnel had sliced through the supply feed and the pilot and most of the crew were steadily losing consciousness. Only the rear gunner, with a turret still largely open to the elements, had remained unaffected and was sufficiently compus mentus to alert his skipper. The problem was quickly rectified, and the navigator, Dan Cruden, brought them safely home.

Tragedy was to befall Swales a week later over Pforzheim. In the intervening period, the squadron raided Dortmund and Monheim (February 20/21) and Duisberg (February 21/22) without incident, save for the loss of Lancaster PB652, damaged beyond repair and later struck off charge. Over Pforzheim, Swales' aircraft was attacked by nightfighters and severely crippled, losing two engines. On his way home, and over friendly territory, he ran into cloud. Without a DR compass and with many of his instruments u/s, he gave the order to bale out. Although the crew managed to make it out in one piece, Swales was too low to jump himself and attempted a crash landing. At the last moment, the aircraft hit some high tension wires, and smashed into the ground, bursting into flames. The following morning, Swales' charred remains were still at the controls, a booted foot jammed in the rudder pedal. He was recommended for an immediate Victoria Cross.

February ended with attacks on Essen, Kamen and Mainz. Essen was a most unsatisfactory affair, being covered in 10/10ths cloud. The defenders showed that they weren't beaten quite yet, making life most uncomfortable for Flying Officer Allen by trying to shoot him out of the sky. In the end they managed to hit the port outer, causing it to burst into flames, and put shells through the bomb doors and port wing. Lancaster ME381 lived to fight another day.

Flight Lieutenant Berney was posted to Little Staughton in February along with several other pilots and crews: Pilot Officers Quine, Dighton, Folkes and Haines. Another new skipper was Squadron Leader Pat Carden, a pre-war regular who held the DFC from his first tour. Carden had joined the RAF in 1932, initially serving as an instructor at the Central Flying School at Upavon. He had been released for operations in 1942 completing his first tour with 15 Squadron at Mildenhall. He arrived at Little Staughton via 35 Squadron at Graveley, and already had more than 50 operations to his credit.

Squadron Leader 'Min' Mingard – one of the 'old contemptibles' – was posted out, and Harry Manley, an Australian who had joined the squadron from 550 Squadron in the summer of 1944, was promoted flight commander in the rank of squadron leader.*

March proved a month of 'firsts' and 'lasts' for the squadron. Several new names appeared on the target maps, primarily synthetic oil plants (SOPs) as well as a few old favourites such as Cologne and Essen that were bombed for the last time. After two months of comparatively 'light' casualties, the crew were also reminded about just how dangerous the Germans could still be, losing 14 men in the space of 10 days.

The first crew lost was skippered by 23-year-old Flying Officer 'Johnnie' Gould, and their story was especially tragic. Returning home from an attack on Chemnitz on March 6, their mission only partly completed, Gould seemed unperturbed that the bomb bay was still loaded with flares. Flying in loose formation with Flying Officers 'Hal' Mettam and George Harvey, Gould steadily lost height as they crossed the English coast and continued his descent towards Little Staughton. At 3,000ft, disaster struck. There was a blinding flash, followed by a shattering explosion as the illuminator flares fused and then detonated in the bomb bay. Rather than being 'safe' as they should have been, somehow they had become 'live'. The aircraft immediately dived into the ground killing all on board with the exception of the rear gunner, Bill Hart, who was the only one with sufficient time to bale out. The average age of the crew had been little over 20, the youngest being the 19-year-old flight engineer, Sergeant Arnold Denbigh. The telegrams were duly sent out the next day.

---

* Before the war's end, Harry Manley DFC left 582 Squadron to crew one of the first Lancastrian delivery flights for Qantas.

The next night there was further tragedy. Flying Officer Lewis Austin, a 33-year-old air gunner from Worthing, was flying as mid-upper gunner with Squadron Leader Vivian Owen-Jones on an attack on Dessau with nine other aircraft from 582 Squadron. Flak was intense, hitting the aircraft of Flight Lieutenant Art Green and causing the pilot's escape hatch on the Lancaster of Flying Officer Wright to blow off, making two holes in the perspex panel. Flak also struck Lancaster PB591 'N' nuts, tearing great chunks out of the starboard wing and striking Lewis Austin in the mid-upper turret, killing him instantly. The aircraft too never flew with the squadron again.

On March 15/16, Flying Officer William Underwood DFC and his crew disappeared without trace. There were three targets for the squadron to choose from that night: Rauxel Tor, Misburg and Hagen. The new CO was in charge at Rauxel Tor and oversaw a successful attack with main force well up with the markers and bombing accurately as instructed. One of the two aircraft sent to Misburg, Lancaster ND709 that had taken over the letter 'N' Nuts, was forced to turn back when the nav two became unconscious as a result of petrol fumes. During the devastating area attack on Hagen, six Lancasters and four Halifaxes were shot down, including the Lancaster ND849 'P' Peter flown by William Underwood. Underwood and his men had the unhappy distinction of being the last full crew to be lost on operations.

The last attack in March took place on the 27th, when a force of 14 Lancasters led by Wing Commander Coulson marked the ancient town of Paderborn with Wanganui for a main force of 254 aircraft that promptly laid waste to the area in less than 15 minutes.

Even with Bomber Command and the war now in the home straight, the pace of operations seemed to increase, with crews called for raids on Merseberg Leuna and Lutzkendorf (April 4), Hamburg (April 8), Kiel (April 9), Leipzig (April 10), Nuremberg (April 11), Kiel again (April 13), Potsdam (April 14), Heligoland (April 18), Bremen (April 22), Ingolstadt (April 24) and Wangerooge (April 25).

With peace in sight, there was one further cruel twist that the squadron had to endure, the death of two more of its aircrew in tragic circumstances. Flying Officer Robert Terpening DFC and his crew were on a training exercise when disaster struck: flying into a snow cloud, the aircraft iced up and they suddenly lost power on both port engines. Although Terpening fought with the controls, the aircraft (Lancaster PB983) spun in and crashed, killing the pilot and his rear gunner, Pilot Officer John Watson DFM, and seriously injuring the rest of the crew. Terpening, an Australian, had been one of the pilots on the Cologne/Gremberg operation who had been shot down, and his faithful gunner had been awarded the DFM for fighting off repeated attacks from German fighters. Sadly they had fought their last fight together.

LIFE IN BOTH HANDS

The story of Flight Lieutenant Frank Lloyd DFC,
pilot, 582 Squadron

Frank Lloyd joined 582 Squadron from Ludford Magna, another skipper 'poached' from 101 Squadron as a pilot with Pathfinder potential. Almost immediately he was in the thick of it. Indeed even before his first operation with the squadron his aircraft was nearly knocked out of the sky on a practice bombing sortie. The writing was perhaps already on the wall when he took off one afternoon to attack the synthetic oil plant at Merseberg Leuna.

> "We were on our bombing run, and suddenly the whole world seem to explode in my face and for a few seconds – it might have been one second – I didn't know what had happened and lost all control of the aircraft."

Flying Officer Frank Lloyd was on his 18th trip, his 14th since joining 582 Squadron in November 1944. He'd been assigned to 'B' Flight, now under the command of Wing Commander Johnnie Clough since Brian McMillan's departure, and was on his way to bomb the synthetic oil plant at Merseberg Leuna along with 572 other Lancasters and 14 Mosquitoes from 1, 5, 6 and 8 Groups. 582 Squadron was contributing 10 aircraft to the show, and Frank had on-board a very experienced navigator in the form of Squadron Leader David Mansell-Playdell, assessing Frank and his crew as a future master bomber.

The approach to the target had gone without incident. Frank could hear the master bomber, Squadron Leader Charles de Wesselow quite clearly, and sensed his disappointment at arriving to find the oil plant covered in 10/10ths cloud. Only four hours previously the target had already been hit, but there was little evidence of this now. De Wesselow called for Wanganui flares which in the relatively light winds, drifted slowly down, thus helping to keep the bombing concentrated on the aiming point. At least one large explosion could be seen as Frank attacked at 18,000ft, dropping his 4,000-pound Minol bomb and smaller 500-pound general purpose bombs bang on target.

The heavy concentration of bombers compacted in such a small space at such short intervals meant the risk of collision or being hit by friendly bombs from above was very great. Squadron Leader Danny Everett, a legend amongst the legends of Pathfinder force, fell victim to one such misfortune, his rear turret being severed by a bomb dropped from above, taking his rear gunner with it to his death. Frank Lloyd was similarly struck:

"The control column began to vibrate violently in my hands. I looked at my altimeter and it was going round and down as though we were in a stall. I shouted out to the crew on the intercom to bale out. Des Lamb, my original bomb aimer from OTU (he had since become my nav two) shouted across to me 'Skip it's the starboard engines' and I looked. Both port and starboard engines were loose in their mountings and it was this that was causing the vibrations.

"I knew we had been hit heavily, but I also thought that I could save her. The crew, however, was already making preparations to abandon the aircraft. I shouted back 'grab Tim' – our flight engineer – and Des just grabbed him before he went. David Mansell-Playdell, however, had already gone and it was too late to stop him. Tim would have been next. Des pulled him back and shouted: 'Skip says feather 3 and 4' and that stopped the vibration. One of the bombs had gone through the fuel tank (number one) on the right wing and there was a bit of damage to the aileron control.

"When I finally levelled off I was at 4,000ft. At that time I didn't know we had one bomb come through the mid-upper position (just in front of the gunner) that had made a hole the width of the fuselage. I had assumed that both gunners had gone because I hadn't heard from them. When we were half way back Phil (the wireless operator) said he needed to go to the toilet, but then he told me he couldn't get to the Elsan because of this hole, but that he could see Happy (the mid-upper) and Shorty (the rear gunner) standing by the rear door singing songs. They had actually jettisoned the door, ready to go. Of course they had to shout to one another across the hole.

"I told Phil to maintain silence. I was praying that we wouldn't be attacked by enemy fighters because I wouldn't have been able to take any avoiding action. There was snow on the ground that could have helped the two gunners if they had wanted to jump, but they decided to wait and see how it went. Instead of going to Staughton we headed for Manston and as we crossed the coast, I told Phil to send the message. I thought of my girlfriend (who later became my wife) and I thought 'I know where she lives but I don't know her address!' I thought it didn't really matter as I reckoned I was going to die, but that thought soon gave way to a belief that I could keep the aircraft flying and land in a field if I had to. My only problem was that with two engines I couldn't afford to overshoot.

"There was low stratocumulus up to about 800ft. I asked Manston if they could shine the searchlights at the base of the cloud to help guide me in. I told the crew to go to crash stations. Manston coned the base for me so I just headed for it. My flight engineer Tim was next to me. I went just to the top of the cloud, flew for a minute, turned left down wind and could see the runway lights, and went a bit further downwind than I would normally. I told Tim just before landing to go to his crash station as didn't know the extent of the damage. As soon as I could see the runway, I knew I would make it. Fortunately the aircraft held together and we made it down safely, although I had quite a bit of difficulty taxiing to dispersal.

"When I took my gauntlets off later I had blisters fully the size of my palms on each hand, caused by the continual vibration through the control column. It didn't matter. I was alive."

The ORB for January 14/15 suggests nothing of the drama that night for Frank and his crew. His logbook entry, however, is more revealing: 'Hit by five bombs, one on starboard outer, one between starboard outer and starboard inner, one through number one starboard fuel tank, two through fuselage forward of mid-upper gunner, starboard aileron control u/s. Both hands blistered. Back on two port engines, starboard inner loose on mounting. B/A (bomb aimer) baled out over target. IAS 110. Height 2,000ft.'

Deservedly, Frank was awarded an immediate DFC, the citation stating:

"Seconds after the bombs had been released the aircraft was badly hit. The control column was wrenched from Flying Officer Lloyd's hands and the bomber went into a steep dive. Before this pilot could regain control considerable height was lost. It was then found that both the starboard engines had been rendered unserviceable. The starboard aileron had been severed, one of the petrol tanks had been hit and its contents lost, whilst in the fuselage a three-foot hole had been torn. In spite of this, Flying Officer Lloyd flew the badly damaged aircraft to an airfield near the English coast and landed it safely. This officer displayed the finest qualities of captaincy, great skill and resolution."

John Clough adds:

> "Lloyd was hit by a bomb load and suffered the worst damage I ever saw. He had one engine completely removed so that there was just a bare bulkhead with a few bits of wire and pipes and things sticking out of it, he had a hole abaft the mid-upper turret top and bottom through which one could have dropped a full sized coffin without touching the sides, and I mean dropped it on the flat, not on end. And the rest of the aeroplane was covered in holes as if a madman had been let loose with an axe, the result of a canister of incendiaries falling on him. Mansell-Playdell was lying in the nose and was able to roll out into the night. He must have been very put out when Lloyd somehow got his aircraft out of the spin and made off for Manston. He had blisters on the palms of his hands the size of half crowns. I saw his aircraft at Manston where I went to collect 'R' Robert after landing there with no brakes, because the starboard inner became defunct and the brakes went flat as a result."

It was not the first, nor the last time that Frank Lloyd had shown fortitude, resilience, even stubbornness in the face of adversity. Although not a rebel, Frank was inclined towards rebellious actions, even from an early age.

At 14, at grammar school in Widnes, he so enraged the deputy headmaster as to provoke him into telling the head 'either that boy goes or I do'. He was encouraged to leave before he was obliged to do so, and was placed in the engineering shop within the Widnes Foundry and Engineering Company where he found himself constantly in fights with other apprentices. He'd always wanted to join the navy but his father refused. The RAF was an option, and on May 15, 1939 he signed on as a boy entrant wireless op:

> "I'd wanted to be a Halton apprentice and discovered I'd joined the wrong bit! I spent 12 months training as a wireless operator by which time the war had started. One day I was playing rugby for the station (Sealand) and there was no score with only a few minutes left to play. I was playing in the centre and dropped a goal to win us the game. The CO was a big fan, clapped me on the back and I blurted out: 'please sir I want to be a pilot'. He told me to come and see him in the morning which I did, although I had to get past a very supercilious Basil Rathbone-type adjutant who refused to believe the CO wanted to see me. I told the CO that half of the pilots weren't as bright as I was, and he decided to give me a chance to prove it. A couple of weeks later, a signal arrived requesting LAC Lloyd to report to Padgate."

Trouble, however, was never far away. On the train to his medical, he met up with two older cadets who fancied a drink. Eleven and a half pints later, and Frank was rather the worse for wear. Fortunately his medical was not until later in the afternoon, by which time he had just sobered up long enough to pass. Training followed ACRC at St John's Wood, and 12 hours in a Tiger Moth at Desford was sufficient to convince his instructors that they had their man (he flew his first solo on October 8, 1942). Then it was off to Oklahoma, and an intoxicating experience (in more ways than one) to become a pilot proper, flying the PT19a. As under officer in charge of a section, he received his wings from Wing Commander H A Roxburgh AFC before returning to the UK, via Harrogate to Peterborough.

> "I was due to go to a ground attack squadron, but one day a young sergeant pilot asked me if I fancied going to the low flying area for some mock dogfights in our Miles Masters. I went and we got lower and lower until he misjudged his height and hit the ground. We didn't have any radio so I flew home and reported the crash. Of course I was summoned before the wingco and had to tell him the truth. He told me that I had no discipline. I agreed, and so was packed off to Sheffield."

Sheffield was where all of the 'naughty' boys within the RAF were sent, as well as those suffering from loss of nerve. There was never any suggestion that Frank was such a case. Fortunately he was a good runner as well as rugby player, which again endeared him to the CO, and so he had a relatively easy time of it.

Ultimately, Frank was sent to HCU Lindholme having completed the first part of his multi-engined training on Oxfords at Windrush, a satellite of Little Rissington, and then OTU flying Wellingtons where he 'crewed up'. His bomb aimer was Des Lamb, six months older than Frank, tall, with a moustache, and one for the girls; 'Timber' Woods was his flight engineer, a rather dour man and an introvert; his navigator, 'Wally' Edwards was also rather serious-minded, but this was more because of his age (29), and the fact that he was married, in peace-time he had been a greengrocer. Phil Axford, from Anglesey, was his 'sparks', and the two gunners were Doug Satherley, an instrument maker for the Bristol Aircraft Company nicknamed 'Shorty', and Arthur 'Happy' Mummery who looked constantly miserable.

After 1 Lancaster Finishing School (LFS) the crew was posted to 101 Squadron, Ludford Magna where they were quickly in the wars – before they had even flown their first operation:

> "On October 1, 1944 we took a Lancaster up to the practice bombing range. All was going well, and we were on our bombing run when suddenly there was a bump and a flash and the aircraft started shaking. I didn't know what

had happened. Happy had gone for a pee and when he finished he came on the intercom and said: 'Skip, my turret has been smashed to bits by a bomb'. If he hadn't needed the loo at that moment, he would have been dead."

Operations proper started four days later with Frank flying a 'second dickey' with a Flying Officer James to Saarbrücken. His first trip with the crew – which had been joined by a German-speaking special duties operator by the name of Van Geffen – was on October 14th – two trips within a 24-hour period to Duisberg. Already, however, Frank was getting restless, and when the opportunity came to volunteer for Pathfinders, he seized it with both hands.

Frank arrived at 582 Squadron in time for the squadron's later attack on Castrop-Rauxel on November 21/22, which he noted as 'a good prang'. Further attacks followed to Neuss, Duisberg (twice), Heimbach, Karlsruhe, Merseberg, and two trips to Cologne. He was on the fateful Cologne/Gremberg raid which he recorded succinctly in his logbook as involving 'big chop' and spent Christmas Day at West Raynham having been diverted because of the weather.

> "I never understood what happened in the Cologne/Gremberg raid. I was told in the briefing that we were not to weave under any circumstances, and that we had to bomb on our leader, which I did. When we got back to base I remember saying to Bob Cairns, who had been flying on my wingtip, why was everybody weaving? He didn't know either, as he had flown straight and level. At the debriefing they said that an order had gone out to break formation, but I know I never received it."

David Mansell-Playdell joined the crew as third navigator for three trips on the bounce, including the near disaster at Merseberg Leuna. "David never spoke to me again after that," Frank says. One night, Frank also managed to 'lose' his flight engineer, but not in quite the way he planned:

> "We were told one morning that we weren't going to be on ops that night. This was apparently on the direct orders of Bennett himself. There was a party on in the mess and I was enjoying myself when the ops officer came around and said 'you'd better get some sleep as you're on ops at 2.30am'. But I said – 'Bennett says we're not on ops tonight' and took no notice of him.
> "Then a couple of hours later he came up to me again and said: 'Lloyd, go to bed you have a briefing at 2.30', and said he was serious. I had my wife and my sister with me, and realised he wasn't joking so took the two girls

home. On the way back to Bedford we got a puncture. I dropped them off and headed back to the station, and then got another flat. I mended it eventually, but obviously I was now very late. The gate I used to break back into camp was on the opposite side to the briefing room, and when I got there the tyre was flat again. I just left the car and ran, and got to the briefing room just as the briefing started.

"All of my lads were asking me where I'd been, but there was another problem. Tim wasn't back. Tim's mother lived in Kettering; as we weren't on ops and it wasn't far to go, he had asked me whether he could nip home and see his mother. I said he might as well stay the night, but told him to be back first thing in the morning. Anyway, he didn't make the briefing. I spoke to Des and said: 'you know how to get the gear up and down, and the flaps don't you?' And he said he could if he had to. I told him that Tim was away and I couldn't contact him. Then I asked Des if he was happy to go without him. He wasn't all that happy but he agreed to go.

"I said to a guy who wasn't operating, that when Tim got back to tell him to go straight out to dispersal and stay there until we landed, otherwise we would all be in trouble. That night we were the last to land, and a good 15 minutes behind all of the rest. The CO at the time had introduced a table to demonstrate how much fuel we all used, and how efficient we could be. I wanted to be the best, and so wasn't in a rush to get home. Poor old Tim was having kittens. He thought we'd got the chop. We told him all about the trip so he could come with us to debriefing, and just in case anyone asked us any questions. They never did find out. Tim told us later that it was the worst few hours he had ever spent."

Frank flew 15 more trips with 582 between February 1 and April 22, 1945. Over the Prosper benzol plant at Bottrop on February 3/4 they were coned by searchlights and attacked by a marauding nightfighter, fortunately without success:

"We were on our bombing run when I heard Happy on the intercom telling me that he could see a bandit coming in from the starboard quarter. His voice grew louder and more urgent until at last he shouted 'corkscrew port'. I shouted for the bomb doors to be closed, put the nose down and started taking evasive action. Then we got coned by searchlights. A master beam would find you, and then before you knew it, lots of other smaller searchlights would be pointed at you. It was like lying on top of a bed in a shop window, totally naked."

Frank also remembers the briefing for the raid on Dresden, a raid that has since become infamous:

"I never remember the raid like they say; I've certainly never been haunted by it. I do remember that we were told at briefing that the German civil servants had sent all of their families to Dresden, to get away from the bombing. I never gave it a thought, and I don't recall anyone expressing any concerns at the time. I think the general view was that the Germans hadn't cared about women and children when they had bombed London, so why should we? What I also remember was that our port outer went u/s after two hours, so we were a little late getting back."

February ended for Frank with an uneventful trip to Pforzheim, in which he reported 'heavy flak'. March started with a long-haul to Chemnitz in which Johnnie Gould was killed. His very last trip, with the exception of various Exodus sorties, was to Bremen, from which he returned with his bombload intact.

Rated 'above average' as a heavy bomber pilot, throughout his time on 582 Squadron, Frank flew a number of different Lancasters, but always refers to one in particular: 'P' Peter.

"I had been complaining about my aircraft to our Chiefy, and had made quite a lot of noise about it in the mess. The aircraft simply wasn't giving me the performance against the settings that it should. Coulson (Group Captain Stafford Coulson) wouldn't listen. Then one of the new pilots* took my aircraft up and was lost. I was delighted, because now I would get a new aeroplane. Sure enough, a nice shiny new Lancaster arrived, and I was only too loud in telling everyone how great it was and how right I was about the previous Lanc. I should have kept quiet; Coulson gave me his aircraft and took the new one for himself, so I was no better off!"

Awarded his permanent Pathfinder badge on June 5, 1945, he was posted to 97 Squadron, RAF Coningsby.

---

* Believed to be William Underwood, lost in ND709 'P' Peter on March 15/16, 1945.

LEADING THE WAY

The story of Flight Lieutenant Reg Cann DFC,
nav one, 582 Squadron

Reg Cann was another who need not have gone to war, having been in a reserved occupation with the Admiralty. Originally destined to become a pilot, an accident late in his training meant he was re-mustered as a navigator, a role he found infinitely more rewarding, giving instructions to his 'driver', Bob Cairns. Pretty soon they found themselves accelerated through the ranks of the Pathfinders, from supporter to visual centerer, deputy master bomber to master bomber, at the vanguard of those 'leading the way'.

Reg Cann will never forget the night in February 1945 when they went to bomb Dresden. Not for the horror that the attack has since invoked following post-war, retrospective analysis, but simply because it was the first time as a navigator on operations that he had got really lost!

His skipper, Flight Lieutenant Bob Cairns, had started engines at 22.11hrs and taxied to the end of the runway, waiting for his turn to go. With a green from control, he released the brakes and eased the throttles forward, accelerating down the tarmac with 3,000rpm and +9 inches of boost keeping the aircraft level with a light touch on the rudder bars until the Lancaster (PB179 'Z' Zebra) finally became airborne. The time, 22.23hrs.

At his navigator's table, Reg was thoroughly occupied, working closely in partnership with his fellow navigator, Johnny Crew:

> "We sat alongside each other, with me on the left, shut away behind a curtain with a light over our desk. Johnny was the nav two, and operated the sets – Gee and 'Y' (H2S). I'd ask him for a fix, and he would work one out for me, calculating the longitude and latitude. It made life much easier. We would be working continuously. There were so many things to concentrate on. Bob always used to fly extremely accurately, trying wherever possible to keep a constant speed, height and course (on the DR compass). If there were a change of course, I would allow time for Bob

to make a rate one turn. That way we were able to remain on track."

Within 20 minutes they had climbed to a cruising height of 10,000ft, with an indicated air speed (IAS) of 155 knots. Forty minutes later they began climbing again to get above cloud, rising to 16,000ft and then 17,000ft, where the temperature outside was –22 degrees.

> "As navigators we worked to 10ths of a minute, and would keep three minutes in hand for every hour we were in the air. So, for example, if it was still two hours to the target, then we would keep six minutes in hand so that we could lose/make up time as required. To lose time we would simply dogleg by flying two sides of an equilateral triangle; making up time was considerably more difficult."

Problems started for Reg at 00.33hrs when their 'Y' set went u/s, and flak started heading their way. Slightly ahead of schedule, and less than 50 miles from the target, he began losing time by flying a dogleg until identifying the aiming point at 01.27hrs, and commencing their bombing run. The master bomber's instructions were difficult to hear, but Cairns could just make out an instruction to overshoot the green markers by two seconds. A large area to the north-east of the aiming point was covered in fires from an earlier attack, and their own four 500-pound and single 4,000-pound bombs fell accurately onto the city.

With bomb doors closed, Reg gave his pilot a course to steer for home, increasing speed to an IAS of 160 knots. All went well for about an hour, then all hell broke loose:

> "With our 'Y' set u/s, the only proper fix I had managed to get was Dresden. What we didn't know, was that the wind conditions had changed dramatically, and we were being blown off track. First of all we were coned; the searchlights were switched on and seemed to be all over the place, and then every gun in the area opened up on us, blowing us all over the sky. Taffy looked out and said 'there's a town down there'. I said 'there can't be' but there was. It was Nuremberg, and we were the only aircraft there. Bob threw the aircraft into a dive and we managed to get away fast. The only consolation was that at least I was able to get a positive fix. We were nine miles off track!"

Bob Cairns continued his evasive tactics, diving and then climbing for more than six minutes before he was at last able to lose the searchlights and resume a course for home. The remainder of the trip was uneventful, and they landed back at base at 06.29hrs, after a flying time of more than eight and a half hours.

Dresden was Reg's 33rd operation, and his 25th since arriving at 582 Squadron with the crew on August 23, 1944. Originally from Gosport, Reg had grown up fascinated by stories and tales of derring-do from the First World War pilots and their aircraft, and at the outbreak of war was in a reserved occupation, working in an Admiralty department in Portsmouth Dockyard.

> "I had decided to join up, and was sent for my aircrew medical in Oxford. I had a chitty from the Admiralty to say that I could not be enrolled without their prior permission. I didn't reveal this, and so I was accepted into the RAF."

Reg took some time before he was finally washed out as a pilot, his postings including 4 EFTS Brough (September 1942) and on to 31 EFTS and 36 SFTS in Alberta, Canada, having crossed the Atlantic unescorted on the liner *Aquitania*:

> "I had done a little over 100 hours in Tiger Moths and Oxfords before doing an Oxford no good on take-off. I had forgotten to tighten the throttle nuts, the result being that I ended up off the runway in a field on my nose. Not surprisingly, I was dumped. This was the first big set-back in my life. Until then, it had all been a breeze. I thought I was invincible. Canada was all a tremendous adventure, so perhaps this did me a bit of good."

Re-mustered as a navigator, Reg took to his new task with relish, deciding on balance that he found navigating more interesting than driving:

> "There was always something happening, something to do. You told the pilot the course, the speed and the height, and he had to do as he was told."

Still in Canada, he attended 2 AOS in Edmonton between May and October 1943 before coming home to finish his training at 8 AFU Mona (Anglesey), acclimatising to UK conditions, and then on to 28 OTU Wymeswold.

> "I was meant to get crewed up at OTU but it didn't quite work out that way. There was a navigator at another OTU in Peplow, a Canadian who had been washed out as an alcoholic, which meant that a crew needed a replacement. I went over to 83 OTU to take his place, and it was here that I met Bob Cairns. Bob was a Scot, very dour, very calm, an excellent pilot and skipper. Nothing seemed to

faze him. I flew with some crews later where they used to chatter incessantly. We didn't have any of that. We flew in absolute silence, and only spoke when it was absolutely necessary to do so."

From OTU, the crew – complete with their more sober navigator – passed on to 1667 HCU Sandtoft (nicknamed 'Prangtoft' for obvious reasons) and then 1 LFS Hemswell before being posted to 625 Squadron, Kelstern on July 21, 1944.

"When we arrived, it was a real thrill to be on an operational squadron. Until that time, we had only been training and it all seemed a little artificial but these chaps were really doing it. This was exciting and daunting in equal measure."

Their new squadron had been formed in October 1943 as part of 1 Group, and was now under the command of Wing Commander Douglas Haig DSO, DFC. Reg was operational four days after arriving, and had his first real taste of combat on July 25 over Stuttgart when they were attacked by enemy fighters on no fewer than three occasions:

"I remember that when Bob went into a corkscrew, everything came flying off your navigator's desk and you ended up scrabbling around trying to find it all again. And then when you were on the floor and the pilot had stopped throwing the aircraft all over the place the skipper would come on intercom and say: 'Where are we Reg?'

"One of the devices we used was an air position indicator (API) which was linked to a gyro compass in the rear of the aircraft with repeaters to the pilot, me and the bombsight. It gave you your position in the air from the last time you set it. So if you had the wind velocities you could effectively work out where you were. It all worked well unless the gyro toppled, in which case you had to make your way to the back of the aircraft to re-set it, and you could only do that if you had a 'fix' either visually or from Gee or 'Y'."

In all, Reg completed eight trips at 625 Squadron before moving to 582 Squadron:

"Bob was keen to go on to Pathfinders, and consulted us about it. To be honest, I wasn't that keen. I couldn't see the attraction in even more training, but neither did I want to be the one to split the crew up. We went off to NTU, where

I undertook a number of cross-countries with a highly experienced navigator instructor watching my every move. For me it was all very exacting; for the rest of the crew, I think it was a doddle!"

At Little Staughton they were allocated to 'B' Flight, commanded by Brian McMillan, and given a second navigator, Johnnie Crew, a Canadian. Reg's first trip on September 10 was as a 'spare bod':

"I was flying with Flying Officer Finlay who in turn was the deputy master bomber. I remember stooging around the target for a little while and thinking 'this is novel'. No one liked spare bods or being a spare bod; it disrupted the crew."

Their first trip as a full crew started the next day, September 11, to Castrop-Rauxel. Over Osnabrück on the 13th they had the satisfaction of seeing their bombs strike the target but were then hit by heavy flak in the fin, rudder and tailplane, as well as taking damage to the starboard inner nacelle and the fuselage. Fortunately they made it home safely. The following month, whilst attacking Stuttgart, they were again set upon by nightfighters on three separate occasions:

"Willie (Ritchie) in the rear turret began blasting away at them and he could see the tracer rounds clearly in the night. I cannot remember what the gunnery leader's instructions were about nightfighters, but I do know that we took a very aggressive stance. If we saw an enemy nightfighter then we would open fire straight away. We always attacked, in the hope that we would scare him off and he would go and look for someone less troublesome.

"Taffy once asked me to come out from behind my curtain and have a look at what was going on below. 'Oh my God' I thought. Before I had heard it, and felt it, but now I could see it. I never looked out again."

By October 28, Bob Cairns had been 'promoted' to deputy master bomber, a role he fulfilled two days running for the attack on ground positions in and around Walcheren (Domberg). On December 6, Reg once more had to occupy the guest seat in somebody else's Lancaster, this time one flown by Flight Lieutenant Freddie Gipson. Reg explains:

"It was the first and only time I had ever said it was pointless to go on. We lost an engine very early into the flight and so were well behind schedule. I was having to cut corners to make up time, but even then we ended up over the target six minutes late."

Tonsillitis meant Reg wasn't flying the day the squadron took off to attack Cologne/Gremberg, but happily the rest of the crew made it back in one piece, with Reg there to greet them:

"Percy (Ansell), the wireless operator, was waving at me though a large jagged hole where the astrodome should have been."

Reg celebrated his 30th trip with a faulty distributor, and being forced to jettison their bombs over Mannheim. By now, Wing Commander Johnnie Clough had taken over as officer commanding 'B' Flight and their regular bomb aimer, an Australian, had been replaced by Flight Lieutenant Colin Hailstone. Colin was a second-tour man:

"Our bomb aimer was getting a little bit flak happy. Every time he saw an aircraft going down he would get a little excited. It was very disconcerting. On one night, Taffy cut off his oxygen supply to keep him quiet. At least that worked for a time."

Generally, morale on the squadron remained high, especially with the arrival of Stafford Coulson who was both well-known and respected amongst the crews. The only dampner was the suicide of Flying Officer Mellor.

"He was a young, dark-haired lad, and a bit of a loner. His death was very bad for morale, but was the exception rather than the rule. I recall a couple of air gunners who got to their aircraft and couldn't go on, but again such incidents were far from typical."

Attacks followed on Bonn, Goch, Chemnitz, Duisberg, Essen, and other targets in the Ruhr, destroying the last of Germany's manufacturing and industrial capacity. Very heavy flak was encountered over Mitzberg on March 15, and the next day they were again tasked with being deputy master bomber for an attack on Hanau. By now, the war had a little over six weeks to run, and on March 22 they were selected as master bomber for a visual attack on Dülmen.

Dülmen, between Munster and Wesel, was an important road centre and home to a major fuel storage depot used by the German air force. Cairns, flying with his deputy Flight Lieutenant Jimmy Brown, was able to identify the aiming point with ease and put their

TIs down accurately but not all of the 582 Squadron supporters and a mere handful of the 106 main force Halifax crews were on time to take advantage. Bob ordered the visual centrers to hold on to their TIs until the main stream had caught up, and in the meantime called upon main force 'to hurry up'. It was a full seven minutes after the first markers went down and the first handful of bombs were dropped that the main force finally arrived, and Bob ordered them to bomb the upwind edge of the smoke that was now beginning to obscure the aiming point. The bombs by now were beginning to find their mark, and two enormous explosions were seen in the target area. Cairns, in Lancaster ND 709 'N' Nuts headed for home.

On March 24, with Wing Commander Stafford Coulson as master bomber, Reg navigated his skipper to Sterkrade, where they had been given the duty of 'longstop' for the attack on densely packed marshalling yards:

> "Our role was to oversee the operation and, with our own troops so close to the target on the ground, to ensure that no bombs fell beyond or before a particular point. We orbited the Rhine to the target and back, but with no marking or bombing required, and no need to cancel any earlier marking, we brought our bombs back."

His last successful attack in anger occurred on the afternoon of April 11, the target being the marshalling yards in Nuremberg. Their role was one of the most difficult and respected – primary visual markers – and theirs were the first flares to be dropped, right on target. The aiming point was obliterated and not a single aircraft lost.

On April 22, Bomber Command gathered more than 750 Lancasters, Halifaxes and Mosquitoes to pound what was left of the city of Bremen, in preparation for an assault by the British XXX Corps. The bombing was to be on the south-eastern suburbs of the city, where the spearhead of the attacking force would strike. The squadron contributed 14 of its crews to the operation, but all of them were forced to abandon the mission over the enemy target on the orders of the master bomber.

> "The Germans still weren't beaten," Reg says. "Opposition was still pretty fierce, and although we had to abandon our attack I know that some aircraft were lost."

Reg is correct: although overall losses were tiny by comparison to earlier raids on the target, the German defences still accounted for the loss of four Lancasters and the lives of 12 men from 153 and 218 Squadrons.

A Pathfinder tour stretched to 45 operations. Reg completed his by dropping parcels of food to the starving Dutch civilians in one of the squadron's numerous Manna flights. He remembers clearly how much pleasure it gave them, and how he could see people emerging from their houses and waving frantically skywards. His final operation – number 47 – was an Exodus sortie in June returning POWs from Lübeck to Wing, Buckinghamshire. Their Lancaster was adorned with chalk slogans celebrating the prisoners' return, and their rewarding role as glorified taxi drivers.

Reg remembers his time on the squadron well, but also the need to get away from the base and people whenever he could:

> "The mess could get a bit claustrophobic, and I used to try and get away from Little Staughton as much as possible to be where 'normal' people lived. We had an old Ford 8 that we used to run on 100 octane, so you can imagine what that was like. We all used to pile in and head off for Bedford; a load of 20-year olds together. Great fun.
>
> "As officers we had a bat-woman who made our beds but little else. Her ambition was to find an American and marry him. I often wonder if she did."

One of the last entries in Reg's logbook is a flight on April 26, 1946. The passenger is Air Commodore Patch MBE. The flight is from St Mawgen to Hendon. In brackets are two words: Cup Final!

After demob, like many of his colleagues Reg decided to put it all behind him and forget about it. Bob Cairns went on to pilot one of the Lancasters that flew Harris on his tour of Brazil and South America. Reg went back to the Admiralty, from whence his journey had begun. He is nonetheless proud of what they achieved, and happy to smile about the time he got lost coming back from Dresden:

> "A navigator is never lost, he merely knows his position with uncertainty."

PATHFINDER VC

The story of Captain Ted Swales VC, DFC,
pilot, 582 Squadron

Edwin 'Ted' Swales was one of that select band of fighting men from the Commonwealth who answered the King's call to defend the Empire against the evil tyranny of fascism. Originally a soldier, he fought in the desert and at El Alamein before transferring to the South African Air Force (SAAF) and joining the elite 582 Squadron. He had nothing to prove, but constantly pushed himself and those that flew with him until he attained master bomber status, and was briefed to lead the attack on Pforzheim on February 23, 1945.

Before the war, Pforzheim, in the Land of the Baden, had been the chief centre in Germany for the manufacture of gold and silver ornaments and jewellery. Its population of 78,500, swollen no doubt by evacuees, had managed to avoid the attention of Bomber Command for more than five years, but all that changed on the night of February 23, 1945.

As if to confirm the cosmopolitan mix of Colonial and former-Colonial types helping to win the war for the Allies, the eight skippers briefed to attack the town that night included a New Zealander, Flight Lieutenant Nairn; an Australian, Flying Officer 'Hal' Mettam; an American, Flying Officer Oswald Interiano: an Irishman, Flight Lieutenant Paddy Finlay; and three Brits, William Underwood, Frank Lloyd and Jimmy Brown. Tasked with the master bomber role was a South African: Captain Ted Swales.

Ted Swales was one of the more remarkable squadron characters in the context of a remarkable body of men. Born in Inanda, Natal on July 3, 1915 – the second of four children – Swales moved to Durban in 1919 on the early death of his father. From his earliest school days at Durban High School, Ted was more interested in his sport than academic life, especially rugby, but he eventually matriculated and embarked on a career in banking, joining a branch of his local Barclays.

Always one seeking adventure, he enlisted in the Natal Mounted Rifles, roughly the equivalent to the Territorial Army, in June 1935, completing his term of service four years later with the rank of warrant officer II. With war looming, he quickly rejoined his unit, that by now had fallen under the aegis of the 2nd South African Infantry Brigade, and volunteered for service overseas. He saw active service in Kenya (which was under threat from the Italian army), Abyssinia and Egypt, taking part in the Crusader offensive, the Gazala battles, and El Alamein. A desire to get off the ground and into the air prompted him to join the South African Air Force (SAAF) to which he transferred on January 17, 1942, being posted to 75 Air School, Lyttleton near Pretoria. Training was delayed somewhat, but after the obligatory square bashing (which after seven years in the army must have been irksome) he started training proper at 4 AS, Benoni in October, making his first solo by the end of the month. In February 1943 he reported to 21 AS, Kimberley, for two-engined conversion (flying Oxfords) before finally achieving his 'wings' and his commission on June 26, 1943.

Ted Swales turned down the offer of instructing to "go north" – leaving South Africa on August 27, 1943 on a journey that went via South America and took 10 weeks before finally arriving in the UK. Another six months of intensive training in England went by (including 6 AFU Little Rissington and 83 OTU, Peplow) before he was posted to 'B' Flight of 582 Squadron for operational duties. Interestingly Swales was posted directly to a Pathfinder squadron before having any experience as a Bomber Command pilot, or indeed any operational experience in any other command.

Ted's first trip was on July 12, 1944 to Thiverny, and two more followed to Mont Cordon and Cagny in quick succession. He nearly came to grief on his way back from Kiel at the end of July when, short on fuel, he diverted to the Handley Page factory in Radlett, Hertfordshire, and attempted an emergency landing. Unfortunately he misjudged his approach, and Swales and his flight engineer were both injured in the crash that resulted. The aircraft, Lancaster JB417, was permanently damaged and struck off charge.

The South African's operations then followed a similar pattern to his contemporaries: short trips to France, long hauls to Germany; attacks on troop concentrations and oil installations. Always keen to learn, Swales would question others on the squadron almost incessantly, and not just about the job or the war but also about history, science and farming. Groomed as a future master bomber, he would make a point of seeking out the most experienced crews for their advice, and not just the pilots but also the flight engineers, navigators and gunners, such was his desire to learn everything about the role.

He suffered too the similar mishaps: bombsights malfunctioning, H2S sets going on the blink, engines overheating. On one occasion he was obliged to return early when his canopy blew off shortly after take-off, only to receive a severe reprimand from his CO for failing to press-on. He told his friend Johnnie Clough in confidence that he would never turn back again. It was a prophetic statement.

On a daylight to Duisberg he suffered more than most. Flak forced his flight engineer to feather both port engines, and with his starboard outer also misfiring it was touch and go whether he would make it back in one piece. Severed hydraulic lines meant no flaps or brakes on landing, and in the end he was forced to bring the Lancaster to earth with his undercarriage retracted on the outskirts of Brussels. All of the crew got out safely, and were picked up by an Anson and flown back to Little Staughton. The aircraft, PB485 'J' Johnnie was wrecked. It had lived for only 23 hours.

Promoted captain, by December 23, the date of the daylight to Cologne/Gremberg, he had flown 33 trips. It was over Gremberg that he won the first of his immediate awards for gallantry. The citation for his DFC tells the story succinctly:

> "This officer was pilot and captain of an aircraft detailed to attack Cologne in December 1944. When approaching the target, intense anti-aircraft fire was encountered. Despite this, a good bombing attack was executed. Soon afterwards, the aircraft was attacked by five enemy aircraft. In the ensuing fights, Captain Swales manoeuvred with great skill. As a result his gunners were able to bring effective fire to bear upon the attackers, one of which is believed to have been shot down. Throughout this spirited action, Captain Swales displayed exceptional coolness and captaincy, setting a very fine example. This officer has completed very many sorties during which he has attacked a variety of enemy targets."

The two gunners – Flight Sergeants Bryn Leach and Jack Smith – were similarly rewarded with the DFM. The awards were gazetted, ironically, on February 23, 1945, the day they were briefed for Pforzheim, Ted's 42nd and final trip.

The crew that night had one or two changes from Swales' regular team. In the rear turret was Pilot Officer Al Bourne. His account of the raid is a testimony to the bravery of all of the men who flew that day, and especially the bravery of their skipper.

> "My posting to 582 Squadron came in October 1944. After the loss of my first Canadian crew with 433 Squadron and surviving a fatal crash, the previous six months had been a series of operations flying as a 'spare' with 425 Squadron (Les Alouettes) and then 405 Squadron at Gransden Lodge. Until I joined with the Swales crew it had been more of the same at Little Staughton. Before the Cologne raid (December 23, 1944) I had the undoubted distinction of flying with Flight Lieutenants Hemsworth RAAF, Morgan, Pengilley, Owen-Jones, and Group

Captain Cribb, then squadron CO.

"After a depressing Christmas at Little Staughton, due directly to the loss of at least five good crews and personal friends on Cologne, I was detailed to crew with Captain Ted Swales. Having completed well over 35 ops by this time I still felt somewhat of a 'sprog' on joining the highly-regarded Swales crew. We were a pretty mixed bunch of Commonwealth types: Swales was from South Africa, Archie Archer (nav one), Clive Dodson (bomb aimer), Bryn Leach (mid-upper gunner) and Gerry Bennington (flight engineer) were all RAF, with 'Whisky' Wheaton (nav two) and Bert Goodacre (wireless op) RAAF, and myself (rear gunner) RCAF.

"On February 23, 1945 we were briefed to be master of ceremonies (sic) on the marshalling yards at Pforzheim, a watch-making centre which was believed to be assembling V2 warheads. The raid, with approximately 600 (sic) aircraft taking part, was to last for 20 minutes, with a deputy MC to orbit us in case the MC got the chop. Met gave a forecast of between 5-6/10ths cloud over the target which meant the marking could be visual or blind and on the return flight a warm front would move in giving thick fog and poor visibility.

"On arriving at Pforzheim and orbiting the target for the second time, I noticed some movement low on our starboard side. It overtook us at high speed so couldn't be a Lanc. I made a mental note to watch the starboard side. Several minutes passed while I continually rotated the turret, then when the skipper started to broadcast to main force I was cut off from the aircraft intercom.

"At that moment, an enemy aircraft dropped rapidly astern of us and seemed to rise slightly at approximately 20 degrees low on our starboard quarter at a range of less than 400 yards. 'Fighter starboard – Go!' I called on the intercom then realised there was no response to my call for a corkscrew to starboard because the pilot could not hear me whilst he was transmitting. Immediately I began flashing my starboard 'fighter call light' to warn Ted visually of our plight. At no more than 200 yards I opened fire with all four guns, at the same time I felt the aircraft shudder and go into a starboard corkscrew as the fighter opened up with his cannon. As we levelled with the Me (Messerschmitt 410) still close on our tail, cannon shells straddled each side of my turret scoring hits on both rudders and inner engines. As the rudder surfaces disintegrated, they looked for all the world like washing on a line on a windy day.

"With both inboard engines hit, I realised that our hydraulic power for the turrets and guns was gone. In all this time I had heard nothing on the intercom but the sound of my own breathing. Soon the Me410 grew enormous from my position as either he soared above us or we began to lose height, every detail of our attacker was clearly visible.

"Realising that my guns were still pointing upwards and to port, I determined to have one last crack at him and stuck my thumb into the opening under the rear seat of the upper Browning to trip the firing mechanism. After a few rounds, the gun stopped firing and sparks seemed to fly off the underside of the enemy telling me I was hitting, but to what effect I didn't know. At this time Bryn Leach, my gunner partner, let out a shout and only then did I realise that as our attacker rose into view from the stern, he had also opened fire to good effect.

"A call from the skipper to check our status confirmed that nobody had been injured but, with both inner engines dead, we were losing height at an alarming rate. While we still had some height, Ted decided to make a last broadcast to the incoming main force. After passing instructions for the aiming point it was decided to make for the Schaffhausen salient in Switzerland, it being the nearest friendly base. It would also mean internment for the duration of the war. After heading this way for some twenty minutes, the skipper found that, while we could only maintain between six or seven thousand feet and the fuel state was good, he could with some difficulty hold a steady course. A discussion with all crew members took place on whether to turn for home or to carry on to Switzerland and internment. After estimating the duration of power from our batteries and the loss of all blind flying instruments when they gave out (the generators being on the dead engines), the navigator reckoned that we might just make it through the front forecast for our return to base before we lost our flying instruments. The vote was unanimous 'Let's head for home!'

"The next hour was a nightmare as 'M' Mike slithered violently from side to side and rapidly lost much needed height, the skipper fighting the controls to stay in the air. Several times during this period, through breaks in the fog, we saw what looked to be V2s rising ahead of us. When this happened a number of times, we realised that this was the horizon as we banked steeply and slewed around in the sky.

"By this time, with the blind flying panel useless, we

were down to less than 2,000 feet and Archie's estimate put us over the German border and into France.

"Now, with feet braced against the bulkhead and arms embracing the control column, Ted gave the order, 'Prepare to abandon aircraft'. As the crew in the nose prepared to exit via the forward hatch I left my turret still wearing my helmet and joined Bryn and Bert ready to leave by the main door. Then the urgent call came over the intercom 'Jump! Jump! I can't hold her any longer'. I signalled to Bert who moved quickly and plunged out, I followed seconds later and Bryn gave a sign that he was OK.

"From a deafening roar to complete cotton wool-wrapped silence was the immediate effect as my 'chute opened and the sound of the aircraft receded. The descent could have taken only seconds from the altitude of under 2,000 feet. Tugging on the shroud lines to stop the pendulum motion I heard the noise of engines growing louder. Oh no! It can't happen, not my own aircraft chewing me up before I get down!

"I remembered that 'M' Mike had been in an almost uncontrollable orbit when we abandoned and it could possibly happen. Seconds later there came a tremendous explosion and a flash as the aircraft struck the ground somewhere below. By the light from the burning plane I landed in the mud of a ploughed field, sinking in over my boot tops. Minutes later, by the use of our aircraft whistles, the crew gathered, without Ted, at the fiercely burning remains of our aircraft.

"A quick check round showed that we had all landed safely except for Whisky who had badly sprained his ankles. This was the result of leaving the hatch feet first instead of rolling out head first in the approved manner. As for myself, Bryn claimed that he was still shovelling the bulk of my parachute out of the hatch after I went out. Vaguely I remember a parachute instructor saying count a slow three or a fast ten – or was it the other way round? In any case, thanks to Bryn's quick thinking I made a clean descent.

"Archie, having a working knowledge of conversational French, made contact with some local people and found that we were close to the town Valenciennes, bordering on Belgium. With the Americans having advanced through the town a day or two earlier, a tactical wing of the army air corps was nearby and proved a great help by returning us by B17 to our home base on February 24, ready to press on again without our skipper, Ted Swales. After spending the remains of the night at the US base we returned to see the smouldering skeleton of our aircraft with Ted's body still strapped in position."*

Ted Swales was dead. In the operations record book, the adjutant first typed in the 'Details of Sortie or Flight' column the words: 'Missing. Last heard of over the target'. With the safe return of the crew to Little Staughton, the raid report was amended to state: 'Crew afterwards returned except pilot, Capt Swales E E'.

Within 24 hours the extent of Ted Swales' bravery was known. The commanding officer, Stafford Coulson, sat down to compose the 'particulars of meritorious service' for which the recommendation of a Victoria Cross – Britain's highest award for gallantry – was being made. Coulson gave a full account of the raid, and Ted's part in it. He wrote:

> "Throughout this difficult and hazardous return journey, Captain Swales made it plain that he was determined to bring his aircraft and crew back without further damage, in the best interests of operational flying. When he found that this was no longer possible in toto, his only thought was for the safety of his crew. This latter was only ensured by his complete disregard for his own safety and his acceptance of certain death for himself."

Stafford also cited two other examples of Swales' bravery: the attack on Duisberg, when again he brought his crew safely home, and the daylight to Gremberg for which he received an immediate DFC. The date was February 27, 1945.

The commanding officer's recommendation was endorsed by the station commander (and former 582 squadron commander) Peter Cribb. He wrote:

> "This is undoubtedly a superlative example of heroism and self sacrifice. There can be no doubt that Captain Swales, fully aware of the risks involved, made a most determined effort to ensure the success of his mission [...] Making up for his lack of experience by his resolution and tenacity, he has risen quickly to the status of master bomber, and it is in this capacity he has best demonstrated his qualities of heroism and unflinching devotion to duty. Having thus terminated a brilliant career by giving his own life that seven others might live, I most strongly recommend that he be awarded the Victoria Cross..."

The final word came on March 2 from Donald Bennett himself, who

---

* It is suggested that their vanquisher was Hauptmann Gerhard Friedrich of II./NJG1.

made a point of stressing the success of the attack in which Swales died:

> "PRU (photo reconnaissance unit) cover of the target has subsequently proved that the attack was one of the most concentrated and successful of the war. He showed heroism beyond praise in sacrificing his own life in order to ensure the safety of his crew."

100 UP!

The story of Flight Lieutenant Ted Stocker DSO, DFC, engineering leader, 582 Squadron

Only a handful of officers and men who arrived at 582 Squadron upon its foundation in April 1944 were still there at the war's end, 13 months later. One of the most illustrious, and undoubtedly the most experienced, was Flight Lieutenant Ted Stocker, the engineering leader, believed to be the war's only surviving flight engineer DSO and DFC. His operational record spanned four front-line squadrons, and he chalked up more than 100 operations. Officially. Like his last commanding officer, however, not all of his trips necessarily feature in his logbook.

Ted Stocker was born near the naval dockyards of Sheerness, Kent, the son of a farmer. Neither the navy, nor farming, held much interest to the lad, but from the very earliest days he had a fascination for aircraft, happily wiling away his hours reading W E Johns and watching the aeroplanes swoop and land at the emergency landing ground in Laysdown.

> "I had a cousin in the RAF and so talked to him about joining the apprentice scheme at RAF Halton after I left school. I took the exams and was offered a place, but the school principal wasn't very happy with me. It didn't matter; I joined as part of Entry 37 in January 1938, and became one of Trenchard's 'Brats'. I was officially classed as a Fitter 2E, and we tended to provide a good number of flight engineers to the squadrons. Not many of us survived."

With the possibility of war edging closer, and then being declared, Ted's course was shortened from three years to two years and four months, something they achieved by cutting out all of the sport and fitness in the curriculum. He passed out an AC1, somewhere in the middle of the pack, and was posted to the experimental research and aircraft evaluation base at Boscombe Down.

"This was the time immediately after Dunkirk and I spent four weeks in the MT section. Of course at Dunkirk the RAF lost much of its transport, and a large number of its mechanics, and so as 'engine fitters' we were considered the nearest thing. I didn't have a license and couldn't drive, but remember being told by the chiefy to move the lorries around the yard which I did without question. One of the vehicles was a 1917 Leyland petrol bowser – that's how short of modern equipment we were.

"It was an interesting time to be at Boscombe. I was there when the first Short Stirling came in for evaluation with 'Pop' Watts as the flight engineer. Pop had been a World War One balloonautic and a member of Alan Cobham's Flying Circus, and later I was to serve under him and then be his boss at 35 Squadron. Other aircraft came and went: Spits and Hurricanes fitted with the first cannon; a Mohawk that fired its guns through the propeller arc. I can tell you I became quite expert at changing propellers! It was a wonderful way of learning about aircraft in a very short space of time."

Ted's hankering, however, was to be a pilot. Since his first flight in an Avro Tutor as an apprentice, his desire had been confirmed. To be a pilot he needed to be at least an LAC (leading aircraftsman). Ted was still only an aircraftsman 1st Class, but in his quest for promotion, he did rather too well, and as a corporal the powers-that-be wouldn't let him go. Instead he took advantage of a request for flight engineers, and took off for No. 8 flight engineers/air gunnery course at Evanton, near Inverness, arriving on May 24, 1941.

"God knows why we had to do air gunnery to be a flight engineer but we did. There were 12 of us on the course: 10 are dead, one's blind and there's me. Survival was the name of the game. You stayed alive you got the gongs."

Ted's first posting was to 76 Squadron, but they didn't seem to have any aircraft when he got there and he was immediately posted to 35 Squadron. He could not help but be impressed by the squadron's three commissioned pilots, all of whom went on to greater fame: Flight Lieutenant Cheshire; Flying Officer Cribb; and Pilot Officer Cresswell. Within days he had his first flight in a Halifax (his pilot was later shot down during an attack on La Pallice) and flew his first operation on October 11 with Sergeant Williams at the controls. It was a six hour 20 minute trip to Essen that passed without incident. The same could not be said, however, for his second trip:

"It is important to remember that the Halifax was originally designed as a relatively short-range bomber, and after Dunkirk there were some major modifications to ensure we could reach targets in Germany flying from bases in the UK, rather than France. The Halifax I and the Halifax II also had different fuel capacities.

"We were briefed to go to Nuremberg, and at the briefing, our CO, Wing Commander Robinson, made a big point of saying that he did not want any of us landing away from base, which was becoming a habit. By my calculations, however, given the air miles and the fuel load, there was no margin for error whatsoever, and so I mentioned it to the wingco. He tartly replied that 'Group must know what they're doing'. Unfortunately, they didn't.

"I kept the throttle settings and speed constant for maximum fuel efficiency on the way out and on the way back. Although we got within sight of the airfield coming home, it was clear that we weren't going to make it, and so we set about preparing to bale out. (Cresswell, it should be noted, only managed to get as far as Dover)."

Ted and his crew had the added complication of carrying a second pilot, a skipper from 58 Squadron where they flew the twin-engined Whitleys:

"We used to carry the Whitley skippers as co-pilots before they did the conversion course. Being used to his own aircraft, this fellow had put on a full Irving suit – the big Irving top, the big Irving trousers – and he was a big lad himself. The pilot gave the order to bale out and this fellow sat in the hatch with his legs dangling over the edge. He then tried to dive through head-first, the end result being that he got stuck with his bottom stuck up in the air. Len Thorpe, our wireless operator, was due to go next, and so climbed back up the steps to where the co-pilot's position was, and jumped straight down onto this fellow's backside and the pair of them went out like a cork out of a bottle!

"By this time the rest of us were too low to bale out. We might have got out, but the skipper's parachute pack was missing, and so we went straight in. There were three of us left in the aircraft when it crashed and we went down in an untidy heap in a field. The squadron sent two ambulances, one for the bodies, and one for the wounded. When they got there and found out that we were all unhurt, they left us to make our own way back!"

Ted completed four ops with 35 before being moved to 102

Squadron, which at that time (January 1942) was converting from Whitleys on to the Halifax. The chief flying instructor (CFI) of 102 Squadron Conversion Flight was Squadron Leader 'Wally' Lashbrook DFC, DFM, himself a former Trenchard Brat, who suggested Ted put in for a commission. Stocker flew with the CO (Wing Commander Bintley) and a flight commander (Squadron Leader Griffiths) but missed the 1,000 Bomber raid when his own skipper, Flight Lieutenant Welsh, had ear trouble. By June he had a regular captain by the name of Hank Malkin (later DFC and Bar, AFC), and by August had flown 15 trips.

> "Hank was a warrant officer and one for the popsies," Ted recalls. "It was Hank who decided that he wanted to go to Pathfinders, and so I decided I would go too. It was thus that we found ourselves back with 35 Squadron which by then had become the first of the Pathfinder squadrons."

Many of Ted Stocker's adventures whilst with 35 Squadron are well documented in those squadron's records. The trip to Milan where 'Robbie' Robinson called him urgently to the front just so he could show him how beautiful Mont Blanc looked in the moonlight; the flares that ignited in the bomb bay over the North Sea en route to Hamburg that Ted jettisoned with only seconds to spare; the emergency landing at Tangmere when he fell unconscious as a result of eating too many baked beans.

In the autumn he went to the air ministry for his commission board interview, heeding Squadron Leader Lashbrook's advice.

> "I had been on ops the night before the morning interview, and arrived a little late, looking a little bit dishevelled and tired. The interview panel was made up of some very senior officers, most of whom I figured had never seen a shot in anger. One of them said to me quite severely: 'where were you last night?' So I told him the target. The uncomfortable silence that followed was punctured only by the sound of the officer's ego deflating, and I sailed through the rest of the interview. I got my commission."

Ted flew 47 operations on Halifaxes – not unusually flying with some of the Pathfinder 'greats': Gordon Carter, Julian Sale, 'Dixie' Dean – and including a number of hairy trips when they were lucky to make it home. Over Lorient in January 1943, the port outer engine had to be feathered over the target, and the port inner stopped on landing; over Berlin in March they were hit by heavy flak, wounding the mid-upper gunner, losing two engines and damaging the rudder controls. Despite being coned for 25 minutes, they still made it back in one piece. Stocker was untouched, save for a small hole in the sleeve of his jacket – the one and only time he was hit in combat.

A trip to Pilsen with Flight Lieutenant Paxton proved amusing:

> "It was quite an uneventful trip. We went over the target, we dropped our bombs and nobody fired back or did any damage or anything. So I put my head down, checked the instruments, and filled in the log sheet. We were clear of the target then – so I peered through the astrodome to have a look at the exhausts, see that they were all the right colour. As I looked out, I said quietly over the intercom, 'Navigator, if we are going home why is the Pole star on the port side?' There was a little hush that lasted a good 10 seconds before all hell broke loose. The Pole star on the port side meant that we are going east, and by my reckoning heading east from Czechoslovakia was not the best way home!"

On June 19, 1943, on the way back from Le Creusot at low level, the bright moonlight was such that they could see clearly a train and a flak ship below and the gunners gave both a squirt to make them feel better.

Officially now coming to the end of his tour, On July 13, 1943, the *London Gazette* promulgated his DFC, the citation mentioning how his sound knowledge 'has on occasions greatly assisted his captain in making a safe return to base.' Pilsen is one of the targets mentioned, although the degree of assistance given is not!

Pathfinders had started out operating with four different types of aircraft, and three different types of heavy bomber. Towards the early winter of 1943, Bennett set about rationalizing his equipment policy, to determine once and for all whether his squadrons would use the Lancaster, or the latest Halifax IIIs. On October 5, Stocker and Bennett were alone in a Halifax III when the final decision was made in favour of the Lanc:

> "The Halifax III was a powerful beast, but could also burn a great deal of petrol in a very short space of time and so the Lancaster was preferred."

Christmas 1943 came and went and the New Year brought a new squadron after only the briefest of rest periods. Further training was given to Ted in January 1944 when he attended Pathfinder NTU and after one week was posted to 7 Squadron, Oakington. Again his habit of flying with senior officers was continued, his logbook detailing trips with Wing Commander James Tatnall DSO, OBE, DFC, the CO, and Squadron Leader Richard Campling DSO, DFC. It was a period of firsts. After one practice on the range on his first trip in a Lancaster, he dropped his first bombs in anger over Leipzig:

> "On a Pathfinder Lancaster it was different to the rest of Bomber Command in that the flight engineer actually had two roles: Don Bennett said 'any idiot can aim a bomb and drop it so the engineers can do it!' So that was that. Instead of a navigator and a bomb aimer, we had two navigators sat side by side to improve the quality of the job and make it easier, and to ensure that we arrived over the target at the right point and at the right time. As soon as we got there, the pilot would say: 'engineer, get down the nose and aim the bombs' – it was as simple as that."

Ted crewed permanently with a rather dour Welshman, Flying Officer Davies, who was a good bit older than the rest of them, but also a damn fine pilot. For some of his time at 35 Squadron, Ted had been engineer leader. His new squadron already had its own section leader, and so Ted's services were not required. He had completed 55 trips by the time he, his skipper, crew and indeed his entire flight was shunted off over the border from Cambridgeshire to Bedfordshire to form the nucleus of 582 Squadron.

Officially, Harold Siddons (who had been a 'Brat' on the 38 Entry course immediately after Ted) was the engineer leader, but almost immediately – given his experience and operational record – Ted found that his expertise was being called upon:

> "As engineer leader we had to look after everything and anything that related to engineers. I had an office, a desk, and a chair, and any information that might affect my section came my way. At a personal level, I would keep a check on them all as individuals, help them if there was a problem. I had a sort of mentoring role: I would check their logs, and make sure that they were being kept accurately, and be there to give advice. On Pathfinders, most of the flight engineers – indeed most of the aircrew generally – were very experienced and very capable, so there wasn't that much to do. Later, when Peter Cribb joined us as CO, I would often be consulted along with the adjutant and flight commanders as to who would be flying that day.
>
> "I knew Cribb well of course, or as well as wartime standards allowed. He was Oxbridge and then Cranwell educated and very bright. (After the war he lectured in nuclear physics.) His family was from Bradford, and I believe had made their money in wool. I stayed with them on a number of occasions and they always made me feel

most welcome. When we were at 35 Squadron, we would regularly go to the pub, and it was on his instigation that I got myself a motorbike and would nip over to the American airbases and borrow their films."

Ted was operational from the outset, and in early June, his skipper was in charge of the attack on the airfield at Laval. Laval was home to one of the Luftwaffe's crack fighter/bomber groups, III./SG4 under the command of Major Gerhard Weyart, one of the most experienced leaders at that time. The gruppe had started life as III./ZG2 in April 1942 flying the Me109, before converting to the Fw190 in the summer of that year. Weyart had had a torrid time of it lately, being shunted from one airfield to the next often at very short notice, and losing several of his pilots to marauding Mustangs whilst in transit. The last of his aircraft (from the 7th Staffel) had arrived at Laval on June 6, albeit that two had been shot down whilst trying to land. Bad weather had limited the gruppe's operations, and on the 9th the kommandeur himself had to make a forced-landing near Falaise. Had he known what was about to follow, he might have been tempted to stay where he was.

The 582 Squadron aircraft arrived over the airfield shortly before 02.50 and immediately set to work. Flight Lieutenant Davies was in the hot seat as master bomber, and having identified the target both visually (he could clearly see the woods and the road north-east of the airfield) and by the green and red TIs that had already been placed (by his deputy), he dropped his own bombs and yellow TIs to confirm where the main force should bomb. Ted, with his clear crisp English accent was preferred over Davies' broad Welsh dialect, and so it was Ted who then proceeded to issue the orders to main force as to where to bomb.

"We were down at about 3,000ft and so I gave the instruction to main force to come down below the cloud so they could see the target. I had seen the first of the green TIs fall and could see them burning in the middle of the airfield. I could also see the red TIs burning slightly to the north-west. We therefore approached the target with the wood slightly to our starboard and dropped the yellow TIs across the roads along the north-east edge of the base, by the aircraft dispersals. Main force seemed to be ignoring my instructions; I couldn't get them to come down. There was a little light flak (Bob Wareing's Lancaster ND817 'S' Sugar was hit in the starboard wingtip), but it didn't trouble us much."

The failure of the main force to obey instructions directly impacted on the effectiveness of the raid. Many were distracted by the fires that were burning close to the woods, and the temptation to undershoot meant several of their bombs fell on the town rather than the airfield, and many more were scattered harmlessly in the open countryside. It had been far from a successful encounter, but for Ted several invaluable lessons had been learned.

A further lesson was learned the following month when he had the pleasure of taking part in one of the very first 'Heavy Oboe' experiments, with no less a man than Wing Commander George Grant, DSO, DFC – CO of 109 Squadron – sharing the driving seat with his regular skipper:

> "In a Heavy Oboe, the 582 Squadron pilot flies the aircraft to the target, and then swaps with the 109 Squadron pilot for the actual 'run'. On this occasion it was Grant who got into the left-hand seat for the attack. The diabolical thing is that whilst he is on the run, there is no intercom, nothing, just a deathly hush. You have earphones but cannot hear; a microphone but cannot speak. I don't know how long it lasted, perhaps five minutes, but it seemed like half an hour or more.
>
> "If you can imagine being sat there, flying straight and level with people firing guns at you, not able to warn anyone, and just hoping that nothing hits you until the bombs go. And then thank god we are back on intercom and the gunner can at least say that there is something happening out there. I think the boys in the Mosquitoes had a better deal with Oboe because they were a lot higher up, but in Lancasters, Oboe was no fun at all."

Ted's last flight with Davies was to Lisieux, an eventful trip in that the nav two was slightly wounded. There then followed an extended period when Ted found himself as a 'spare bod', flying with all manner of skippers: Spooner, Goddard, O'Donovan, Magee, Hockley, Finlay, Brown, Nairn, Interiano ("He gave me a lift to Manston to see my Mum,"), Berney, Cairns, Mettam. It was with Flying Officer 'Hal' Mettam, then on his 13th trip, that Stocker clocked up his 100th operation (amounting to 452 operational hours) at which point he was recommended for an immediate Distinguished Service Order. The 'particulars of meritorious service' for which the recommendation was made related to an earlier master bomber attack on Wanne Eickel, two months earlier:

> "On October 12, Flight Lieutenant Stocker volunteered to be bomb aimer and flight engineer to the master bomber for a daylight attack on the oil works at Wanne Eickel in the heart of the Ruhr. The attack was opened by a well placed TI aimed by Stocker and the master bomber

continued to circle the area for 10 minutes, during which time the aircraft was under almost continuous fire from many heavy guns and was hit in several places. A further bombing run was directed by Flight Lieutenant Stocker with equally satisfactory results and throughout he assisted the master greatly by his accurate commentary on the bombing and by his indifference to the opposition.

"Flight Lieutenant Stocker's conduct on this occasion was exemplary and in accordance with the high standard of courage which he has shown on a great many occasions in his long operational career."

Whilst Wanne Eickel earned him his DSO, perhaps Ted's most memorable trip was his 86th on October 3, 1944 when he broke the sea wall at Westkapelle.

"I was flying with Group Captain Peter Cribb, 582 Squadron CO at that time. It was a daylight raid, and we were briefed to bomb the island of Walcheren on the Scheldt Estuary. The idea was to make the island uninhabitable for the Germans by knocking a hole in the sea wall. It wasn't a big raid as far as aircraft was concerned. We stayed over the target for a couple of hours and they were sending in 50 main force aircraft every 20 minutes or so.

"We put the markers down on the sea front and gradually the bombers knocked a hole in the sea wall and eventually the water came flooding in. The best bit was that the last wave of bombers included 617 (Dambusters) Squadron with their 'special' bombs called Tallboys. The Dambusters were part of 5 Group, and obviously there was quite a rivalry between them and us. The dyke was breached before they arrived, so I had great fun in telling them to go home. One up for Pathfinders!

"It was also an interesting trip because there was only one anti-aircraft emplacement at Westkapelle, right on the tip of the island, and earlier – between I think the first and second wave – we lobbed a few smaller bombs in their general direction. We had the pleasure of seeing the brave Hun get on their bicycles and cycle down the main road straight through the middle of Walcheren Island to the mainland. That was very satisfying, seeing the Germans doing a runner."

Another 'experimental' trip with Peter Cribb also sticks in his mind:

"Someone had come up with the idea of attaching a smoke

generator to the bomb bay of a Lancaster such that the Pathfinders could lay down a smokescreen. We flew over to Wyton to give it a try. No one, however, had thought to check what happens to the airflow through a Lancaster. It creates an area of low pressure around the rear turret, so what happened when we turned the smoke machine on was that it came out of the back and then immediately back into the aircraft through the rear, along the fuselage and into the cockpit. Within moments we couldn't see a thing as smoke was everywhere. It was panic stations all round as we put on oxygen and opened the windows!"

Unofficially, Ted took part in the squadron's '10-hour cross-country' to bomb Hitler's home at Berchtesgarten; although the pilot, Group Captain Cribb, aircraft (PB 969 'Z' Zebra) and bomb load (four 2,000-pounders), is written in green ink, the target is scribed in his logbook in pencil, such that it could be rubbed out later. It was Ted who dropped the bombs that did the damage that officially cannot be accounted for. The last 'formal' operations included a number of 'Manna' trips – dropping food for the Dutch in Rotterdam.

"We did some of those from Little Staughton, and then we started the Exodus trips, bringing home the prisoners of war. I had a service motorbike and I put that in the back of a Lanc when we went to Lübeck on May 8. I sat on the end of the runway acting as air traffic control. We were the first in in the morning and when the last Lancaster left in the evening we stopped what we were doing, picked up our quota of POWs and we flew back. We then had the privilege of flying back over England on the evening of VE Day when bonfires were lit all over the country. It was a magnificent sight! I didn't actually get a drink because my logbook says that we didn't land until the morning of the 9th which was probably sometime after midnight."

By the war's end, Ted Stocker had flown 108 operations, and survived. Modestly he describes his time at 582 Squadron as a 'holiday' compared to some of his earlier experiences. That's not to say this period was not without its dangers:

"I stayed alive when other people were dropping dead all around me. It's amazing, I went through a hundred odd raids and the worst damage I had? They'd made some holes in my jacket with flak. But, remember – I was the lucky one. For every one that was lucky there was an awful number that were unlucky."

SQUADRON COMMANDER

The story of Group Captain Stafford Coulson DSO, DFC, commanding officer, 582 Squadron

Stafford Coulson described himself as an ordinary, run of the mill RAF officer, and an extremely lucky man. But it was not always the case. Originally a fighter pilot and professional airman, Stafford found himself stranded in Singapore at the start of the war, an idyllic posting that meant he missed out on the excitement of the Battle of Britain and the early fighter sweeps over northern France. A transfer from Fighter to Bomber Command, and a posting to Pathfinders, at last gave Stafford the excitement he had been looking for.

Of all the tactics deployed by the Pathfinder force, Wanganui sky marking was nearly always the least satisfying for the crews taking part. Accuracy was often doubtful, even with the most skilful of set operators, and results hard to discern. It was strange, therefore, that it actually accounted for one of Wing Commander Stafford Coulson's most successful trips as a master bomber, when he fully destroyed the town of Paderborn in less than 15 minutes.

It was March 27, 1945, and the war had less than six weeks to run. Bomber Command was almost running out of targets, but there were still a few pockets of resistance and hurdles for the Allied forces to overcome before total victory could be assured. One such final target was the old city of Paderborn that stood in the way of the American troops in their attempt to complete the encirclement of the Rhine. Stafford, flying Lancaster PB956 'N' Nuts with Ted Swales' old crew, was leading 14 aircraft from his squadron out of a total force of 268 Lancasters and eight Mosquitoes tasked with the town's destruction:

"The attack was scheduled to be a Musical Parramatta, but the Met Mosquito (a Mosquito from 1409 Flight sent ahead of the force to report on weather conditions over the target) broadcast 10/10ths cloud and so I gave the order to use Wanganui which meant we had to be ready to bomb as soon as the skymarkers went down. It was the least satisfactory, but in this instance accounted for one of my

most successful attacks. Like Dresden it was a daylight
raid, and we coolly wrote off a German town in less than
a quarter of an hour. We razed the town to the ground and
boy did it burn."

At 17.10hrs the Met Mosquito broadcast cloud tops at 3/4,000ft
and light cirrus at 23,000ft. Five minutes later, Stafford checked
with his deputy (Flight Lieutenant Paddy Finlay), and gave the
basement as per the flight plan and indicated a blind attack,
repeating at regular intervals the words: 'This is a blind attack.'

The first sky markers (in the form of green smoke puffs) were
dropped by Flight Lieutenant Anthony Harte-Lovelace – a relative
newcomer to the squadron although an experienced bomber pilot
who had earned the DFC at 578 Squadron for 'a notable tour of
operations'. Others followed, with Coulson instructing main force
to come in and bomb the centre of two smoke puffs that he adjudged
bang over the aiming point. In all, seven skymarkers went down,
and in the space of four minutes a large number of main force
aircraft completed their bombing runs and headed for home. Smoke
began to mushroom though the cloud, indicating the target had been
well and truly hit, forming a pall of smoke about one mile in
diameter. The marking was so accurate that the town was totally
destroyed, its narrow streets helping the fires to spread and
contributing to its rapid destruction.

The raid was the second successful master bomber attack led by
Coulson in less than a week. Over Sterkrade on March 24, in a
Musical attack, he had finally coaxed 155 Halifaxes from 4 Group
to do as they were told and bomb an excellent group of Oboe
markers that they seemed to be wilfully ignoring, some bombs
undershooting the target by over a mile. A few carefully chosen
words seemed to do the trick, and the target – the marshalling yards
jammed pack with military freight – were totally destroyed.

Two trips in rapid succession were unusual for a squadron
commander with his long list of responsibilities but Stafford had
always been one to lead from the front. It was a lesson he had
learned early on:

> "When I was posted to the great 40 Squadron flying
> Hawker Hinds, long before the war, I never saw my flight
> commander or squadron commander get in the air. I took
> it for granted that they were there to administrate. They
> were quite old people by my standards. It never dawned on
> me until people like Don Bennett, Basil Embry, Harry
> Broadhurst, Gus Walker and Sid Bufton turned up, that
> you led your flight commanders, your pilots, your crews by
> example, and by finding out what it was like. This was
> Bennett's forte which he brought to Pathfinder force."

Stafford Coulson had been born in 1916, and from his very earliest memory had always been interested in flying:

> "At the age of eight I managed to get a flight in an aeroplane with the St Austell Aviation Company. I had a photo taken with two school friends, three small heads poking out of the rear cockpit hole. I decided, even then, that I must join the RAF; there was nothing else for me. My parents must have listened, for I was given many opportunities to see aeroplanes – early Hendon air displays and aeroplane books for Christmas. This was curious because my father, a surgeon and a very capable horseman, was not mechanically minded and my mother was dead scared in a car so she didn't give much of an impression that she would care to see me in the RAF! Nevertheless, when I finished school (Charterhouse) I applied to go to Cranwell.
>
> "Cranwell was not like it is today where the starting standards are extremely high. Then you were interviewed by patronising old chaps who set you at ease and recorded your achievements as reported by your last headmaster. The interview went well. I had been racing a motorcycle for a year, so I played the technical side as hard as I could and it worked. I felt my school record would let me down, having put up an enormous number of blacks and generally being a bloody nuisance. After giving me 10 of the best, my headmaster said: 'I believe you want to go into the RAF. You seem to have just the qualities required.'
>
> "I was staying in Northampton with a friend who had also applied to go to Cranwell when one Saturday his mother came into the room to say that I had been accepted, but Mark, my friend, had not. Mark did finally enter on a short service commission but was killed early in the war."

Stafford arrived at Cranwell with 28 others in January 1935, and was immediately impressed with the luxury of his accommodation. On the first morning they drew clothes and were shown around their new 'home'. The next day they were taken up, Stafford's instructor being a fighter pilot from the 'great' 19 Squadron flying Bristol Bulldogs.

> "I thought at the time that there was nothing more beautiful or effective than a Bulldog. Flying training was done in an Avro Tutor and was very thorough. There was the initial stage, moving on to the operational stage, and finally air armament where we fired guns and did things like that. It was a marvellous time, excitement every

minute of the day and always something new. The
instructors, many of whom became well known – and
some already famous like Leonard Snaith who had been a
member of the High Speed Flight in 1931 – were among
my heroes. My contemporaries included Peter Wykeham-
Barnes (who went on to become chief of air staff) and Peter
Jolliffe, my best friend, who was killed flying a MkIV
Blenheim with 254 Squadron in Norway."

Stafford 'passed out', and was posted to 40 Squadron in
Oxfordshire to fly Hawker Hinds. It was, by any measure, a
wonderful time to be in the RAF, a time of hilarious parties and
good friends, and getting away with murder careering around the
countryside from pub to pub on four wheels or two – the latter being
Stafford's preferred mode of transport. From 40 he went to 34
Squadron in Lympne, Kent, converting, in July 1938, to the
Blenheim twin-engined fighter/bombers. With war clouds now
gathering Stafford was given command of a Blenheim delivery flight,
tasked with delivering 32 new aircraft to Singapore:

"There was a view at the time in the air ministry that if a
war was to start, then it would start in the Far East so we
were sent overseas. Our briefing wasn't up to much; they
gave us Dunlop car maps to follow, and told us to make
our way to Singapore! We encountered a monsoon and the
worst flying conditions I had ever witnessed, losing three
crews on the way. Fortunately I had an excellent navigator,
and it taught me how important the relationship between
the pilot and navigator was. Singapore was just the best
posting, but when war came, it was terribly frustrating."

Unfortunately, whilst abroad, Stafford was taken ill with an ear
infection, and it was some time before he was again posted fit to fly.
He undertook a three-month journey home by sea via The Cape,
staring at the same piece of water for what seemed like an eternity,
reaching England in May 1941. Fortunately, in the five years he had
been in the RAF he had made many friends, and these friends
allowed him surreptitious flights in a variety of aircraft to keep his
hand in, before being posted to Canada as a flying instructor. He
spent nearly three years in Nova Scotia instructing single-engined
types to convert to twin-engines, taking part in the odd anti-
submarine patrol in the flying school's Hudson and stooging around
in dated Blackburn Bothas where at night the engines used to glow
in the dark.

It was a frustrating time for a man keen to get back into action,
until at last he was posted home and passed as medically fit in early
1944.

"My main aim was to get into the Pathfinders. Although most of my experience was on fighters, and I was a damned good shot, I had missed the Battle of Britain so had not seen much action. We had read in the papers what the bomber pilots were doing, and the Pathfinders in particular, and it impressed me. I thought I was in for another up-hill battle, but it wasn't the case. Bennett seemed to know of my shenanigans, and if anything I think it helped me. They took me readily. Nobody even asked me for interview, I was just told I was going to Pathfinders."

The shenanigans to which Stafford refers do not only relate to his time at Cranwell or Singapore, but rather his gratuitous exploitation of his many friends and contacts, among them Wing Commander 'Tubby' Baker:

"I used to go and see Tubby when he was in command of 635 Squadron at Downham Market and he would let me go along with him on a trip or two. Of course none of this was official. They were 'non-recordable' jobs as we used to call them.
    "My first 'formal' posting was to 35 Squadron flying Lancasters. This was where the 'real' trips began. I stayed about five months until I completed a tour. The squadron at that time was commanded by 'Dixie' Dean, and I was one of the flight commanders. As an interlude, I also spent some time at OTU at Finnmere near Bicester, where the chief flying instructor was an old friend of mine from Singapore. I also managed to get a few daylight trips in on B25 Mitchells."

Whilst at 35 Squadron, he remembers one incident particularly vividly:

"I came into my flight commander's office one day and two Australians – 'Bluey' Osmond and Frances Tropman* – who were a pretty funny lot, were both lying on the floor holding each other, without moving. They had this stunt where they would squeeze each other until they passed out."

Coulson's first official Pathfinder operation was on May 27, 1944, a relatively modest trip to St Valéry en Caux. This was followed

---

* Ironically, 'Bluey' Osmond DFC & Bar and Frances Tropman DFC were both shot down on the same night, February 21, 1945, by which time they had completed 70 and 62 ops respectively. Tropman was flying with Stafford's regular crew, all of who survived to become POWs.

four days later with an attack on Isigny, in which his crew acted as 'illuminators'. He flew six sorties in July, five in August, and five again in September, and by the end of the year had logged no fewer than 34 operations. Dixie Dean put him up for a DFC, describing Stafford as:

> "...a captain of exceptional ability who always shows the keenest desire to fly against the enemy wherever possible. He has now completed a good number of operations involving the dropping of vital markers and through his tenacity on the target, and leadership of his crew, has attained a high degree of accuracy and reliability. As a flight commander he sets a very fine example to his crews and has played a big part in achieving a high standard of reliability and precision in the squadron..."

Coulson's record of operations and leadership were sufficient to persuade Bennett he had the right man to take over from Peter Cribb, himself a former 35 Squadron flight commander, as commanding officer of 582 Squadron. Again he wasn't called for interview, but was simply informed of his posting. Stafford arrived on 582 Squadron at the end of 1944, assuming command officially on January 10, 1945, although he had been with the squadron some weeks previously to ensure a smooth transfer of responsibilities. The disastrous trip to Cologne/Gremberg that had decimated the squadron prior to Christmas had severely impacted on morale – or at least so Stafford had been led to believe:

> "Cribb had an appointment at group and we were due to meet for lunch, so I decided to stay and have lunch in the mess. I asked for something to be fetched for me only to be asked who I was! I gave the man a bit of a rocket and told him to jump to it and then made my way to an armchair by the fireplace to read a newspaper. A few moments later, there was a blinding flash in front of me, and for a moment I couldn't work out what had happened. Then it dawned on me that someone (it was actually the gunnery leader and principal joker in residence by the name of McQueen) had set fire to my newspaper, and at much the same moment I realised that any problems with squadron morale seemed to have been over-exaggerated."

He found the role of squadron commander an exacting one:

> "As a flight commander, the relationship with your men was much more intimate. You had day-to-day contact with crews. As a commanding officer, you were much more

remote, and you had to do everything. If anything went wrong, then it was my fault. If it went right, then you simply wouldn't hear about it. What you had to remember was that whatever you thought you knew, Bennett always knew 10-times more than you did! He would ask questions of you that would bowl you over. He was a very cold-blooded man, but we enormously admired him, especially as he had himself been shot down and got back."

One of the issues Stafford had to deal with was making sure none of his pilots or crew put others at risk, either because they were 'flak happy' or simply could no longer cope with the stresses and strains of operational life.

"Generally the standard of aircrews – and groundcrews of course – was very high at 582 Squadron, right the way through. All of us had at the back of our minds that we were the guys making the whole thing work. It was such a hard job; such a difficult job. Indeed I don't think anyone has ever really conveyed just how complicated and demanding a job it was. Many think we just staggered around until we found the most likely place, then chucked down a couple of flares and that was that. Well let me tell you, if you've ever seen a load of TIs going down from close range then they're more frightening than bombs! We were good but we weren't arrogant. If it had been easy then we would have been lots of overbearing twits.

"Morale tended to be very high, although there were a few incidents. O'Donovan, for example, a nice chap who flew straight into the church steeple. The enquiry had just happened when I arrived, and it was quite clear that he was getting flak happy. I only ever sent one crew back that had been posted to me. If I suspected something wasn't right then I used to fly with them and see for myself. There was one trip we went on to the Ruhr. Going out, flak was everywhere, as solid as an umbrella. By jiminy they could chuck it out, although it wasn't so bad the closer you got. Well this pilot just flew right through the lot and kept asking me what was going on. I got rid of him straight away.

"With any cases of LMF you had to try and let the guys down gently. No one I knew ever went purposefully sick, although I did have one mid-upper gunner go berserk on me on the way to the target. I had to get the navigator to pull him down from the turret and hold him down until he'd stopped screaming and could control himself. Of course I had to report him when we got back. This man was very experienced. Three aircraft had fallen to his guns on previous tours, and had I known him longer then maybe I would have seen the signs earlier and could have chucked him out before it got to that stage. You couldn't afford to have unstable or unreliable personalities in your crew."

Fortunately for Stafford, he was blessed with flying with a number of the very best throughout his operational career:

"My rear gunner was a Yorkshireman and as tough as old boots. He never took the credit for anything he did. If he shot down a fighter he would say it was because of my expert flying. He was the right 'type'; never made a fuss. Completed three tours, amounting to over 100 trips. I also had a brilliant H2S set operator. He was very modest. Whilst I was at 35 Squadron, we flew as a blind marking crew and he was one of the very best. His error rate was less than 200 yards from the aiming point and that was quite remarkable. He was later shot down, but survived I believe to rise to high rank in the foreign office."

During Stafford's tenure as CO he had a number of duties to perform, including writing the citation for Ted Swales' Victoria Cross:

"Ted was such a jolly nice chap and had a fine crew, very well trained. He wasn't what you would call a squadron 'character' – he wasn't that type – and apart from his uniform he didn't really stick out. But he was just very good at what he did and really stuck to the task. I wrote the recommendation for his VC and it was accepted just like that."

Stafford also oversaw a series of actions that was to become known colloquially as the 'Staughton War'. The 'War' was in effect an escalation of the rivalry that had existed between 582 Squadron and 109 Squadron who shared the Little Staughton base. The arrival of a new 109 Squadron CO, Wing Commander Dickie Law, seemed to be the catalyst for a new series of increasingly mad-cap stunts, including setting fire to the wing commander's office in-tray and dropping a target indicator down the office chimney. Things really came to a head when a home-made bomb was being planted in the CO's office and exploded in the would-be terrorist's hands, resulting in a brief period of hospitalisation.

"The worst thing about being squadron commander was

that you couldn't fly as often as you wanted. I didn't like briefing my chaps for a trip I wasn't on. The best thing about my time as CO was the ability to have a laugh, the biggest laugh of all being when we shoved the TIs down the 109 Squadron CO's chimney!"

Such incidents of fun were just harmless pranks, fully understandable on a squadron of men, many not long out of school or university, who in-between the perils and dangers of operations had a very real need to let off steam. It was also understandable given the risks the Lancaster bomber crews experienced commensurate to their Mosquito counterparts.

"The 109 boys didn't get the fighters or flak like we did, but they were still excellent pilots, and the standard of navigation was also very high. Some of them went to Berlin twice in one night, which meant they were able to have their eggs, bacon and chips twice! One pilot, a friend of mine, came back once and his navigator had been killed. When he went in for his post-op meal, he asked for double of everything as he wasn't going to let his navigator's meal go to waste."

During his five months in command of 582 Squadron, Stafford managed nine official trips: Wiesbaden (February 2/3), Chemnitz (February 14/15 with John Clough's crew), Essen (March 11), Rauxel Tor (March 15), Oslebshausen oil refinery, Bremen (March 21), Sterkrade (March 24), Paderborn (March 27), Lutzendorf synthetic oil plant (April 4/5), and Heligoland (April 18), where he also reported seeing a submarine. The last six were all in the role as master bomber.

His preference was for Newhaven attacks:

"Newhaven attacks on a clear night were my favourites. The illuminators went in first, and they probably had one of the worst jobs, and were always experienced crews. They had to fly straight and level for about 80 seconds in full glare of the flares. Then as master bomber I would discuss with my deputy which of us would mark the aiming point, and whether we needed to use one of the primary visual markers. Again that was another exciting moment. After flying for hours in silence, you would call your deputy and hear his voice coming back to you in the night. It was important that you made contact, because either he or you could have been hit or even shot down on the way in. There would be perhaps three of you with a full load of reds and greens, and they looked marvellous as they went down. Then I would issue instructions to the main force about what TIs to aim for, and call in the visual centrers to re-mark the target every minute until the attack was over."

Although the operations record book for 582 Squadron lists Stafford's last attack as being on Heligoland, there is at least one other raid in which he was involved in and which his role – and that of his 'crew' – is not mentioned in any history books. Officially they did not take part. Unofficially they did.

"The war was obviously coming to an end and whenever we got back from the pub we would go straight to the ops room to see if there was anything we had been called for. Many were what we called 'tidying up' trips. Then one day Bennett called for a master bomber, deputy master bomber, primary visual markers and visual centres all from 582 Squadron, with the target being a crack at Hitler's house. To us this was absolute heaven. So we waited. But then no orders came. Worse than that, we had been stood down and someone else had been ordered to go. I wanted to know what had happened to my trip to Berchtesgarten. The biggest bash of the lot, and we were going to miss it.

"We weren't on operations, so we decided to invent one. If we couldn't go legally, then we would just go illegally, and went off to get together a crew of volunteers. Of course they all jumped at it: Dudley Archer said he would navigate, Ted Stocker was the bomb aimer, the gunnery leader McQueen went in the rear turret, we had the signals leader as wireless op and decided to go without a second nav or mid-upper.

"I phoned group as I had a confidante up there, and although he could give me the H-Hour he couldn't tell me the route, so we had to make one up. As long as we were there on time, everything should be all right. I had a chat with the armaments officer and he found me some 2,000 pounders that weren't on the inventory and we winched those on board. Nothing was going to stop me. Common sense didn't come into it.

"We flew the direct route, right across France and straight in, west to east. We had no fighter escort, and were flying in broad daylight. By the time we arrived, we could see the mountain covered in smoke. Stocker put the bombs bang on the target, and got an aiming point photograph that of course officially doesn't exist, because we weren't there.

"Whilst we were out, Bennett obviously got wind that

something was up and phoned the squadron. Our simple, honest adjutant was asked by Bennett where I had got to, so he told him I was on a 10-hour cross-country exercise. Not surprisingly he hit the roof."

Stafford's official tenure as CO 582 Squadron came to an end on June 21, 1945 when he was succeeded by Wing Commander Emile Mange. He had flown 47 Pathfinder sorties amounting to 260 operational hours. The real total, however, was never recorded. He had also added a DSO for his courage and leadership both in the air and on the ground. Fittingly the citation was written by Peter Cribb, and paid particular reference to Stafford's personal leadership:

"He arrived at a time when heavy losses had just been sustained and a fall in morale might well have been expected. This was in no way the case. In remarkably short time the spirit of his crews was unsurpassable and the many newcomers had been moulded into the squadron and were producing results of which they were justly proud. He has commanded the respect of all ranks by his continuous readiness to take his place at the head of his squadron whenever a tough fight was anticipated. His own irrepressible spirits have been reflected in his officers and men, and welded them into a loyal brotherhood who worked with a will to achieve a common end."

His departure from Little Staughton was by no means the end of his flying career, however. He had the honour of being station commander at RAF Scampton, the first Vulcan station, before retiring from the RAF on September 30, 1965. He then spent the next 16 years in the Queen's messenger corps.

In many ways, Stafford considered himself no different from any other bomber pilot during the period. He had a few, not very exciting, skirmishes, and was occasionally knocked around by flak, especially in the Ruhr. He loved flying and could handle a Lanc probably better than most and knew how far he could go without breaking it. But above all, Stafford Coulson considered himself a lucky man, often in the right place at the right time:

"I am an extremely lucky man, possibly more lucky than many. The truth is, I had a clean and pleasant war, causing trouble for other people."

Chapter Six

A Squadron at Peace

May – September 1945

On April 30, 1945, Adolf Hitler, Führer of Germany, committed suicide, and the war seemed all but over. A large pocket of western Holland, however, remained in German hands, and the population faced the very real prospect of starvation. A truce was arranged with the local German commander and Lancasters of 1, 3 and 8 Groups were permitted to drop food to the grateful Dutch. These were Manna operations, and kept 582 Squadron busy throughout the first few days of May.

On Sunday May 6, one of the last battle orders was posted on the flight commander's notice board. It comprised five pilots: Coulson, Cairns, Haines, Coombes and Carter, with Flying Officer Allen in reserve. Briefing was at 10.00 hours, and meals an hour later. Officer commanding flying was Squadron Leader Owen-Jones. The next day, General Eisenhower accepted the unconditional surrender of all German forces on all fronts, effective from 00.01 hours on May 9. Peace had at last arrived.

With peace came some practical issues, including bringing home the thousands of captured Allied servicemen that were in prisoner of war camps dotted around Germany. For these operations the planners again decided upon a biblical reference – Exodus – in which the squadron was again heavily engaged, flying several sorties between the 8th and 26th. Many of the pilots – with their squadron commander's blessing – also took their groundcrews on trips over Germany to witness the devastation that they had helped to wreak.

The squadron arranged a VE-day flypast, and some joker threw a fully-clothed dummy out of the rear turret, causing considerable upset amongst the local populace. Training continued: cross-country and bombing flights, air sea firing, beam approaches, even formation flying. The war in Europe may have been over, but Japan had yet to be defeated, and Bomber Command was in the process of bringing together Tiger Force to go to the Far East. Some couldn't wait to go, and were genuinely disappointed if their names weren't in the frame. Others had had enough, and kicked their heels impatiently, waiting their turn to be demobbed.

June arrived and with it a new CO. Stafford Coulson, the squadron's last wartime commanding officer handed over the reins to Wing Commander Emile Mange. Mange was yet another experienced Pathfinder, a former flight commander with 635 Squadron, Downham Market. With 635 he had won the DFC in November 1944 after 41 operations, one of which was the raid in which his contemporary, Squadron Leader Ian Bazalgette VC, was shot down and killed. By the end of the war he had completed another 20 sorties, 280 operational hours in all, and added a Bar to his DFC. His CO, Wing Commander James Fordham, described him as 'a most skilful and courageous pilot...' who had shown himself as '...a worthy leader of men....'

The 8 Group commander, Donald Bennett, had also handed over command to Air Marshal Sir John Whitley KBE, CB, DSO, AFC & Bar who visited the squadron in July. It provided a welcome distraction from the humdrum existence of peacetime squadron life, and he complimented the station on its smart turnout. By now, decisions at the air ministry were being taken as to the squadron's future, decisions accelerated by the dropping of the two atomic bombs on Japan and the end of the Second World War.

On August 7, several of the crews were engaged in operation Dodge, repatriating British troops from Italy. (Each Lancaster could ferry up to 24 soldiers plus kit at a time; nearly 100,000 troops in all were flown home between August 1945 and the beginning of 1946.) By the end of August, squadron strength had been reduced to 94 officers and 135 NCOs. Eight New Zealanders were still on the books, but all of the other Dominion aircrew had long-since been posted or sent home. On September 8, there was no flying, and the CO played host to the squadron's farewell party. Two days later the squadron was officially disbanded, and the aircraft flown in batches to Mepal and Wyton for use in other squadrons.

582 Squadron had been formed on April 1, 1944 and flown continuously until the end of the war. Such was the demand for their skills that they had chalked up some 2,157 Lancaster sorties (officially at least!) dropping a little over 8,029 tons of bombs. The crews had between them won one Victoria Cross, 10 Distinguished Service Orders, 146 Distinguished Flying Crosses, 22 Bars to the DFC, 47 Distinguished Flying Medals and one Bar.

But success had come at a cost: 39 Lancasters had been shot down or lost as the result of accidents in 165 raids. Many more aircraft had been damaged, patched up and repaired, continuing to provide loyal service to the squadron and its crews until finally being confined to the scrap heap.

But the real price paid was in the casualty list: 153 killed on operations – including men such as Harold Heney DSO, Arthur

Raybould DSO DFM, John Hewitt DFC, Stuart Little DFC, John Weightman DFC, Owen Milne DFC, William Underwood DFC, and of course Ted Swales VC DFC – pilots with irreplaceable experience who between them had flown more than 300 heavy bomber operations. Then there were the equally tragic losses of 15 further aircrew in accidents, including William Shirley, Johnnie Gould, and Robert Terpening DFC, highlighting the dangers faced by World War II airmen not just in enemy combat, but often when apparently 'safe' over English soil.

Whilst death and tragedy was an ever-present threat, the spirit of the squadron remained undinted, even in its darkest hour following the disaster at Cologne/Gremberg, a testimony to the strength and character of the station and squadron commanders who opted to lead from the front. It was also a reflection of the Pathfinder ethos.

At some time during its existence, an unknown songwriter penned a squadron ditty to be sung to the tune of 'My Darling Clementine.' More than anything, perhaps, the chorus captures the humour and spirit of 582 Squadron, Pathfinder force:

"What a squadron, what a shambles
But there's lots for them to do
Bags of training in the daytime
Ops at night, for 582!"

Appendix One

Roll of Honour

Bernard Wallis	23.04.44
Henry Collins	
Henry Falloon	
William Squibb	
John Sturgeon	
George Lyall	
Joseph McGinn	
Frederick Bertelsen	4.05.44
Reginald Lovegrove	
James Ritchie	
Glenwood Schwerdfeger	
Edward Slattery	
Ronald Mansbridge	
Geoffrey Clyne	
Charles O'Neill	4.05.44
James Mansfield	
Stanley Hewitt	
James Ingham	
George Coon	
Frank Holmes	
Stuart Little DFC	25.05.44
Wilfred Truman	
John Flynn	
Gwynfor Jones	
Alfred Oram	
Bernard Webb	
Neville Rawlinson	
Harold Heney DSO	28.05.44
Leonard Cudlipp	
Ronald Lamb	
Stephen Brown	
Frank Webb	
Francis Ross	

Allan Harrington

Arthur Raybould DSO, DFM   6.06.44
Gerald Ramsey
Arthur Feeley DFC
Arthur Grange
Henry Kitto DFM
John Papworth DFC
Dennis Johnson DFC

John Hewitt DFC   15.06.44
Vincent Crosby DFM
Harry Wilson DFM
Robert Clenahan DFC
Denis Flynn DFC
Walter Smith DFC
Gilbert Cottrell
Albert Bouch DFM

Norman Tutt   16.06.44
Sidney Parr
Harold Harris
Richard Ames
Paul Long-Hartley
William Williams

John Austin   29.06.44
Robert Chelu
Douglas Coole

Donald Manson   6.07.44
John Geeves
John Stapleton
Ero Salomaa
Alan Fretwell
Douglas Eggleston
Edward Smith DFM

John Weightman DFC   20.07.44
James Gresty
George Macarthur
Edgar Pratt

Raymond Rember   24.07.44
Leonard Whybrow
Edward Radcliffe
Ronald Smalley
Keith Hibbert
James Tweedie
Dennis Phillips

Philip Dicerbo	26.07.44
Reginald Lewis	29.07.44
William Bunting DFM	
Donald Margach DFC	
Geoffrey Taylor	
William Waldron	
Alfred Baines	
David Craggs	
Edwin Hawker	8.08.44
Reginald Blaydon DFM	
Robert Campbell	
Wilfred Gaughran	
Bernard Pullin DFC	13.08.44
John Broad	
Walter Parfitt	
Kenneth Archibald	
Allan Farrington	30.08.44
George Bradley DFM	
Alfred Strout	
Lorne Tyndale	
Henry Silverwood DFM	
Douglas Stevens	
Charles Stewart DFM	
John Goddard DFC	8.09.44
Howard Baker	
William Daniel	
George Lythgoe	
Jack Beecroft	
Robert Newton	
Victor Davis DFM	11.09.44
Graham Nixon	16.09.44
Michael Lamb	
Kenneth Durrant	
Herbert Wilkins	
Arthur Robson	
Robert Fishpool	
John Norris DFM	
William Shirley	23.09.44
Desmond Evans	
Frank Hill	
Duncan Smith	
George Burch	

Colin Mitchell
William Alston

Lawrence Croft   29.10.44
Eric Dawson DFC
Kenneth Hodgson
Rex Mahoney
Robert Pocock
William Roberts
David Wilson
Wilfred Witty

Abel Mellor   11.11.44

Frederick Grillage   3.12.44

Jack Kinman   12.12.44
Harry Mawson
Michael Gisby
Albert Plimmer DFM
Patrick Hughes DFM
Ernest Evans
Stanley Wright
Sidney Trevis

Arndt Reif   23.12.44
John Paterson
Kenneth Austin
Peter Uzelman
George Owen

Kenneth Hewitt

Owen Milne DFC
Albert Carter DFC
Bert Nundy
William Dalgarno

Peter Thomas
Vivian Hobbs
Frederick Campbell

Nicholas McNamara   17.01.45

Edwin Swales VC, DFC   23.02.45

John Gould   6.03.45
Arnold Denbigh
Ross Barnett
Glen Torr

Ellis Hemsworth
Gerald Ralph

Lewis Austin   8.03.45

William Underwood DFC   15.03.45
William Goodwin
Richard Robson
John Lewis
Richard Cantwell
George Murray
Gordon Willer

Robert Terpening DFC   28.04.45
John Watson DFM

Appendix Two

Aircraft Losses

22.4.44	ND737	Hit a church steeple and crash landed at Woodbridge. Pilot Godfrey O'Donovan
23.4.44	JA933	Ex-7 Squadron aircraft with 352 flying hours Pilot Bernard Wallis shot down over Lâon
4.5.44	JA968	Shot down attacking Montdidier. Pilot Freddie Bertelsen KIA
4.5.44	ND910	Montdidier as previous. Pilot Charles O'Neill KIA
25.5.44	ND816	Shot down over Aachen after 121 hours. Pilot Stuart Little KIA
28.5.44	ND814	Lost on attack on Rennes after 111 hours. Pilot Harold Heney KIA
6.6.44	NE166	Missing following raid on Longues. Pilot Arthur Raybould KIA
10.6.44	ND714	Etampes. NB – no loss and no aircraft mention in squadron ORB for this date
15.6.44	NE172	Douai. Pilot John Hewitt KIA
16.6.44	ND502	Target Lens. Pilot Norman Tutt KIA
29.6.44	ND921	Shot down over Blainville-sur-l'Eau. Pilot Splinter Spierenberg POW
6.7.44	NE169	Lost on raid to Wizernes. Pilot Donald Manson KIA
24.7.44	ND931	Shot down over Kiel. Pilot Ray Rember KIA
24.7.44	JB417	Overshot and written off landing at Radlett. Pilot Ted Swales
29.7.44	ND810	Shot down attacking Stuttgart. Pilot Reginald Lewis KIA
8.8.44	ND817	Mare de Magne. Pilot Bob Wareing POW
13.8.44	ND969	Lost over Rüsselsheim. Pilot Elmer Trotter POW
30.8.44	PB202	Shot down on way to Stettin. Pilot Allan Farrington KIA
8.9.44	PB123	Missing over Le Havre. Pilot John Goddard KIA
11.9.44	PB184	Shot down over Castrop-Rauxel. Pilot Tiny Shurlock unhurt
16.9.44	PB378	Lost over Kiel. Pilot Graham Nixon KIA
23.9.44	PB512	Spun in and crashed near North Weald, Essex. Pilot William Shirley killed
7.10.44	PB511	Wrecked, Little Staughton, after only 17 hours. NB – no mention of this aircraft on this date in ORB

12.10.44 ND880   Crash landed at Manston and caught fire on return from Wanne Eickel. Pilot Jimmy Brown. No one hurt

29.10.44 PB630   Lost over Walcheren after 40 hours. Pilot Lawrence Croft KIA

3.12.44   PB629   Shot down over Heimbach. Pilot Art Green unhurt

12.12.44 PB554   Missing over Essen. Pilot Jack Kinman KIA

23.12.44 PB120   Shot down on daylight to Cologne. Pilot Walt Reif KIA

23.12.44 PB141   Cologne as previous. Pilot Reg Hockley POW

23.12.44 PB523   Cologne as previous. Pilot Peter Thomas KIA

23.12.44 PB371   Cologne as previous. Pilots Bob Palmer and Owen Milne KIA

23.12.44 PB558   Cologne as previous. Pilot Robert Terpening unhurt

17.1.45   NE130   Zeitz. Pilot Patrick McVerry unhurt. Rear gunner killed

20.1.45   PB182   Crashed landing at Oakington. Pilot Flying Officer Keely RAAF

22.2.45   PB652   Duisberg. Damaged beyond repair. Pilot 'Windy' Gale

23.2.45   PB538   Pforzheim. Pilot Ted Swales KIA

6.3.45   PB475   Crashed near Chesham, Bucks on return from Chemnitz. Pilot Johnnie Gould killed

15.3.45   ND849   Missing following attack on Hagen. Pilot William Underwood KIA

28.4.45   PB983   Crashed at Deenthorpe. Pilot Robert Terpening killed

Further losses (operation 'Dodge'):
4.9.45   PB954   Crashed on take-off, Bari, Italy. No injuries reported

Appendix Three

The Loss of the Star Tiger

After the war, Donald Bennett continued to push the boundaries of aviation, and had a particular ambition to be the first to survey new passenger and trade routes to South America. As chief executive of British South American Airways (BSAA), he commanded the first commercial flight out of the newly opened Heathrow Airport flying an Avro Lancastrian to Buenos Aires. The aircraft was called Star Light; indeed all Avro Lancastrians and Yorks then flown by BSAA bore names with a 'star' prefix in keeping with the company's 'starline' call-sign.

Lancastrians and Yorks were admirable workhorses, but had already been seriously left behind in the technical and practical stakes by the growing number of US aircraft entering the commercial airline world, notably the Lockheed Constellation. Bennett looked to Avro for the answers, and specifically to its new Tudor airliner.

The four-engined Tudor had experienced an unhappy birth. Originally ordered by the British Overseas Airways Corporation (BOAC), it was an interim type using the wing design from an Avro Lincoln fixed to a modern, pressurised circular section fuselage.

BOAC demanded so many modifications to the design, that its development became somewhat of a fiasco. Bennett took matters into his own hands and flew the type to Jamaica for extensive hot weather performance trials, pronouncing himself more than satisfied with the results. Not all of his crews, however, felt the same way. The aircraft's heating system had a tendency to malfunction, especially at high altitude, and the disproportionately high tail-fin and rudder, made necessary to rectify earlier aerodynamic issues, made the airliner difficult to handle in a crosswind. An early Tudor design had also crashed on take-off, killing Avro's chief designer, Roy Chadwick, even though a subsequent enquiry concluded the accident was not caused by a design fault.

Notwithstanding these difficulties, Bennett ordered six of the aircraft in total: four Mk IVs – the re-vamped Tudor I with a longer fuselage and space for 32 passengers; and two Mk IVBs which could carry 28 passengers. For crew, Bennett turned to the best in the business, and the best in his mind were those who had been under his command in No. 8 Group. All of his captains were experienced airmen, and all held first class navigator's licenses. Counted amongst their ranks was Brian McMillan.

McMillan, the former 582 Squadron flight commander, was the chosen skipper for one of the first Mk IVs to be delivered, called Star

Tiger. By January 1948 the aircraft had already made 11 return journeys across the Atlantic, amounting to 575 hours in the air since its initial test flight two months earlier. For its 12th journey, the aircraft set off from Lisbon to Kingston, via the island of Bermuda, stopping over to refuel in the Azores. The weather, however, was so bad, that McMillan decided not to risk going on, and to stay overnight. Another BSAA skipper, Frank Griffin, had the same thought, and the pair met in the met office the following morning to receive the latest weather reports. "There's a strong wind," Griffin later recalled saying to McMillan. "I can make it in the Lancastrian, but I don't know about you." Nevertheless, McMillan opted to go, and they agreed to fly at no more than 2,000ft throughout the journey to avoid the worst of the weather, and to permit drifts to be observed on the surface of the sea in daylight hours.

Griffin and McMillan also decided upon another precaution. Griffin would fly ahead, such that he could pass back weather information to Star Tiger, and McMillan would take off an hour later. This they did: the Lancastrian getting away at 2.22pm on January 29, and Star Tiger following at 3.34pm.

The journey ahead was daunting: nearly 2,000 miles across the open Atlantic, one of the world's longest civil aviation journeys. The Tudor had a range of 2,900 miles – more than enough to reach Bermuda safely, even in a strong wind. In theory at least.

The weather was foul. Star Tiger began to rise and fall alarmingly, and the two 'Stargirls' – some of the first air-hostesses, Sheila Nicholls and Lynn Clayton, sought to re-assure the passengers. One needed no such re-assurance – the former leader of the allied air forces in the desert, Air Marshal Arthur 'Mary' Coningham. He was himself an expert pilot and navigator, and veteran of long-distance flights across Africa and the Sudan. He had every sympathy with the crew on the flight deck, but was not inclined to interfere.

The two aircraft flew on, maintaining radio contact with each other and Bermuda. After 10 hours in the air, the gap between the two aircraft had closed. Griffin's navigator obtained a fix that suggested they were more than 60 miles north of their intended track; McMillan, meanwhile, had passed the point of no return, committed to making his landfall in Bermuda. Star Tiger's co-pilot and first officer Cyril Ellison, obtained his own fix and gave his pilot a new course to steer into the teeth of a strong wind. Still there was no need to be overly concerned. He had flown through worse. At 3.00am, McMillan reported his position, giving his estimated time of arrival in Bermuda at 5.00am. Griffin put in one last call and added: "See you at breakfast."

Star Tiger's radio operator 'Tucky' Tuck contacted Bermuda for a radio bearing, depressing his transmitting key so Bermuda could home in on it and, after a little delay they were given a bearing of 72 degrees. The aircraft acknowledged receipt of signal at 3.15am. Bermuda called Star Tiger at 3.50am but received no reply. Thinking that they may have switched over to direct radio contact with Bermuda approach control, there was a delay whilst that assumption was checked. Bermuda again tried to raise Star Tiger 15 minutes later and then once more at 4.40am. Only then was a state of emergency declared.

For five days, 26 aircraft flew 882 hours between them looking for survivors or signs of a crash. They found nothing. Star Tiger, her crew and her passengers, had simply disappeared. The loss of Star Tiger prompted a comprehensive investigation conducted under the authority of Lord MacMillan and his MacMillan Committee of the civil air ministry. The official recital was impressive of what could not have happened to her:

> "There would accordingly appear to be no grounds for supposing that Star Tiger fell into the sea in consequence of having been deprived of her radio, having failed to find her destination, and having exhausted her fuel."

Whatever occurred, it was concluded that it did so extremely rapidly:

> "There is good reason to suppose that no distress message was transmitted from the aircraft, for there were many radio-receiving stations listening on the aircraft's frequencies, and none reported such a message... the weather was stable, there were no atmospheric disturbances of a serious kind which might cause structural damage to the aircraft, and there were no electrical storms."

The aircraft was also deemed not to have been off course; following the broadcast bearing from Bermuda, with the winds prevailing, Star Tiger would have been brought to within 30 miles of Bermuda where she could not have failed to have found the island, brightly lit up.

Engine trouble as a cause was also ruled out since at this late stage in her flight, without the added weight of her fuel, Star Tiger could have flown safely on three, or even two engines instead of the four she had. Considering the evidence, the Committee concluded soberly:

> "It may truly be said that no more baffling problem has ever been presented for investigation. In the complete absence of any reliable evidence as to either the nature or the cause of the accident to Star Tiger the Court has not been able to do more than suggest possibilities, none of which reaches the level even of probability. Into all activities which involve the co-operation of man and machine two elements enter of a very diverse character. There is the incalculable element of the human equation dependent upon imperfectly known factors; and there is the mechanical element subject to quite different laws. A breakdown may occur in either separately or in both in conjunction. Or some external cause may overwhelm both man and machine. What happened in this case will never be known and the fate of Star Tiger must remain an unsolved mystery."

It remains a mystery to this day.

Glossary

ABC	Airborne Cigar – transmitter carried by 101 Squadron aircraft to jam German nightfighter communication frequencies
ACRC	Aircrew Reception Centre
AFC	Air Force Cross – awarded to officers for feats of outstanding airmanship
AFU	Advanced Flying Unit
AS	Air School
Bullseye	Night affiliation exercise often in support of bomber operations
CAOS	Combined Air Observer School
Corkscrew	Evasive manoeuvre to alter rapidly the height and direction of an aircraft to avoid nightfighter attack
DFC	Distinguished Flying Cross – awarded to officers for acts of courage on operations
DFM	Distinguished Flying Medal – awarded to NCOs for acts of courage on operations
DR (Compass)	Distance Reading
DSO	Distinguished Service Order – awarded to officers for outstanding acts of leadership
Feathering	Altering the pitch of the propeller blades to face the thin edge into the wind
Flak	Anti-aircraft fire (from the German FliegerAbwehrKanonen)
Gardening	Mining operations
Gee	Medium range navigation aid, using ground transmitters and an airborne cathode ray tube receiver
Hang ups	Bombs that failed to drop usually owing to electrical/ mechanical failure
HCU	Heavy Conversion Unit
H2S	Airborne scanning radar and target location aid showing a reflection of ground detail displayed on a cathode ray tube. Also known as 'Y'
ITW	Initial Training Wing
LMF	Lack of Moral Fibre
Main force	The bulk of an attacking force, usually comprising those squadrons outside of PFF
NCO	Non Commissioned Officer – flight sergeants, sergeants etc
Newhaven	PFF technique based on visual marking and backing up
Nickel	Leaflet drops over enemy territory
NJG	Nachtjagdgeschwader – literally nightfighter squadron
NTU	Navigation Training Unit

Oboe	Ground controlled radar blind bombing device incorporating two ground stations to track aircraft and signal the point at which the bomb should be released. Any PFF attack with the pre-fix 'Musical' (e.g. Musical Parramatta) meant it involved Oboe
OTU	Operational Training Unit
Parramatta	Blind bombing using H2S
PFF	Pathfinder force
POW	Prisoner of War
Scarecrow	Reputed secret German artillery device to simulate an exploding aircraft and so demoralise the attacking force
TI	Target indicator – coloured 'markers' (usually red, yellow or green) to indicate the point at which to bomb
Tractable	Target codename in support of attack on Caen
U/S	Unservicable
V1	Vergeltungswaffe 1 – 'vengeance weapon' 1 – a flying bomb aka a Doodle Bug
V2	Vergeltungswaffe 2 – the A4 long-range rocket
V3	Vergeltungswaffe 3 – a long-range cannon
WAAF	Woman's Auxiliary Air Force
Wanganui	Blind marking technique used to indicate the bomb release point for targets obscured by cloud
Y	H2S

Sources

Personal Interviews/correspondence

Stafford Coulson DSO DFC   Bill Hough
Philip Patrick MBE DFC   David Spier
Revd Les Hood   Bob Pearce
George Hall DFC & Bar   Frank Lloyd DFC
Roy Pengilley DFC & Bar   Reg Cann DFC
Roy Last   Ted Stocker DSO DFC
Bill Heane DFC   John Clough DFC
John Torrans   Charles Steele DFC
Vera Jacobs   Robert Alabaster DSO & Bar DFC & Bar
John Smith DFM   Les Owen

Logbooks

Frank Lloyd   Philip Patrick
Reg Cann   John Smith
George Owen   Ted Stocker

Official Records

Air 27/2052   Air 2/9112
Air 2/9157/49010   Air 2/8829
Air 2/8782/81007   Air 2/8831
Air 2/5867   Air 2/9137
Air 2/8755   Air 40/2378
Air 2/8930
Air 2/9053   WO 208/3349/3323/3334/3351
Air 2/9058
Air 2/9060   ZJ 1/980

Additional Sources

The Illuminator (newsletter of the Little Staughton Pathfinder
   Association – various issues)
Staying On (unpublished) – David Spier
Men and Heroes – via Bob Pearce
My grandfather – a Pathfinder – via Bill Heane
211 Squadron Association – www.211squadron.org
The Little Staughton Pathfinder Association Archive – via Les Owen
The 97 Squadron Association

Published Sources

Heroic Endeavour – Sean Feast

Carried on the Wind – Sean Feast
Flying through Fire – Sean Feast
Bomber Command Handbook – Jonathan Falconer
Pathfinder – Donald Bennett
Pathfinder Force – Gordon Musgrove
The Right of the Line – John Terraine
The Source Book of the RAF – Ken Delve
Flying for Freedom – Tony Redding
It's never dark above the clouds – Syd Johnson
Swifter than Eagles – Barney Hewitt
The Bomber Command War Diaries – Martin Middlebrook
Avro Lancaster – Harry Holmes
Coningham – Vincent Orange
Wings over Olympus – Tom Wisdom
Bomber Command Losses – Bill Chorley

Personal thanks

My thanks to Philip Patrick for graciously writing the foreword, and to my party of veterans who read through and corrected my manuscript. I now have no one to blame for any errors other than myself.

Thanks particularly to Don Clark through whom I was able to meet John Farrington, son of the late Allan Farrington, and his lovely wife Sue. Thanks also to Sandra Silverwood (and her army of helpers, notably Greg Nixon), Jill Saunders and Marty Jacobs.

Thanks to Jocelyn Finnigan, daughter of the late Stafford Coulson and her husband John for their kind and gracious support.

Special thanks, as ever, are due to Richard Robinson, researcher par excellence for this, our fourth collaboration. His efforts were all the more remarkable given that his computer exploded mid-way through the project! My thanks to my good friend and critic Simon Holden for offering that a glossary may help further his enjoyment of my books, and thanks in particular to Victoria, Iona and Alison at the AGA Group for providing cover when I most needed it. (Remember, holidays are not a target.) Finally, to Elaine, Matthew and James for allowing me access to the family computer just long enough to finish the job.

Index

A

Alabaster, 'Alaby' 64-6, 215
Alexander, Bob 47, 142
Allen, F/O 123, 153, 200
Alston, William 69, 206
Ansell, Percy 168
Anderson, Don 54, 57-8
Archer, Dudley 111, 120, 174, 198
Armstrong, F/O 31
Aungiers, Graham 62
Austin, Johnny 38, 42, 204
Austin, Ken 141, 146, 206
Austin, Lewis 154, 207
Axford, Phil 159

B

Backhouse, Horace 63
Baker, Gordon 148
Baker, 'Tubby' 193
Bagshaw, Bill 62
Baldwin, John 12
Bazalgette, Ian 50, 201
Beesey, LAC 23
Bellinger, Les 46
Bennett, Donald 12, 13, 15, 17, 47, 64, 66, 78, 127, 160, 177, 183-4, 190, 193-5, 198-9, 201, 210, 216
Bennington, Gerry 174
Berney, F/L 153, 186
Bertelsen, Freddie 31, 48, 203, 208
Bintley, Sydney 182
Blake, Gordon 95-6
Blaydon, Reg 84, 205
Boehm, 'Vicki' 86
Boland, F/L 150

Booth, Leslie 18
Boots, F/Sgt 35
Botha, Bernhorst 120
Bouch, Albert 34, 204
Bourne, 'Al' 173
Bowyer, Arnold 95
Bradley, George 92, 205
Brandt, Jack 42
Britton, P/O 125
Broadhurst, Harry 190
Brown, Sgt Jimmy 22-24
Brown, F/O Jimmy 68, 116, 124, 126, 133, 168, 171, 186, 209
Brown, Stephen 203
Brownlow, Jimmy 50
Brownlow, Phil 76
Bryan-Smith, Martin 18
Bufton, Sidney 190
Bunting, William 62, 205

C

Cairns, Bob 68, 137-8, 160, 163-5, 167-70, 186, 200
Cameron, Doug 86
Campbell, Johnny 132-6
Campbell, Robert 81, 84, 205
Campbell, Frederick 206
Campling, Richard 183
Cann, Reg 5, 163-170, 215
Carden, Pat 153
Carr, Roddy 12
Carroll, James 149-150
Carter, Edward 17, 18
Carter, Gordon 182
Chadwick, Roy 210
Charlton-Jones, Cecil 20
Chelu, Bobby 38, 42, 204
Cheshire, Leonard 180

Chetham, Charles 18, 118
Clarke, F/L 64
Clayton, Lynn 211
Clenahan, Robert 34, 204
Clough, John 64, 68, 117-8, 122, 151, 155, 158, 168, 172, 197, 215
Cochrane, Ralph 12, 21, 97
Coleman, F/L 34
Collings, Raymond 'Fatty' 16, 70, 76, 96-7, 102, 104-5, 107, 125
Collins, Henry 29, 203
Collishaw, Raymond 87
Coningham, Arthur 211
Coole, Douggie 38, 42, 204
Coombes, F/O 123, 200
Corran, Graham 71-2, 75
Corrion, Norbert 31
Coryton, Alec 12, 21
Cottrell, Gilbert 34, 204
Cousens, Alan 29
Coulson, Stafford 5, 10, 148, 150, 154, 162, 168-9, 177, 189-99, 200, 201, 215, 217
Couvert, André 41
Cresswell, Keith 180, 181
Crew, Johnny 163
Cribb, Peter 63-5, 67, 78, 91, 99, 110-11, 115, 124, 148, 174, 177, 180, 184, 187-8, 194, 199
Croft, Lawrence 118, 206
Croney, Don 119
Crosby, Vincent 34, 204
Cruden, Dan 152

D
Dagger, Ted 54
Dalik, Ed 133, 136
Daniels, Pat 17
Davis, Victor 'Davy' 69, 105, 205
Davies, F/O 184-6
Davies, Tom 54
Dawson, Eric 118, 206
Dawson, 'Hoppy' 25, 27
Day, Art 46
Dean, 'Dixie' 182, 193, 194

Denbigh, Arnold 153, 206
Dicerbo, Philip 'Jock' 62, 71-2, 74, 76, 205
Dighton, P/O 153
Dimbleby, Richard 89, 112, 118
Dockar, Frank 124
Dodson, Clive 174
Drew, Alan 25
Drünkler, Oblt 38
Dunnicliffe, Charles 17-18, 33, 43, 63-4, 96, 105

E
Edwards, 'Pookie' 86
Edwards, 'Wally' 159
Ellison, Cyril 211
Embry, Basil 190
Everett, Danny 156
Evins, Dr 83-4

F
Farrington, Allan 5, 67, 85-93, 205, 208, 217
Feeley, Arthur 18, 26, 34, 204
Finlay, Michael 'Paddy' 71, 77, 152, 167, 171, 186, 190
Flynn, Denis 34, 204
Flynn, John 109, 203
Foley, Bill 38, 42
Folkes, P/O 153
Fordham, James 201
Foulsham, James 62
Fresson, Noel 17
Friedrich, Gerhard 177

G
Gale, 'Windy' 151, 209
Gaughran, Wilfred 81, 84, 205
Geeson, Bill 42
Geoghan, S/L 48
Gibson, Guy 9
Gipson, Freddie 31-32, 67, 167
Glennie, Bill 88-9
Goddard, John 31, 67-68, 98, 186, 205, 208
Goodacre, Bert 174
Goodwin, Gordon 7, 25

Gorman, Jack 105-106
Gostling, Alec 124
Gould, Johnnie 59, 120, 153,
  162, 202, 206, 209
Grange, Arthur 'Bud' 54, 55, 204
Grant, George 57, 61, 186
Green, Art 120, 133-4, 154, 209
Griffin, Frank 211
Griffiths, S/L 182
Grillage, Freddie 120-121, 132,
  135-6, 206

H
Haig, Douglas 166
Hailstone, Colin 168
Haines, P/O 153, 200
Hall, George 5, 18, 44-52, 81,
  128, 215
Harris, Arthur 'Butch' 9, 11-13,
  15, 21, 26-7, 66, 116, 119,
  137, 138, 170
Hart, Bill 153
Harte-Lovelace, Anthony 190
Harvey, George 148, 152-3
Hawker, Edwin 80, 84, 205
Hazlehurst, Bill 105-106
Heane, Bill 5, 94-101, 108, 215
Hemsworth, Hugh 117-9, 128,
  173
Hemsworth, Ellis 207
Heney, Harold 26-27, 32-33,
  201, 203, 208
Hetherington, John 88-9
Hewitt, John 34, 202, 204, 208
Hewitt, Kenneth 122, 143, 146,
  206
Hewitt, Stanley 203
Hill, Alan 82-3
Hockley, Reg 122, 129, 139,
  143-4, 146, 186, 209
Holden, Dave 54
Holl, Fred 95
Hood, Les 5, 36-43, 45, 215
Hough, Bill 5, 132-138, 215
Hughes, Patrick 121, 206
Hughes, Ron 95
Humphrey, Jimmy 25, 27, 55, 57,
  58

Hunt, Gordon 119

I
Ingalls, Ross 18, 63
Interiano, Oswald 123, 131, 171,
  186

J
Jacobs, Hadyn 'Taffy' 25, 27, 69,
  102, 105, 106
Jacobs, Vera 5, 102-7, 215
James, F/O 160
James, Ray 124, 126
Jehan, Vic 143, 146
Johnson, Dennis 34, 204
Johnson, Syd 30, 216
Jolliffe, Peter 192
Jones, Freddie 71-2
Jones, Gwynfor 109, 203
Joyce, William 106

K
Kelly, F/O 152
Keely, F/O 150, 209
King, Bob 80, 84
King, Dennis 37
Kinman, Jack 101, 116, 121,
  128, 206, 209
Kitto, Henry 34, 204

L
Laere, Can 31
Laere, Jean 31
Lamb, Des 156, 159
Lamb, Michael 205
Lamb, Ronald 203
Lanning, Bill 152
Lashbrook, Wallace 'Wally' 182
Last, Roy 5, 71-78, 215
Law, 'Dickie' 196
Leach, Bryn 173-175
Lee, 'Wally' 22, 25, 27
Le Good, 'Speed' 151
Lenz, Ken 105, 106
Little, Stuart 'Sam' 32, 108, 109,
  202, 203
Lloyd, Frank 5, 148-149,
  155-162, 171, 215

Lockhart, Guy 24

M
Macarthur, George 110
MacLachlan, Tommy 5, 32,
   108-114
MacLennan, Jack 70, 141, 145
Magee, Clyde 29, 34, 186
Mahaddie, Hamish 78, 127
Malkin, Hank 182
Mange, Emile 199, 201
Manley, Harry 153
Mansell-Playdell, David 149,
   155-6, 158, 160
Manson, Donald 61, 204, 208
Marical, Francis 82-3
Marks, Jimmy 63
Mathers, Bart 66
Mathers, S/L 43
McComb, Tommy 109
McGinn, Joseph 29, 203
McKeown, 'Mac' 132-3
McMillan, Brian 19, 25, 48, 49,
   67, 76-7, 79, 81, 92,
   116-7, 120, 139, 155,
   167, 210-11
McNamara, Nick 149-150, 206
McVerry, Patrick 120, 149-150,
   209
Mellor, Abel 119, 168, 206
Mettam, 'Hal' 151, 153, 171,
   186
Middleton, Rawdon 21-22
Miller, F/O 123
Milne, Owen 69, 121-2, 137,
   144, 202, 206, 209
Mingard, Norman 67, 94-5, 97,
   99-101, 108, 111, 117, 134,
   136, 153
Minogue, P/O 109
Mood, 'Willie' 133-134, 136
Morris, Jeff 41
Moye, Ken 95
Mummery, Arthur 'Happy'159
Myatt, Trevor 149-150

N
Nairn, F/L 120, 149, 171, 186
Nathan, Bernard 67-8
Naylor, Dennis 133, 136
Nettleton, John 24
Nichol, Tommy 46
Nicholls, Sheila 211
Nixon, Graham 66-9, 205, 208
Norris, John 69, 205

O
O'Donovan, Godfrey 30, 62,
   115, 186, 195, 208
O'Neill, Charles 31, 203, 208
Oram, Alfred 109, 203
Osmond, 'Bluey' 193
Owen, George 141, 146, 206
Owen-Jones, Vivian 129, 154,
   173, 200

P
Palmer, Robert 9, 121-2, 209
Papworth, John 34, 204
Parrott, 'Pip' 143, 146
Patch, A/C 170
Paterson, John 141, 146, 206
Patrick, Philip 5, 8, 19-28, 55,
   64, 69, 102, 215, 217
Paxton, F/L 183
Peacock, Doug 67, 117
Pearce, Bob 5, 139-147, 215
Pengilley, Roy 5, 18, 27, 53-60,
   67, 173, 215
Pillot, M. et Mme 84
Plimmer, Albert 121, 206
Plonczynski, P/O 23

Q
Quine, P/O 153

R
Rampling, Kenneth 23
Rasmussen, Axel 93
Rawcliffe, Sgt 66
Rawlinson, Neville 109, 203
Raybould, Arthur 27, 33-4, 55,
   202, 204, 208

Rayner, Paddy 124
Reid, Dave 124, 126, 128
Reif, Walt 68, 70, 118, 122,
   139-141, 143-144, 146, 206,
   209
Rember, Raymond 30, 62, 204,
   208
Renault, M. et Mme 41-42
Rice, Edward 12
Rieger, Herbert 18
Ritchie, 'Willie' 167
Robinson, Basil 64, 95, 181-182
Rodley, Ernest 23
Rogers, Alan 71-2, 75
Roxburgh, W/C 159
Rupp, Bruno 92-3
Russell, George 121

S
Sage, Johnny 22, 25
Sale, Julian 182
Satherley, Doug 159
Schild, Emile 83
Scott, 'Doc' 54
Sellick, Boyd 133
Sexton, Robert 34
Shirley, Roy 143, 146
Shirley, William 69, 131, 202,
   205, 208
Shurlock, 'Tiny' 35, 69, 102,
   105, 208
Siddons, Harold 18, 38, 42, 120,
   184
Silverwood, Geoffrey 92
Silverwood, Henry 92, 205
Simmonds, Reg 105-106
Sisley, Alan 51
Spierenberg, 'Splinter' 18, 35, 37,
   38, 42, 110, 120, 208
Smith, F/O 69
Smith, Duncan 205
Smith, Edward 204
Smith, Jack 173
Smith, Sgt Jimmy 24
Smith, John 5, 124-131, 215
Smith, Tony 139, 143, 146
Smith, Walter 34, 204

Snaith, Leonard 192
Somerville, 'Slim' 56
Spier, David 5, 139-147, 215
Spooner, Bill 77, 115, 186
Steele, Charles 50, 215
Stevens, Douglas 92, 205
Stewart, Charles 92, 205
Stewart, Len 46
Stocker, Ted 5, 18, 116, 130,
   137, 179-188, 198, 215
Street, Joe 32, 108, 109-11,
   113-14, 118
Strout, Alfred 92, 205
Swales, Ted 5, 35, 62, 100, 122,
   130, 134, 151-152, 171-178,
   189, 196, 202, 206, 208, 209
Swann, S/L 131

T
Taggart, Lloyd 46, 48
Tatnell, James 183
Terpening, Robert 122, 152, 154,
   202, 207, 209
Thomas, Peter 68, 77, 122, 206,
   209
Thomson, Tom 71-2
Thorby, Warwick 149-150
Thorn, Alex 128
Todd, F/O 125
Torrans, John 5, 79-84, 215
Tovey, Phil 46
Tropman, Francis 193
Trotter, Elmer 65-6, 208
Truman, Wilf 109, 203
Tuck, 'Tucky' 211
Tutt, Norman 34, 61, 204, 208
Tyndale, Lorne Vincent 92, 205

U
Underwood, William 123, 154,
   162, 171, 202, 207, 209
Uzelman, Pete 141, 146, 206

V
Van Geffen 160

W

Walbourn, Derrick 19, 25, 26, 33, 48, 55, 58, 61, 68, 91, 110, 115, 118
Walker, Clive 18
Walker, Gus 190
Wallis, Bernard 29, 203, 208
Wareing, Bob 18, 62, 65, 79-80, 84, 185, 208
Wasse, Kenneth 20, 22
Watson, John 154, 207
Watts, 'Pop' 180
Webb, Bernard 32, 108-9, 203
Weightman, John 18, 56, 59, 61-2, 81, 110, 202, 204
Welsh, F/L 182
Wesselow, Charles de 151, 155
Weyart, Gerhard 185
Wheaton, 'Whisky' 174
Whitley, John 201
Williams, Philip 66, 68, 70, 116
Williams, Sgt 180
Williams, William 204
Wilson, David 206
Wilson, Harry 34, 204
Wisdom, Tommy 85, 92, 216
Woods, Tim 159
Woods, 'Timber' 16, 58
Wright, F/Sgt 34
Wright, F/O 154
Wright, Stanley 206
Wykeham-Barnes, Peter 192
Wynyard, Jim 87, 89

Y

Yeulett, Russ 122